SMOKESCREEN

OTHER BOOKS BY PHILIP J. HILTS

Scientific Temperaments
Memory's Ghost

SMOKE SCREEN

THE TRUTH BEHIND THE TOBACCO INDUSTRY COVER-UP

PHILIP J. HILTS

Addison-Wesley Publishing Company, Inc.
Reading, Massachusetts   Menlo Park, California   New York
Don Mills, Ontario   Harlow, England   Amsterdam   Bonn
Sydney   Singapore   Tokyo   Madrid   San Juan
Paris   Seoul   Milan   Mexico City   Taipei

Many of the designations used by manufacturers and sellers to distinguish their products are claimed as trademarks. Where those designations appear in this book and Addison-Wesley was aware of a trademark claim, the designations have been printed in initial capital letters.

Library of Congress Cataloging-in-Publication Data has been applied for.

ISBN 0-201-48836-1

Jacket design by Jean Seal
Set in 11-point Electra by Pagesetters, Inc.

123456789-MA-0099989796
First printing, May 1996

Addison-Wesley books are available at special discounts for bulk purchases by corporations, institutions, and other organizations. For more information, please contact: Corporate, Government, and Special Sales Department, Addison-Wesley Publishing Company, Reading, MA 01867, 1-800-238-9682.

To Kay and Len Hilts, with love

Contents

Acknowledgments

The Robert Wood Johnson Foundation, the Kaiser Family Foundation, and the Harvard University School of Public Health, Center for Health Communications made this work possible with their support. The *New York Times* permitted me to work this story for two years, and at the *Times*, unlike other institutions, the company lawyers were enthusiastic and supportive at all turns. I want to thank my agent, Gloria Loomis, editor Henning Gutmann, and many others at Addison-Wesley for their help and their efforts to get the book into print. And the work would not have been possible without the aid and comfort of Carisa Cunningham, my wife.

Author's Note

This book is not so much about smoking and smokers as about corporate behavior. I was enamored of the habit myself for ten years; I would probably still be smoking if my wife, when she became pregnant and had to quit herself, hadn't asked me to join her in protecting our first child. Yet I am still drawn to the tobacconist's shop and will sometimes go in just to let my nasal passages swim.

1

CANCER AND CRISIS

Falsehood is invariably the child of fear. . . .
— Aleister Crowley

It was a cold morning, December 15, 1953, in New York City, at the elegant Plaza Hotel on Central Park. A group of men, the key figures of their industry, were nervous as they headed for a meeting room with their aides at their sides, like generals preparing for war. The meeting was private, neither noted by industry analysts nor discovered by reporters, but it was a pivotal moment in this history of this trade, and less fortunately, a pivotal moment in the public health profile of the nation.

The product that these men and their companies had made so profitable was tobacco, *Nicotiana tabacum.* It could fairly be described, taking the long view of business history, as one of the most saleable commodities on earth. It is also a purely American product in its origin, development, and domination of the world market. Perhaps the best simple description of it from a business point of view comes from a typically brash American, Warren Buffett, an investment specialist who is reputed to be the richest man in America. "I'll tell you why I like the cigarette business," he said. "It costs a penny to make. Sell it for a dollar. It's addictive. And there's fantastic brand loyalty."

The cigarette trade in the United States had climbed from nothing over sixty years: At the end of the last century less than one in a hundred Americans used cigarettes regularly, but by 1950, an astounding 50 percent of the adult population smoked them. Cigarettes were sent by the carload to soldiers at war;

government hospitals distributed them free to patients; and as late as 1966, the Congress voted to send 600 million cigarettes to the victims of a terrible flood in India as a form of relief.

In 1953, this hugely successful and popular industry found itself suddenly in crisis. Tobacco stock prices had taken a sudden drop. People had unexpectedly begun to abandon the habit out of fear. Consumption peaked at 416 billion cigarettes per year in 1952 in the United States, and now was quickly dropping, for the first time in memory, and the drop was very large, down to 384 billion in less than two years. It seemed possible to the executives at the hotel that they were near the end of the industry as they had known it.

As we reconstruct the moment, we know they had worried for some time about the health hazards of cigarette smoking. They had commissioned some research of their own, and found that cigarettes could cause extreme irritation to living tissue. (One scientist they hired began a series of toxicity tests by putting a single drop of tobacco-smoke extract on rabbits' eyes, just to begin to find out the level of irritability of cigarette tars. He had to stop the project after finding that a single drop was so toxic that it caused massive sores and the complete loss of the eye. He said it was the most toxic substance he had ever seen. That was reported to the companies in the 1940s.) They had also watched as, from 1929 onward, university scientists and doctors began unearthing evidence that tobacco tar was toxic.

Until 1952, the companies' chief concern was not really one of human health. It was marketing, selling a "smoother" product that would cause less coughing and throat distress to customers. In this regard, tobacco was one of the chief beneficiaries of two young and vigorous industries in America, advertising and public relations. The companies ran a substantial amount of advertising on the topic of health, to counteract growing public concern. This may have made things worse, as the companies used such lines as "not a cough in a carload" and "Doctors recommend Camel." One television ad showed a woman being interviewed on a sober set with dramatic lighting:

Q: Mrs. O'Brian, is it true that you visited a famous throat specialist every week for a thirty-day period, and that he carefully examined your throat each time?

A: It is.

Q: Is it true that you smoked Camel and only Camel during that thirty days?

A: That's true.

Q: Will you tell us what the doctor told you?

A: He said there wasn't any sign of irritation to my throat from Camel.

Then, matters got much worse. Until this century, lung cancer had been a very rare disease. Dr. Alan Blum recalls that when Dr. Alton Ochsner, a pioneer of tobacco and health studies, was in medical school in 1919, he was summoned with his entire student class to an autopsy being performed one day. It was the autopsy of a man who had died of lung cancer, and the chief surgeon believed that the students would never get another chance to see such a case. As a surgeon 17 years later, Dr. Ochsner began seeing a stream of such cases, and became alarmed.

Over 50 years, lung cancer had gone from a rare disorder to a raging epidemic, from fewer than five cases in every 100,000 men to 75 per 100,000, from a handful of deaths at the turn of the century, to more than 18,000 per year in 1950 from lung cancer alone. (That number would shoot up to over 110,000 per year in the following two decades.) Epidemiologists worried about the rise, and cigarette smoking became an ideal target of study. In studies of more than 40,000 men patients, it appeared that the disease was 10 to 30 times more common among smokers than among non-smokers. They also saw in the data the signature of a toxin: the number of cancers in the population of smokers went up in direct proportion to the number of cigarettes smoked per day, the dose-response relationship. An examination of lung tissues added certainty, when it was found that smokers' lungs not only blackened with years of smoking, but that the lungs of 93 percent of smokers carried abnormal, possibly pre-cancerous cells; in non-smokers, only 1 percent had such abnormal cells.

In private papers, tobacco company executives noted these findings with some alarm. They made an effort to parry them, but the public's attitude was shifting. Already, 40 percent of the population believed smoking caused lung cancer. The staid *Reader's Digest* ran a damning story in 1952 entitled "Cancer by the Carton." It did seem logical, after all, that drawing hot black char into the lungs hourly, coating the sensitive and vital membranes of breathing with sticky particles, ought to do something serious. Then, too, there was the evidence of the street, subway and neighborhood: hacking and wheezing smokers.

What brought the tobacco executives to the emergency meeting at the Plaza, however, was the publication of an article in the December, 1953, issue of the journal *Cancer Research*. In it, Drs. Ernst Wynder and Evarts Graham and their colleagues at the Sloan Kettering Institute in New York published a slim paper describing experiments in which painting smoke condensate from cigarettes onto the susceptible skin of mice produced cancerous tumors. The smoke induced not a few cancers, but tumors on the skin of 44 percent of the animals, a huge number by experimental standards. And human lungs, after all, are also made of skin. For the first time, the health dangers of cigarette smoking were on the front pages of newspapers.

Within days of the appearance of Wynder's paper, the chief executives of the biggest tobacco companies in the industry, who had never before met to make policy, grimly greeted one another. The last time men of equivalent titles in the business met was in 1939; that time, the government successfully prosecuted them for price fixing. If the government knew of the Plaza meeting, the executives might well have been investigated again for collusion. But they had little choice.

In those years, the leaders of the market were the same as they are now: Philip Morris and R.J. Reynolds. Today, the total tobacco company business in the U.S. is about $45 billion a year. The number of companies sharing in that wealth has dwindled, and there are five giants left. Philip Morris is the largest, with about 43 percent of the American market. Reynolds is not far behind, with about 28 percent. Brown and Williamson is third, with about 11 percent of the market (to which one can now add about 7 percent of the market from American Tobacco, which B&W just acquired). The two smallest in the group are Lorillard at about 7 percent of the market, and Liggett & Myers at 2 percent.

All the leading companies agreed to an emergency plan in 1953: Philip Morris, Reynolds, Brown and Williamson, American Tobacco, U.S. Tobacco, and Benson and Hedges. Only Lorillard declined to participate, on the grounds that the companies should remain silent rather than mounting a P.R. campaign.

On the morning of December 15, four chief executives were present, and leading the meeting. The bold and outspoken Paul D. Hahn, president of American Tobacco, was the strongest voice of the group. From Philip Morris came O. Parker McComas; from Benson & Hedges, Joseph F. Cullman; and from the U.S. Tobacco Company, J. Whitney Peterson.

The minutes of the meeting at the Plaza show that, after they settled in their places that morning, the executives first agreed that the matter was "extremely serious" as the minutes say, and "worthy of drastic action." They spoke of the sense of crisis, "that salesmen in the industry are frantically alarmed and that the decline in tobacco stocks on the market has caused grave concern, especially since tobacco earnings will be much higher next year because of the termination of excess profits taxes."

The industry might have to acknowledge the hazard and make themselves ready to regulate tobacco much as alcohol or other drugs.

Or, perhaps not. John Hill of the firm of Hill and Knowlton, the largest of the emerging "public relations" firms from the aggressive new industry which sought to shape feelings rather than facts, was present at the meeting. He suggested a bold move: the industry could, instead, mount a public counter-attack against the scientists.

He had already met with R.J. Reynolds, which had considered a campaign of its own. He had also spoken to the fiercest of the tobacco executives, Paul D. Hahn of American Tobacco. Hill came away with the conclusion that, first, it would be important to assuage the public worry. He wanted the companies to make a statement saying that they were honestly concerned with the public welfare. He also wanted them to go further and say that they would never knowingly market a product which was harmful.

The tobacco men were defensive. They had been accused of callousness and disregard of the health of their customers; yet their scientists had told them that the evidence coming in might not be true, or at least could be argued with vigorously in those early years.

They decided, according to the minutes of the meeting, helpfully written down by a Hill and Knowlton staff member, that the first order of business was to establish a joint group funded by all the companies to work on the issues of smoking and health.

Such a group could be in violation of the antitrust rules which disallow them from industry-wide collusion on matters that affect their finances, so say the minutes, "Instead, they prefer strongly the organization of an informal committee which will be specifically charged with the public relations function and readily identified as such."

Paul Hahn of American had wanted to call their new group "The Committee for Public Information." Hill, in turn, suggested adding the word "research" to give it some authority. So, the provisional agency of tobacco defense was named the Tobacco Industry Research Committee (TIRC).

As they warmed to the subject that day, the CEOs said they felt they were being abused by the scientists who were studying cancer. These researchers, they said, were not being honest. They were working not with pure motives, but had "publicity issued in the hopes of attracting funds and support for further research."

The executives countered with what seemed to them obvious: a campaign that attacked directly those who conclude that cigarettes cause cancer. In this case, there was one other public relations firm that had been approached about working for the tobacco companies; that firm had turned them down.

Thus it reads in the minutes, as the Hill and Knowlton scribe writes: the company executives "are confident they can supply us with comprehensive and authoritative scientific material which completely refutes the health charges."

The discussions soon led to the central conclusion that the issue was so important that it would take a large and expensive campaign, sustained over many years, to protect the companies. And, the campaign must be tough, as the minutes say: "The industry should not engage in a merely defensive campaign. They should sponsor a public relations campaign which is positive in nature and entirely 'pro-cigarettes.' "

As a parting measure, John Hill warned the executives that if research showed the companies wrong, they couldn't remain on this course. This was agreed to, and so, considering what happened later, the executives on that December morning also affirmed the principle that "public health is paramount to all else."

Thus began the conspiracy. Money was at its center, and public relations forestalled any serious look at the issue or any conscience-searching at the time. The plan was to spend large amounts of money every year indefinitely into the future to pre-vent, not sworn adversaries, but *scientists and public health offi-cers,* from warning people of a potential hazard in the normal manner. There is no case like it in the annals of business or health.

2

CREATING THE DISINFORMATION MACHINE

[The sage] warns the heads of parties against believing their own lies.

— John Arbuthnot, *The Art of Political Lying*

The unlikely moment at the Plaza Hotel grew in import over the following years, and the strategy arrived at, apparently without much reflection, put the industry on its path for the next half century. At that meeting there was no reference to scientific data, or the credibility of the studies. There was no discussion of whether the countervailing opinions were merely doubts or had evidence to support them. Nevertheless, by a little after noon on that day, the top research scientists from the tobacco companies were already beginning to brief Hill and Knowlton about what to say to deny the accumulating evidence against cigarettes.

The campaign, which still continues, has so far expended what in current figures would be more than a billion dollars; it might be the largest and most expensive public-issue campaign ever launched. TIRC and the industry campaign began not with doctors and scientists, but with 38 public relations experts from Hill and Knowlton hired by the tobacco companies, plus associated advertising executives and other contractors.

The tobacco executives themselves appeared incurious about the hazards of smoking and about the science that was trying to outline those risks. To build their defense, they were able to find scientists outside the companies who said cigarettes were very probably not the cause of cancer. Chief among these was Dr. Clarence Cook Little, a founder of the National Cancer Institute, former head of the organization that became the American Cancer Society, and the founder of the Jackson Laboratories in Bar Harbor, Maine. The companies found him in retirement, and available, a true gift to their cause. He was both prominent and knowledgeable. He came from a wealthy and prominent Boston family, and had the easy charm and confidence that comes with status. In an era when cancer was the most feared of diseases, one often concealed from patient and family until death, he worked to demystify it. He ran publicity campaigns urging people to get regular exams and to pay attention to any appearance of lumps or other symptoms. He suggested, albeit erroneously, that cancer could be cured if it could be found early.

His life's chief work was on the genetic susceptibility to cancer; he built a whole laboratory whose mission was to breed mice with susceptibilities to different cancers. Because of this, he had little patience for those who thought cancers were caused by environmental influences such as toxic chemicals or smoke. He felt that some people were predisposed to lung cancer, and so it was their weak genes rather than their smoking which was the source of their lung disease.

Little casually dismissed the growing evidence against smoking; this buoyed the sinking spirits of the tobacco executives. He was also willing to accept direction from public relations people as to the best way to present the pro-cigarette case. And so, he was hired on as the first chief of the Scientific Advisory Board of the newly-formed Tobacco Industry Research Committee.

When he arrived in the job, Hill and Knowlton had some tasks and some scripted lines ready for him. For example, Harry Haller, a publicity man, wrote a memo to Hill and Knowlton, saying some "aggressive moves" were needed to attack columnist Drew Pearson for a recent anti-tobacco column. Haller suggested that Dr. Little should be the one to deliver the message to Pearson, as Little was generally viewed as having some integrity. Dr. Little should be given a statement to make in public, and possibly in private with Pearson, which would say, "the TIRC is a concerted industry effort for thorough scientific study of any possible relationship between tobacco use and human health" and that "very definite plans now being worked out by the Scientific Advisory

Board should certainly allay fears of a few persistently vocal skeptics."

Little was instructed to add: "No evidence within our knowledge has yet established cigarette smoking as a causal factor in lung cancer!" (The exclamation is in the original.) "Research reports have definitely NOT produced to date a fragment of conclusive evidence." In particular, he was to criticize another scientist, Dr. Alton Ochsner, who had published a projection which suggested that lung cancer would continue to increase as a proportion of all cancers, to the point that in about 1970 it would be 18 percent of all cancers. (Ochsner was proved correct.)

In his memo, Mr. Haller said such statements by Dr. Little "could be placed" on Edward R. Murrow's television interview show. A few days later, Dr. Little did appear on the Murrow show, and the following exchange took place:

ARTHUR MORSE: Dr. Little, have any cancer-causing agents been identified in cigarettes?
CLARENCE LITTLE: No. None whatever, either in cigarettes or in any product of smoking. . . .
MR. MORSE: Suppose the tremendous amount of research going on, including that of the Tobacco Industry Research Committee, were to reveal that there is a cancer-causing agent in cigarettes. What then?
DR. LITTLE: Well, if it was found by somebody working under a tobacco industry research grant, it would be made public immediately and just as broadly as we could make it, and then efforts would be taken to remove that substance or substances.

These spare comments are remarkable in several ways. To begin with, the "tobacco industry research grants" did not finance any scientist to test the substances in smoke to see if they cause cancer, so they were unlikely to know such substances even if they were looking at them daily. Instead they supported research giving alternate explanations, like that of Dr. Little and others. Dr. Wynder, of course, had already shown that condensed smoke painted on skin produced tumors. (The agents in smoke were enumerated and named early in the 1960s.)

As for the promise to make industry-funded work public, memos at the time show that the public relations executives and lawyers would screen the scientist's reports before permitting them out. The TIRC gave grants with the intention of avoiding any studies that could be damaging, but still some did turn up damaging conclusions. They did not make those public. In fact, an entire set of research that had the potential for trouble — scores of experiments — was done "off the books" so that it would never be made public. One piece of work, by Dr. Frederic Homberger, almost escaped even these precautions. But TIRC executives soon stripped him of his grant, forced him to remove the word "cancer" from his paper, and then successfully pressured the organizers of the meeting where he was to present his results to cancel a press conference on Homberger's paper. The news of his work did not emerge at the time, and the full story only appeared two decades later when internal company documents describing the harassment were unearthed.

All of this was done by the TIRC. But there was more research being done quietly — without each company knowing what the others were doing — within the company labs themselves. We now have the documents showing the results of that work, and it has proved to be not only good work, but advanced far beyond that of the top university scientists of the time. It was in these tobacco company labs, in less than eight years after Dr. Little's remarks, that company researchers found not just one cancer-causing substance in smoke, but numerous compounds that caused cancer and arrays of others which encouraged cancer growth. The discoveries of these effects were also not made public by the companies; again they emerged only when company documents were obtained 25 years after the events.

All of this was yet to be, and Dr. Little did not know of it when he spoke on the Edward R. Murrow show.

But more important than these points, that televised moment may have been the first time when the industry publicly put forward its most private hope and strategy on the topic of health.

An admission of any hazard of tobacco would have resulted in a catastrophic drop in sales. So, the executives found themselves clinging to every possible doubt, waiting for the last possible moment before admitting to themselves and others what the problem was.

This ultimately was their gamble: they would find out privately what the offending chemical was, and remove it. If they could do that relatively quickly, they would be home free. But even if they could not remove the hazard, then probably the worst they faced was government regulation of the sale of tobacco, as alcohol was regulated. And in the meantime, of course, the profits would continue at the much higher rate of pre-admission days, rather than the lower rate of post-admission days in which millions of people would have quit smoking. The difficulty, of course, though they probably did not see it at the time, was that while this gambling was going on, papers accumulated in their files.

In the winter of 1953–1954, the companies seemingly had passed through the narrow opening in this crisis, between the rocks and out again. They had established a new public relations organization. It would be funded at a high rate, and expected to carry on indefinitely as a permanent feature of the social and intellectual landscape of America. It was larger than the American Cancer Society or the National Academy of Sciences in financial terms, and far above them in terms of single-minded purpose. Its architects made an effort to build in some integrity, but what could not be purchased in this regard had to be bypassed. To this end, Hill and Knowlton's preliminary recommendations for the work of this new agency, this TIRC, included intelligence gathering, advertising, laboratory research, and activities which now have come to be called "dirty tricks," that is, legal or semi-legal attempts to smear the companies' opponents, produce publicity or events which would not seem to originate with themselves, and attempts to disrupt the communications of their opponents by sending their own people to give counter arguments in every possible forum. (Such a program can be particularly effective if the opponents think they are simply scientists working on a question of health, and are unaware that they are enemies who will be watched and targeted.)

Three days into the new year, 1954, the tobacco industry broke into public with its campaign. On one day, January 4, full page ads bearing the black headline, "A Frank Statement to Cigarette Smokers," ran in 448 newspapers reaching 43,245,000 people in 258 cities. This was all the cities over 50,000 population with few exceptions. (But "no Negro newspapers," the internal memos say.)

The copy said, "Recent reports on experiments with mice have given wide publicity to a theory that cigarette smoking is in some way linked with lung cancer in human beings. Although conducted by doctors of professional standing, these experiments are not regarded as conclusive. . . ." The appearance of concern and honesty was clear, and it was the tone that would characterize tobacco company statements to the present day.

The ad stated, "We accept an interest in people's health as a basic responsibility, paramount to every other consideration in our business."

Soon after the blizzard of these ads to the public, the TIRC followed up with a booklet sent to every doctor in the United States. Carefully recasting the issue, it was called "A Scientific Perspective on the Cigarette Controversy."

The lawyers for TIRC expressed some concern that the booklet could create some legal trouble. In a memo dated May 3, 1954, the head of the Law Committee, George Whiteside, wrote that the booklet used quotations of scientists and others improperly, without their permission in what could be described as a commercial advertising document, not a scientific one.

He wrote that he could always just go ahead and argue that it was a scientific booklet, anyway, but said gamely, "It should be said that this argument would be stronger if the 'white paper' included not only all the available scientific material questioning or negativing the relationship of smoking to the increased incidence of lung cancer, but, in addition, fair quotations from the available medical authority claiming to establish such a relationship." In other words, if it were not so totally one-sided it might seem more scientific.

The TIRC's tactics used on enemies were not exactly gentle, either. There was the case of Alton Ochsner, for example, which appears among the internal documents recently extracted from the TIRC and the companies.

Ochsner at one time was the grand old man of tobacco and health research, who had written papers on cigarettes and disease as early as 1929, was writing a book on some of his tobacco research, and continued to have something of a following after several decades of work on the topic.

John Hill expressed his frustration about Ochsner in a memo once, writing, "I know of no way to keep him from writing a book or to keep the papers from reviewing it." But he had did have one idea: suing him. The suit of course could not be filed on behalf of the TIRC, which had to retain a scientific aura. But it could be pursued "through one of the companies or a stockholder in one of the companies" in the form of a libel suit based on the first sentence in Dr. Ochsner's new book: "Cigarettes cause cancer." Hill wrote that "such a suit would give the companies a peg on which to hang an attack upon Ochsner and his ilk in making irresponsible and panicky statements under the cloak of scientific authority."

One executive of Young and Rubicam, which had the advertising account for TIRC, suggested that Roy Norr, the author of the *Reader's Digest* piece, be investigated to find out if he had any puritanical moral views which might be used against him. Harry Haller noted that a college classmate of his was a scientist, and had done some studies on cancer and tobacco which "are in agreement with TIRC." This schoolmate, he said, had been approached, and if he could be put on the board of TIRC, he "wouldn't object to blasting Wynder."

In a memo in July from Hill and Knowlton's Carl Thompson (and marked "highly confidential" and "minimum distribution") to Timothy Hartnett, the chief of TIRC after retiring as president of Brown and Williamson, Thompson spoke of under-the-table payments to writers to write and try to place their pieces in national magazines. In two successful cases, *True* magazine and the *National Enquirer* published articles. (Though by the same author, they carried different fictitious bylines.) The same author was paid to write a booklet called "Smoke Without Fear." Other disguised articles were proposed for *Harper's* and *Cosmopolitan*.

Thompson said that in attacking writers, it would be best to get to them before publication. He noted that one "prominent magazine" deleted a negative reference to TIRC and the tobacco companies after being approached. He said he had gotten advance knowledge of a story by Bob Considine to be published in *Cosmopolitan*, and he boasted that he was able to get "seven revisions and five qualifying additions to the story, which was already in type."

An active intelligence crew was sent out to hear the papers delivered at medical meetings, with responses of some kind attempted when the reports could be damaging. Material was to be developed and passed on to writers on subjects such as "the psychology of how the public is carried away by over-simplified reading of scientific experiments" and "smoking habits of long-lived, distinguished public leaders" as well as "human ills erroneously attributed to tobacco over the centuries." These materials would be passed out, but "none of this material would be for sponsorship or release by TIRC."

Its creators said the core of the TIRC was research, though a skeptic might note that more than 50 percent of its budget was devoted to public relations. Still, the level of research expenditures was large — of the order of a major research university, and all, in theory, focused on the question of the effect of tobacco smoking on health.

Unlike the typical scientific organization, however, the approach to research was far from simple. Most knowledgeable scientists were already trying to examine the question, and their research was completely open to the possibility that it would produce unpleasant answers. Thus, the reasoning put forward by the TIRC was that, since others are working on traditional scientific approaches, they would instead look at "unsuspected" possibilities. Genetics, for example: do people have genetic predispositions to particular cancers, so that it is not the smoke, but the victim's genes that are at fault? Couldn't air pollution account for a significant number of lung cancers? Does smoking enhance mental or physical performance?

As it turns out, the tobacco industry grants show that while a substantial amount of the work funded by TIRC was good science, it had nothing to do with tobacco and health. In one survey of those who received the grants, 80 percent of the scientists said that none of their research, ever, had looked at questions of the health effects of smoking. Of those whose work was somewhat related to the question, the work supports just what other science on the topic shows, that smoking causes disease. In the same survey of grantees, more than 90 percent of the tobacco company's own grantees agreed with each of the following: That most of the deaths from lung cancer in America are caused by smoking, that the smoke from someone else's cigarette is harmful, and that smoking is addictive.

That TIRC was doing its job is clear from numerous memos,

like the one Ernest Pepples of B & W wrote on April 4, 1978: "Originally [TIRC's successor organization, the Council for Tobacco Research, or CTR] was organized as a public relations effort. The industry told the world CTR would look at the diseases which were being associated with smoking. There was even a suggestion by our political spokesmen that if a harmful element turned up, the industry would try to root it out. . . ."

In addition, he wrote, "the industry research has included special projects designed to find scientists and medical doctors who might serve as industry witnesses in lawsuits or in a legislative forum." It has always been difficult to find scientists who aren't convinced that tobacco causes disease; the CTR research program served as a recruiting tool.

As Addison Yeaman, a lawyer for Brown and Williamson and also at one time head of the CTR, said in one CTR meeting: "CTR is the best and cheapest insurance the tobacco industry can buy and without it the industry would have to invent CTR or would be dead."

The tobacco money was available for all sorts of strange research which might help the case for cigarettes, but not available for projects that might hurt the business, as is made clear by one amusing memo in the fall of 1978 to Horace Kornegay, head of CTR. It was written by staff member C.L. Waite. The head of the Addiction Research Foundation in Palo Alto, California, Leonard Cornell, had applied for funds to research the question of what natural substance exists in the body that is mimicked by nicotine. Because all drug actions take place through receptors built to accommodate specific chemicals, it is necessarily true that if nicotine has a drug effect, there must be a natural "nicotine" which the body makes and uses itself. He suggested that Avram Goldstein, an eminent researcher on addiction issues who was the director of the Foundation, could do the industry a great deal of good if he could find a substance to use in cigarettes instead of nicotine, which is known to be toxic in other ways.

The Addiction Research Foundation seemed to get nowhere with its funding request, but Cornell kept writing and calling.

So Mr. Waite wrote a classic memo which must have raised howls of laughter in tobacco company offices:

"1. Mr. Cornell's letter referred to by Ernie Pepples is actually asking the industry for $400,000 to build a laboratory.

2. Mr. Cornell's foundation actually assumes tobacco (nicotine) is addictive and costs the U.S. citizen 42 billion dollars a year!

3. He also believes tobacco causes 300,000 premature deaths each year.

4. And he wonders if this is why we might not be interested."

The odd array of research carried out by TIRC and CTR, though large in quantity, has in the long run been completely irrelevant in the search for the links between smoking and disease. It seems likely that was just what the companies intended.

The tobacco group's research may get low marks as a program to discover the health effects of tobacco, but the public relations program was one of the most effective in the history of the public relations industry. The "no harm from cigarettes" campaign presented to the public worked for forty years, as the government enacted virtually no tobacco regulation that the industry did not want. The steadily growing mass of scientific evidence had, in the public mind, been reduced to a tiresome "debate." No plaintiff, and there were hundreds, ever won a penny from a tobacco company in court.

It may have been one of the most remarkable saves by a PR pitch in the history of that young industry: from a time when tobacco companies had sharply declining sales and a highly suspect product, the companies were soon righted and on course again. As one 1955 memo described the success, "Suspicion is still widespread but the lynching party seems to have been called off, at least temporarily. . . . Even adverse stories now tend to carry modified statements."

The success has endured for forty years: the companies are still largely unregulated in manufacturing and sales, while the rates of disease due to smoking remain higher than any other preventable cause.

The public relations campaign, while designed as a way to protect the companies, eventually became an attack not only on scientific data, and the scientists who produced it, but an attack on science itself. That is, to make their point, the tobacco public relations people needed to devise arguments that attack the credibility of the methods of science and the basis in reason from which they spring.

A chief example is the line devised in 1953, which suggests that connections between smoking and disease are not real, but are "merely statistical." This ignores the fact that the ground of all reason in science is, and has always been, "statistical." It is necessary to observe individual cases, whether they are atoms or cancers, and draw conclusions across many cases. When we say penicillin kills bacteria, we make the judgment based on an experiment in which penicillin kills a substantial number of bacteria in a petri dish. It does not kill all the bacteria all the time. It happens often enough to make use of the information.

The cigarette company executives had been taught by public relations experts and lawyers that the way to deny the hazard of cigarettes is to say that it is not proved. But of course it has been proved, as far as science ever proves anything. It has been proved in the usual sense that anyone uses the word.

But still, it has not been proved in another sense. It has not been proved in the sense that scientists can take the case of a live individual with lung cancer, analyze that person's genes and tissues, and demonstrate that the smoke from a cigarette smoked on a given day, caused certain damage in the DNA repair mechanisms of some lung cell, which then began to behave badly, leading to the accumulation of unrepaired damage, which led to one particular misfiring in which a defective protein was produced, and so on.

This is what tobacco companies mean by "proved" when they use the word in this context. It means science must be able to state every individual biochemical step as a disease is created, and then apply that to a particular individual to find the evidence that the smoker in question, seated in court, did have this sequence of events which led to this tumor pictured in the colored medical photograph, the court exhibit.

If this sort of proof were actually needed, neither science nor any other modern pursuit could exist. This standard, for example, is not the standard the tobacco executives themselves use to decide the fate of their companies. They use statistics to determine where and how to market a particular brand, to determine what amount of what flavoring is needed to give what sense impression to a smoker. They use figures of all kinds in all aspects of their business, none of which meet their created standard of "proof." There is no place in the tens of thousands of pages of research documents I have read from the company files in which they use this standard of proof themselves, for any scientific or other kind of work. It is invoked only in public relations work, and only on the subject of tobacco and disease.

Even the top scientist at British American Tobacco for many years, Sidney Green, wrote frankly in an unpublished paper that company arguments about scientific proof and cause-and-effect, were "disastrous."

"Some might say that the cigarette industry has led the anti-smoking forces up the garden path by emphasizing so much the issue of causality. Scientific proof never has been, is not, and should not be the basis for legal or political action on social issues. A demand for scientific proof is always the formula for inaction on such issues."

He said it is the domination of the industry by lawyers that has led the industry into "public rejection in total of any causal relationship between smoking and disease, which puts the industry into a peculiarly difficult position. . . . Companies while vigorously trying to make their products safer, strenuously deny the need to do so. Industry has retreated behind impossible, perhaps ridiculous, demands for what in their public relations is called "scientific proof."

Thus the tobacco companies' attack is on science itself, or rather, on the idea that we can use science to make decisions. There is never complete certainty at any moment in any science.

Of course, we know perfectly well that company executives are not making actual scientific arguments about tobacco and disease. They are simply making any arguments that might raise any doubt possible.

In the last analysis, for the public, we can say that the effect of the whole campaign can be measured in units of misperception. When it comes time to make decisions about our behavior, about what we permit and do not permit, we depend on our sense of the proportion of things. And it is this which has been attacked. We know some things about how the tobacco pitch has distorted our sense of things. When asked how many people smoke, we guess about twice as many as actually do. When asked to rate the top ten health priorities for the country, we guess that quitting smoking should take tenth place, behind an array of real and imagined hazards, including the installation of smoke detectors, even though while fires in the home cause about 6,000 deaths annually, smoking causes something over 400,000. It is these things that contribute to a lack of broad urgency on the topic.

Sometime around 1964 or perhaps not long after, the evidence which had been just weak enough to be dismissable by tobacco company executives had grown strong enough that any rational soul could see that the companies must change their approach. If not, then they would be destroyed. Perhaps not today, but sometime, when it became clear just what they knew and what actions they did not take.

But this reassessment did not take place. The campaign launched in the Christmas season of 1953 moved ahead, with a public face of solicitude and concern, and a private one of desperation and increasing resignation.

The difficulty became clearer only as time passed and the trail of paper grew. Such an approach, it was found, requires a great deal of trail-covering. Company lawyers began to clamp down on what information was available, not only to the public, but to people inside the companies themselves. Whole areas of tobacco factories were eventually made out of bounds to other employees. Laboratories which had produced literally hundreds of damning experiments had to be shut down. Smokers, of course, were not unaware of the scientific findings of public researchers, and began to sue the companies for damages. Litigation required even tighter control over the company information which could be damaging to the case. The knowledge became a great mass growing in their files, and even included evidence of the expanding cover-up itself.

Perhaps it was confidence born of success that prevented the company lawyers from destroying these papers. Perhaps it was fear of the final legal retribution. Whatever the reason, the documents lay in the files and by the 1980s had to be catalogued for reference in the scores of trials that were current at any given time. Because of some peculiarities of the industry's history, this great archive came to be stored in large part in the vast vaults of Midwestern law offices such as Shook, Hardy and Bacon, the firm that successfully defended the industry against the earliest suits and continues to be chief defender still. There, the paper history lies to this day. We have seen a few scraps of it, enough to reconstruct some parts of the evidence, but the bulk of the tale remains buried.

The first outsider ever to see the tobacco papers that describe some of the unusual story of tobacco and health research was one Judge H. Lee Sarokin of the U.S. District Court in New Jersey, in the spring of 1988. The papers were not allowed in open court, but were read by the judge while they were sealed, at first. After reading them, he wrote that the jury could reasonably conclude TIRC "was nothing but a hoax created for public relations purposes with no intention of seeking the truth or publishing it. . . . The intensity of the advertising and public relations was sufficient to create the desired doubt in the minds of the consumer, and overwhelm or undermine pronouncements as to the dangers. . . . The magazine *Tobacco and Health* 'mailed free to practically every doctor in the country . . . was a blatant and biased account of the smoking "controversy" '." For those remarks, the tobacco companies protested to a higher court, and Judge Sarokin was removed from the case for bias.

Inside the companies, the result of the early strategy was also profound. Out of the pages of the 'tobacco papers' from Brown and Williamson and others, and from the transcripts in court and Congress, a pattern has emerged that the reader will see recurring in the pages that follow: The companies' public persona is entirely that of the salesman, the public relations pitch artist, and the aggressive marketeer.

Beneath it, there is and always has been something else. The companies have hired many scientists, whose job and whose sensibilities are often quite different from the hucksters'. Year after year, when doubts and contrary views came from within the companies, they came from the researchers whose usual go-along attitude broke down occasionally in the face of the facts they had to deal with.

Over the past two years, two figures have emerged in the tobacco wars who seem to represent these two conflicting personalities within the industry. Both men worked for Brown and Williamson, the company that has given us the most complete cache of damning documents to date. One was the chairman and

CEO, a former salesman, Thomas E. Sandefur. The other was the company's chief researcher, scientist Jeffrey S. Wigand. From these two we have completely opposite testimony, and soon the two will face off in court.

But through the history of the companies, whether the sounds came from these two men in particular, and in recent months they often have, both sorts of voices can be heard. They admit, they regret, they hope. The question now is, when will the bluff front be dropped, and frankness prevail, so that society can decide how to handle tobacco in the absence of the campaign of disinformation. It appears possible now, for the first time in decades, that it may happen, that Dr. Jekyll may emerge and Mr. Hyde recede.

CHAPTER

3

THE BURDEN OF KNOWLEDGE

A custom loathsome to the eye, hateful to the nose, harmful to the brain, dangerous to the lungs, and in the black stinking fume thereof nearest resembling the horrible Stygian smoke of the pit that is bottomless.
— King James I, A Counterblaste to Tobacco, 1604

After the crisis of '54, with the scientific and political dogs at their heels, the top companies began a period of sudden discovery. It has been said that the world can only be grasped by action, not by contemplation, that the hand is the cutting edge of the mind. So with the aid of their pursuers, the tobacco companies soon learned more about cigarettes than they had in the previous 100 years of commerce. The cigarette of the early 1950s remained very much like the cigarette of the 1890s. But the conservative companies, roused from their torpor, then began to run hard for the first time since the invention of the cigarette rolling machine, or the discovery of the power of advertising.

What they wanted to do first was to check for themselves, secretly of course, just what the scientific terrorists Wynder and Graham had been doing when they cultivated tumors in animals with cigarette smoke. In fact, one executive for Liggett and Myers, a man with the remarkable name of F.R. Darkis, seemed actually excited by the prospect. Whatever cigarette Wynder had used on his mice, Darkis thought, it was not our cigarettes, not L&M or Chesterfield. So, he wrote hopefully in a 1954 memo just before the companies tried to repeat Wynder's experiments, "If Chesterfield turns out to be negative, and X [used by Wynder] as positive, it would then be possible to say, that by using Dr. Wynder's techniques, Chesterfield did not produce cancer in mice." Imagine the aggressive public relations campaign that he could make out of that!

He added, at the end of the memo, showing just what a naïve conception of the problem tobacco executives had, "if we can eliminate or reduce the carcinogenic agent [singular!] in smoke we will have made real progress."

But there were no trumpets and cymbals heard from the Liggett quarters in 1955 when the experiments were finished. The tobacco company scientists soon found that both Chesterfield and L&M did cause large numbers of tumors in mice. They went a step further and found that tobacco tars caused tumors in rabbits as well. If there was any doubt about whether some companies were willing to use data or lose data, according to their advantage, Liggett's reaction to these findings dispelled that doubt. The results remained secret, and the company scientists slogged on.

(Years later in court, in a landmark case called Cippolone v. Liggett, the issue of these old studies came up again. Kinsley V. Dey, the president of Liggett, was questioned about the tumors caused in the company's mouse painting experiments. Why had the companies done these experiments? The following exchange ensued:

LAWYER: What was the purpose of this?
DEY: To try to reduce tumors on the backs of mice.
LAWYER: It had nothing to do with with health and welfare of human beings? Is that correct?
DEY: That's correct.
LAWYER: How much did the study cost?
DEY: A lot . . . Probably between $15 million and more.
LAWYER: And this was to save rats, right? Or mice? You spent all this money to save mice the problem of developing tumors, is that correct?
DEY: I have stated what we did.

Liggett's partner in research beginning in the 1950s was a company called Arthur D. Little, Inc. ADL was hired to do lab work for the company and continued with basic studies of the hazards of tobacco for several more years. By 1961, the results had gotten only worse. If the data were made public, it would have been the end of the issue for the industry, as everything they did turned out to support the results of the outside "negative" scientists of whom they constantly complained.

In a 1961 paper from Little, stamped "LIMITED, CONFIDENTIAL" which reviewed the results of seven years of work, the matter was put succinctly in the first paragraph:

"There are biologically active materials present in cigarette tobacco. These are a)cancer causing b)cancer promoting c)poisonous d)stimulating, pleasurable, and flavorful."

But still the paper was full of hope. It noted that, although adding chemical treatments to tobacco did not help, nor did inserting chemical reagents in the filters, adding nitrates could cut down the toxicity of cigarettes. Of course, there was the problem that the nitrates themselves were poisonous. Perhaps, the memo suggested, the company could use just enough nitrates to cut down the cancer potential by two-thirds or so. "One-third to one-quarter activity would be a good claim!" the paper crowed. The Little researchers working with company scientists had also succeeded in designing a much safer cigarette, but unfortunately, it was not made chiefly of tobacco and so tasted awful.

The memos from this time do not read as if their authors are deluded or foolish. Rather, they read as if they are obliged to maintain a posture of hope and uncertainty about the evidence before them, and so as they work, they say what is necessary as they carry on with experiments that just might lead them out of the woods.

As it turned out, things were much worse than they imagined, and their belief that the hazardous substances could be removed from cigarettes contained a faulty assumption. It was not fully realized until later that it was not so much the substances in tobacco that made them dangerous, it was that they were *burned*. This turned them into toxic products just before they were drawn into the lungs. In addition, the number of substances which became hazardous on burning was not one or two, but dozens, 43 carcinogens at last count. These could not be removed; burning was the essence of smoking because it released both flavor and nicotine, and it was the essential fact of burning that was hazardous.

Each of the major companies, of course, was going through

the same rapid and disappointing research, all in hopes of escaping the trap the companies had set for themselves.

At Philip Morris, the research director wrote that "at best the mouse work may be indicative" of the hazards but ultimately, "chemical analysis of smoke should give the answer." That was in 1955. By 1961, the company had done that chemical analysis and found 15 cancer-causing substances in cigarette smoke, and another 24 that helped promote tumors. At the end of that 1961 report came the somewhat forlorn plea that, "A medically acceptable, low-carcinogen cigarette may be possible. Its development would require TIME MONEY AND UNFALTERING DETER-MINATION."

This rueful tone appears in the companies' internal documents from time to time after the troubled 1950s, and with it also came the occasional memorandum offering knot-cutting solutions to the Whole Problem.

There was a report in July of 1958, from a Philip Morris scientist, C.V. Mace, to his chief head of research. After noting that "evidence is building up that heavy smoking contributes to lung cancer," he went on to suggest a number of research programs, including one he called "an all-synthetic aerosol to replace tobacco smoke, if necessary. . . . I know this sounds like a wild program, but I'll bet that the first company to produce a cigarette claiming a substantial reduction (say 50 percent less than the present Parliament and Kent) in tars and nicotine, or an ersatz cigarette whose smoke contains no tobacco tars, and with good smoking flavor, will take the market." Dr. Mace went further with his yearning to be free of the evidence: Imagine, he said, what benefits would come to the company that had the "intestinal fortitude to jump on the other side of the fence" admitting that cigarettes are hazardous. "Just look what a wealth of ammunition would be at his disposal" to attack the other companies that did not have safe non-tobacco cigarettes.

"Of course," he wrote, "we would have to be careful to infer that the reason for the change in dress was the continuing evidence linking cigarette smoking with health (problems), and that although the evidence is not altogether irrefutable, we have decided upon this course of action in the public interest."

In 1962, a summit conference on cigarettes and health was held bringing together all the top company researchers under the

British American Tobacco parent—including Brown and Williamson in the U.S. and Imperial Tobacco in Canada.

Since the minutes of the meeting have been preserved, we can listen to the attitudes of the company scientists of more than thirty years ago as they dealt with the issues. They were at a company event, but as the time wore on, you can hear their discomfort with their situation, first surfacing, then being silenced by the voice of business concerns.

Sir Charles Ellis, the most senior scientist present and a man of some reputation outside the company, began with some comments about what they had learned in the laboratory since 1954. It was already clear which compounds were among the bad actors, he said, and these must be taken out. Some compounds cause cancer, he said and others had been found to destroy the cilia in the lungs, perhaps the beginning of emphysema.

He read a letter from Addison Yeaman, a lawyer with the American company, which raised the question whether the companies might be negligent if they "(a) . . . fail to remove the phenols [with a filter], or, (b) . . . fail to warn customers of the product of its potential danger?"

His talk meandered for a bit, and commented on the plight of the smoker: "Smoking is a habit of addiction," he said. "The central fact in this subject is that in sufficient doses, tobacco condensate acts as a carcinogen when painted on the backs of mice, or when injected subcutaneously into rats. . . ."

The chief researchers in the Batco companies that day were unhappy, and were willing to speak at least a bit about what was on their minds.

One Mr. L.C. Laporte got up to say that it was all very well to deny the hazards of smoking to the public, but you could not just tell people, "well these studies are only statistical," and that cancer causation has not yet been proved. He said it would not fly:

"You might have a hard-headed doctor opposite you who would say that your argument had nothing to do with it, that the statistics indicated a connection, and would ask what you intended to do about it? or whether you were just going to sit and wait for years to see if anything happened?"

In a moment of practical philosophy, a fellow named Lynne Reid offered the thought that "No industry was going to accept that its product was toxic, or even believe it to be so, and naturally when the health question was first raised we had to start by denying it at the P.R. level. But by continuing that policy we had got ourselves into a corner and left no room to maneuver. In other words, if we did get a breakthrough and were able to improve our product, we should have to about-face, and this was practically impossible at the P.R. level."

He had already foreseen the coming decades in which, deeply informed of the dangers of tobacco, the companies still would be unable to reverse their public stance. "If we could ease the approach a bit, then when we did make positive contributions we could at least say so without having to crawl behind the door," he said.

Mr. McCormick, the chairman of the company, replied that in Britain they had not yet got themselves in quite that position, though the Americans had. But he said that it was really no use trying to admit the hazard. "It was very difficult when you were asked, as Chairman of a Tobacco Company, to discuss the health question on television. You had not only your own business to consider but the employees throughout the industry, retailers, consumers, farmers growing the leaf, and so on, and you were in a much too responsible position to get up and say: 'I accept that the product which we and all our competitors are putting on the market gives you lung cancer,' whatever you might think privately."

He shrank from the idea of being responsible for endangering the entire company, the entire industry, merely to tell what appeared to be the truth. It was simply an impossible situation.

Sir Charles, according to the minutes, then switched to a more hopeful thought. He began to speak about the positive value of tobacco. The company had begun research on nicotine and how it works in the brain. "It is my conviction that nicotine is a very remarkable, beneficent drug that both helps the body to resist external stress and also can as a result show a pronounced tranquilizing effect. . . . People find that they cannot depend just on their subconscious reactions to meet various environmental strains with which they are confronted: they must have drugs available which they can take when they feel the need. Nicotine is not only a very fine drug, but the technique of administration by smoking has considerable psychological advantages and a built-in control against excessive absorption. It is almost impossible to take an overdose of nicotine in the way it is only too easy to do with sleeping pills." Much work on the positive effects of nicotine was planned, he said.

Dr. Sidney J. Green, chief of research at British American, said it was important to confront the situation to protect the industry. In fact, "he thought we should adopt the attitude that the causal link between smoking and lung cancer was proven, because then at least we could not be any worse off."

McCormick, again the businessman bringing the scientists back to their duty, said this all raised a problem. It was fine to discuss the hazards of smoking, and to think about fixing them. But he asked, if we make safer brands, "how to justify continuing the sale of other brands?"

If the industry made safer cigarettes, "it would be admitting that some of its products already on the market might be harmful. This would create a very difficult public relations situation. The fact was that the industry had slowly been pushed, by Wynder and other people, into the marketing of filter tip brands."

Reid of Australia asked, what are we supposed to say while we wait for our own research to be finished? Maybe we could "at least adopt the attitude that if there were substances in smoke which we felt might possibly be inimical to health, it would be a good idea to remove them. . . ."

Again McCormick jumped in. "How was it proposed to sell such a product, having taken everything out that could be got out?"

Reid said he meant change it only insofar as the flavor was unchanged or better. That was that. The debate was over.

There is nothing which came after those years that added to the tobacco companies' fundamental understanding of the problems with tobacco. They had all they needed in hand already. While company scientists and executives again and again in the years to come wrote hopeful memos about how they might turn the situation around, and expressed the hope that they could admit the problem and go on to new, safe cigarettes, eventually those hopes failed when, as in the Southampton conference, the lawyers and top executives refused to contemplate the move.

I have read tens of thousands of pages of research documents from inside six tobacco companies, and there, scattered throughout the companies are what amount to pleas by the authors of the memos. They want to break out, to bring the companies and their product back into respected society. They do not say it outright, but they show they are tired of hiding in a closet and shouting lies through the door. They are irritated and angry not only at those who criticize them, but at their predicament.

Among the most clear and poignant memos that has come to light is that of Addison Yeaman, the American lawyer for Brown and Williamson mentioned in the research conference in Britain. It was July of 1963, a year after the research conference, and B & W had fresh reports from researchers about a new filter, called "the Griffith filter" after the company's chief researcher. They also had just received detailed scientific reports on nicotine which said that nicotine was addictive, but on the other hand had substantial effects on mood and behavior, creating a "high" that did not feel overwhelming like alcohol or cocaine, but caused a mild lift across many brain systems. It seemed in some ways the ideal drug.

Mr. Yeaman's brief paper is delightful to read not only on its face, but because of the emotions that can be heard running underneath the text, groaning like plumbing in an old house.

As with nearly all tobacco company executives, current and former, no one can talk to him about his paper. I did call him when I first read it. That first call raised my hope; he said he would speak to me if his lawyer was present. But later he reneged.

So all we have to go on, like biblical scholars, is the text itself. In this case, it is five pages, dated July 17, 1963, the year before the U.S. Surgeon General's report that declared smoking, finally, clearly and officially, to cause cancer and other disease. The moment was important. The companies had time to make their public denials, and do much private research, and the lay of the land was clearer than in the days of the Hill and Knowlton gambit. By 1963, at the request of President John Kennedy, the Surgeon General, Luther Terry, had convened a body of the most distinguished scientists and doctors who had not take a position publicly on smoking and health. And, to further prevent bias, Dr. Terry made up a list of candidates for the study commission and asked many parties, including tobacco company representatives, to strike any names they wished, for any reason.

The Surgeon General's committee had been working for a year when Mr. Yeaman sat down to write in the summer of 1963.

There was no doubt what the committee would find; there was a great mass of evidence, more than 10,000 substantial studies, not counting the best work, that is, the material from the companies themselves, supporting the belief that smoking causes much disease. Alternatively, there was no successful line of work showing anything to the contrary.

So Mr. Yeaman and other tobacco executives were a bit nervous as they awaited the Surgeon General's report. Of course, the companies were submitting material to the committee, and making what arguments they could. Liggett and Myers, for example, hired the Arthur D. Little company to write a report from the company point of view.

The ADL report is a remarkable document, because the consultants at first tried to make a credible presentation of the data. In the draft report submitted to Liggett, the paper accepted that smoking directly causes disease: "Basically we accept the inference of a causal relationship between the chemical properties of ingested tobacco smoke and the development of carcinoma. . . ."

It also reported, "All types of smoking are associated with increased mortality from all causes combined. . . . For cigarette smokers who smoke regularly, excess mortality increases with the current number cigarettes smoked . . . excess mortality increases with duration of smoking . . . excess mortality increases steeply with degree of inhalation. . . ." It concluded that cigarettes caused increased death "for coronary artery diseases, for all carcinoma combined, for lung cancer, for genito-urinary system cancers and for cancers of the buccal cavity [mouth and throat]." In addition, it gave a little litany of other trouble caused by cigarettes: "cough, loss of appetite, shortness of breath, nausea or vomiting, blood in stool, pain or discomfort in lower abdominal area, pain or discomfort in chest." Worse, the consultant actually estimated that the number of years of potential life lost due to smoking each year was almost ten times that lost to auto accidents each year.

Needless to say, this document did not make it to the Surgeon General's desk. Liggett executives killed it and submitted instead a paper that, while admitting more than any tobacco company ever has publicly, nevertheless worked to explain away the data. The company submitted it only after obtaining an agreement that it would never be made public.

Addison Yeaman, in his Louisville office, had a different idea. He had just received news of the two large, secret studies on nicotine which showed its positive values, as well as the news of the new filter. The two, he thought, combined to make it possible to change the companies' entire approach to tobacco and health.

"The determination by Batelle [a European lab hired to work for British American Tobacco and sister companies] of the 'tranquilizing' function of nicotine, as received by the human system in the delivered smoke of cigarettes, together with nicotine's possible effect on obesity, delivers to the industry what well may be its first effective instrument of propaganda counter to that of the American Cancer Society, et al, damning cigarettes as having a causal relationship to cancer of the lung." He thought that scientific evidence which showed real, positive benefits from smoking could be a significant weapon in the hands of the tobacco companies. He was suffering from an overload of scientific evidence, from inside and outside the companies, that was uniformly negative. He positively yearned for something else.

The nicotine findings had nothing directly to do with the Surgeon General's report, but "I would submit, however, that the Griffith filter offers the bridge over which the industry might pass from its present terrain of defense to a field for effective counter attack using the Batelle study as the basic weapon. I will assume for purposes of this note that the 'Griffith filter' is one which permits filtration to specification; it filters selectively, both qualitatively and quantitatively. It can deliver taste and nicotine (and nicotine in even more effective form) free of constituent #1 [probably benzo(a)pyrene] to infinity, selectively. I grossly overstate and oversimplify Dr. Griffith's claim deliberately."

He was excited, and began to project an alternative future for the companies. He knew the Surgeon General's report would be damning; after all, the better data at his own fingertips was worse!

"The problem is simple, if the answers are complex. Assume the Surgeon General's Committee concludes (whatever jargon of scientific analysis and to whatever degree specific) that there is real and compelling evidence of a causal — or even a strongly 'predisposing' — relation between smoking and cancer. Cardiovascular disorders will, in all probability, also be found related to smoking. Upon that event, it would seem clear to me that the industry must do two things."

"1. Whatever qualifications we may assert to minimize the impact of the Report, we must face the fact that a responsible and qualified group of previously non-committed scientists and medical authorities have spoken. One would suppose we would not repeat Dr. Little's oft reiterated 'not proven.' One would hope the industry would act affirmatively and not merely defensively. We must, I think, recognize that in defense of the industry and in preservation of its present earnings position, we must either a) disprove the theory of causal relationship or b) discover the carcinogen, co-carcinogens, or whatever, and demonstrate our ability to remove or neutralize them. That means we must embark — in whatever form of organization — on massive and impressively financed research into the etiology of cancer as it relates to the use of tobacco; what constituents or combination of constituents in cigarette smoke cause or are conducive to cancer of the lung. Certainly one would hope to prove there is no etiological factor in smoke but the odds are greatly against success in that effort. At the best, the probabilities are that some combination of constituents of smoke will be found conducive to the onset of cancer or to create an environment in which cancer is more likely to occur."

Making a small confession about previous lies, he said: "The Tobacco Industry Research Committee cannot, in my opinion, provide the vehicle for such research. It was conceived as a public relations gesture and (however undefiled the Scientific Advisory Board and its grants may be) it has functioned as a public relations operation. Moreover, its organization, certainly in the present form, does not allow the breadth of research — cancer, emphysema, cardiovascular disorders, etc. — essential to the protection of the tobacco industry."

This makes clear that if real research will be necessary, then the TIRC simply cannot do it. "I suggest that for the new research effort we enlist the cooperation of the Surgeon General, the Public Health Service, the American Cancer Society, the American Heart Association, American Medical Association, and any and all other responsible health agencies . . . concerned with the question of tobacco and health. The new effort should be conducted by a new organization lavishly financed, autonomous, self-perpetuating, and uncontrolled save that its efforts be confined to the single problem of the relation of tobacco to human health." The very enemies he cites earlier are to be the arbiters. Is there any doubt that, while he knew they were tough, they were also correct?

The course he is suggesting here is also just what the companies promised, and the public thought it was getting a decade earlier with the "Frank Statement to Smokers" and the establishment of the TIRC. Actually, Mr. Yeaman's memo might have been the first frank statement, albeit a little late and held secret until unearthed in 1994.

Here, Mr. Yeaman becomes bold: "Thus to accept its responsibility would, I suggest, free the industry to take a much more aggressive posture to meet attack. It would in particular free the industry to attack the Surgeon General's Report itself by pointing out its gaps and omissions, its reliance on statistics, its lack of clinical evidence, etc. etc. True we might worsen our situation in litigation, but that I would risk in contemplation of the greater benefits to be derived from going on the offensive. My record of advice in this area may well justify the charge of inconsistency, but let me say that so long as the industry does not assume its research responsibility my long-held position would remain unchanged and I would oppose either outright attacks on the Surgeon General's Report or the giving of assurances to the smoking public not supported by research evidence."

He went on, getting more practical, "There is however the problem of what to do until the doctor comes, and this leads me to the second of the two measures I would urge the industry to take:

"2. The Surgeon General's Report will, of course, set off attacks all along the line. Our harsher critics — Senators Moss and Neuberger, the American Cancer Society, et al — will immediately press for all sorts of restrictive and repressive programs:

"a) Public education programs directed particularly at the young.

"b) Much harsher FTC rules in respect of cigarette advertising, with restrictions of the scope and control of content thereof. One might anticipate rules seeking to prevent the use of 'glamour situations', endorsements including those of athletes, prominent entertainment figures, etc., and quite likely an effort to bar tobacco advertising from television and radio.

"c) 'Content' labeling or cautionary legends.

"d) FTC to be given the power of preliminary injunction in respect of cigarette advertising.

"e) Repressive taxation.

"To meet these threats, which will arise not merely at the Federal but at the state level as well, the Tobacco Institute is available. . . . To accomplish anything effective, the Institute needs the leadership of a strong *tobacco figure*, e.g., Albert Clay, Paul Hahn, etc. . . ."

He went on to suggest a clever strategy which, we have seen, has been enormously effective in public and in court. He suggested that one way to blunt the attacks would be, despite the unpleasant taste of doing it, that the companies might issue a warning on packages "such as 'excessive use of this product may be injurious to the health of susceptible persons' and would embody such a legend in pica in its print advertising."

The industry did go on to acquiesce, ten years later, in putting warnings on packages, and successfully argued before the U.S. Supreme Court that the warning relieves the companies of some degree of liability.

"Now at long last I come back to the Batelle report and the Griffith filter," he said. "If Dr. Griffith is no more than on the trail of effective, controlled filtration, we should conduct our planning on the assumption of success. Batelle says: 'The reasons for the pleasure of smoking must be found partly in the relief of anxiety that cigarette smoking brings so constantly, and in such a very short time. This sedative or soothing effect of cigarette smoking and of nicotine is however very different from the "tranquilizing" effect as it was defined by pharmacologists after the discovery of the Rauwolfia alkaloids. . . . Our investigation definitely shows that both kinds of drugs (Rauwolfia alkaloids and nicotine) act quite differently, and that nicotine may be considered (its cardiovascular effects not being contemplated here) as more "beneficial" — or less noxious — than the new tranquilizers, from some very important points of view.'

"Imagine his excitement, in discovering that scientists, who to that moment had done nothing but say tobacco is noxious and dangerous, and he had utterly ignored those warnings, now say that tobacco has not only tranquilizing effects, but *unique* tranquilizing effects. It works more broadly and mildly than what the pharmaceutical companies have come up with.

"Moreover, nicotine is addictive." Now here, you must remember this is a positive attribute. Addictive to Mr. Yeaman meant a dependent population of customers. "We are then, in the business of selling nicotine, an addictive drug effective in the release of stress mechanisms. But cigarettes — we will assume the Surgeon General's Committee to say — despite the beneficent effect of nicotine, have certain unattractive side effects:

1) They cause, or predispose to, lung cancer.

2) They contribute to certain cardiovascular disorders.

3) They may well be truly causative in emphysema, etc.

"We challenge those charges and we have assumed our obligation to determine their truth or falsity by creating the new Tobacco Research Foundation."

This of course was fantasy. He hoped they would create such a foundation. They did not.

"In the meantime (we say) here is our triple, or quadruple or quintuple filter, capable of removing whatever constituent of smoke is currently suspect while delivering full flavor — and incidentally — a nice jolt of nicotine. And if we are the *first* to be able to make and sustain that claim, what price Kent?

"Dare we as a matter of policy make such claims? . . . I would submit that the FTC in the face of 1) the industry's research effort, 2) the truth of our claims, and 3) the 'public interest' in our filter, cannot successfully deny us the right to inform the public."

He then came to the damage done to smokers up to that time. It was a matter of dollars: "As for litigation, it would be my opinion that we would not put ourselves in substantially worsened position and in any event a successful Avalon [profits from the highly filtered cigarette] could be expected to satisfy a number of judgments for damages."

Almost gleefully, he suggested that the company's new research might have to be shared. "Have we an obligation to make our knowledge available to our competitors? If the Griffith claims stand up and when we have perfected the Griffith filter and stocked the necessary machinery, etc., then I suggest there is a strong moral obligation on us to make our knowledge public and free. And think of the kudos. I will be vastly surprised if such disclosure markedly adds to our competitors' knowledge but that is beside the point.

"The point is: On this new terrain, permitting strong offensive action, *we get there fustest with the mostest.*"

This impassioned missive, coming from a company lawyer, is I think convincing. I read it skeptically at first, then I mocked, but by the end I was pulling for Mr. Addison Yeaman, Esq. I thought I could see, played on the screen at the back of his mind, an image of himself, jumping on the table, throwing off the dark cloak he'd been forced to wear, and emerging, not as evil uncloaked, but as the misunderstood hero, to both his colleagues and a suspicious world!

The narrative is chock full of admissions. He believes that cigarettes are hazardous and addictive, and also that the industry has never carried out its moral duty to investigate honestly. He thinks the companies should either do the work and make the admissions, or shut up. He would rather fight honestly and lose a few suits than carry on with business as usual.

Now it may seem remarkable that the leading companies spent so many millions of dollars doing hundreds of studies which prove that cigarettes are highly toxic and cause an array of diseases, but what they were actually looking for was a solution. In at least one case a company researcher has come across a significant hazard of cigarettes, but one not worth studying for commercial reasons. In this case, the company reaction was completely different. The company simply stopped looking into it.

Once launched, the research machinery gathered momentum as it set hundreds of scientists to work obsessively prizing open the biochemical issues. One example from which we have the most complete reports was called Project Janus, of the British American company. Janus, the god facing two ways, reminded the researchers of the two faces of tobacco, although the Janus studies looked mostly at the dark countenance of their product.

The Janus series of experiments alone, though it was essentially devoted to a single topic, nevertheless encompassed building a new laboratory and employing more than 30 workers. It produced about 30 substantial scientific reports between 1965 and 1978. The results were *not* ambiguous. As one company review noted, "over 80% of the mice exposed to a flue-cured blend of tobacco developed tumors. . . ." And in a later review, "Over 70% of mice developed permanent tumors and over 50% developed malignant ones."

With this kind of material in their own desk drawers, it is clearly a testament to the brazenness of company executives that they could step up before Congress, swear an oath, and say, as they did in 1994: It has not been proven. . . .

The days of wanting to know, and of hoping to make use of

their knowledge, were coming to an end. The major companies found out on their own what the trouble was, and that it could not be fixed by simply filtering out the carcinogens and co-carcinogens. Much more radical cigarettes would have to be constructed, and at the major companies there were suggestions of cigarettes with no tobacco at all, or cigarettes with tobacco that was heated but not burned, as well as other radical solutions. Implicit in these proposals is the realization that tobacco flavor could be faked, but nicotine was the essence of the habit and must be preserved. (Perhaps nicotine could even be improved; the companies have spent years looking for other chemicals in the nicotine family which might have the same brain effects but not the dangerous effects on the heart and blood pressure. It is said they have found some candidates.)

As a barometer of the growing worry about what they were finding in their own labs (the concerns never were shown in public) the "tobacco papers" show that the company lawyers began to intrude increasingly in the laboratories. They expressed some alarm at the volume of the negative studies and the way they were flowing freely inside the company research departments. If these documents ever reached the hands of the plaintiffs, they noted, there would be hell to pay.

At last, in Louisville at least, the concern did overwhelm the lawyers and they began desperate acts, assuming courts find they had no right to claim the documents were private.

J. Kendrick Wells, then and now a top lawyer at B&W, wrote a memo on January 17, 1985, after literally years of pleading with the researchers and other executives to keep material tightly held, to make sure lawyers have control of everything. He finally broke down and put to paper a scheme for shipping the dangerous documents out of the country.

The memo was called "Document Retention." He had re-viewed the most damaging biological studies and gave to another executive a list of documents to get rid of: "I had marked certain of the document references with an X. The X designated documents which I suggested were deadwood in the behavioral and biolog-ical studies area. I said that the 'B' series are 'Janus' series studies and should also be considered deadwood.

"I said in the course of my review of scientific documents stored by RD and E [Research, Development and Engineering] a great deal of deadwood had appeared, such as studies of the chemical composition of Canadian tobacco leaf in 1965. [It is not clear that such a boring study was ever among those marked for disappearance.] I suggested that in the context of moving the RD&E facility to the new building and in the context of the building's reference set for smoking and health materials, which contained mainstream scientific materials, RD&E should undertake to remove the deadwood from its files. I said the articles I had suggested were a first pass at removing the deadwood and that RD&E should do additional work to identify and removed deadwood on other subjects.

"I suggested that Earl have the documents indicated on my list pulled, put into boxes and stored in the large basement storage area. I said we would consider shipping the documents to BAT [in England] when we had completed segregating them. I suggested that Earl tell his people that this was part of an effort to remove deadwood from the files and that neither he nor anyone else in the department should make any notes, memos or lists."

This startling admission on paper raises the suspicion that Mr. Wells was not writing the memo voluntarily, that in fact Earl or some other executive had been unwilling to take responsibility for what Mr. Wells was doing, and had asked him to take the blame on paper. Then, should the act ever be discovered, the memo placing the blame on Mr. Wells would also be discovered.

It is not known how much, if any, material was actually dumped overseas in this manner. Worse for the company, developments in the law now have made it unlikely that shipping such files to related but distant affiliates would prevent them from being brought to court, assuming, that is, that the plaintiffs' lawyers could find out they existed. The deadwood memo really seems more an expression of fear and frustration than an effective deceit.

By 1975, five companies had designed and tested successful "safer" cigarettes, including one with a catalyst made of palladium inserted in the filter that would absorb carcinogens, and another that would deliver nicotine in warm air. But by now the companies had come fully round again. They had wanted to strip the hazardous materials from cigarettes, but now found when they had succeeded — it was too late. The companies could no longer afford to offer smokers safer cigarettes.

So each of the top companies put the designs and prototypes in the closet, and closed the door. Gradually, though the companies liked having a rich source of data to use in products and in decision-making, it became obvious that the scientists and their rat labs could no longer offer anything but dangerous data to the companies. As they had decided not to make safer cigarettes, the only place the data could ultimately be used was in court, against them.

So the companies began the dismantling of their scientific establishment.

The elaborate facilities at R.J. Reynolds in Winston-Salem, North Carolina, referred to as the "mouse house," went first. On one day in December, 1970, without warning, the workers at the lab were dismissed, their notebooks were collected by lawyers, and piles of papers were shredded. One man from RJR, Joseph Bumgarner, said he was told that the Surgeon General was already "slitting our throats, we don't need to do it to ourselves" as well.

The British tobacco industry's laboratory at Harrogate was abruptly closed in 1974; that was the end of jointly sponsored research in England.

At Philip Morris, the biology labs were shut down in 1984. Victor DeNoble, a scientist at Philip Morris at the time, said that the only explanation he got was from his superior in the research department, who told him, "that the lab was generating information that the company did not want generated inside the company, that it was information that would not be favorable to the company in litigation." The most important and troublesome trial for tobacco companies to that time, the Rose Cipollone trial in New Jersey, had begun in August of that year.

On the day when the axe fell, April 5, 1984, DeNoble said the department chiefs told everyone not to discuss their work, and were warned not to attempt to publish it. They were told to halt all experiments, kill the laboratory rats, turn off the lab instruments, and give back their security badges by the next morning.

Two of the most active research chiefs in the 1950s and 1960s were Sidney James Green in England, vice president for research of Batco, and in the United States, Robert B. Griffith of B & W. Both ended their careers bitterly, believing both that cigarettes cause disease and that safer cigarettes should be put on the market.

Griffith quit in 1969 because he wanted to "move forward with work on a safer cigarette," according to a report in Louisville's *Courier-Journal*. He was a smoker who had tried to quit and failed. He died of colon cancer, one of the diseases highly correlated with smoking, in 1991 at age 72.

By ten years later, Dr. Green had also quit, and his widow Olwyn Green later told BBC television that he had bitter fights with the Batco board of directors, but she said, "They simply ignored what he told them."

At the time he resigned he sat for a BBC interview, publicly saying what he could not get the company to say: that smoking causes disease: "I'm quite sure it can, and does. . . . I'm quite sure it's a major factor in lung cancer in our society."

He said the industry had failed in its moral responsibility. "The position of the tobacco companies," he said finally, "is dominated by legal considerations. . . . It has retreated behind impossible, perhaps ridiculous, demands for what in PR terms is called scientific proof . . . usually the first reaction of the guilty."

4

NICOTINE FIT

All sin tends to be addictive, and the terminal point of addiction is
what is called damnation.
— W.H. Auden, A *Certain World*, 'Hell,' 1970

Chemical substances tend to be grouped in families according to
the shape of their molecules, and with good reason — what parts
are exposed and whether they are suited to couple with alien
molecules determine their effect in the world. In fact, from a
chemist's point of view, the shape and charge of molecules is the
world as we perceive it. That a table is solid, that a rainbow is
colored are a result of the chemical surface of atoms.

Among the millions of molecules, there are relatively few
that interact with highly-defended territories within the body, and
even more secure areas within the brain.

The family of molecules that is most successful at this is the
family of alkaloids. It makes sense that related plants would produce molecules of similar power, but the alkaloids are an astonishing array of psychoactive substances — heroin, cocaine, nicotine,
caffeine.

Nicotine had been isolated in the 19th century, and experimental work done for decades before the tobacco companies took
up the lab work in the 1930s. Because nicotine was familiar in the
lab for years, the companies' knowledge of its properties was older
and much more certain than that of the other hazards of smoke.

In the tale of cigarettes and lung cancer, we can imagine
that the executives had some hope of escape, and dreamed of
making things all right after cheating for some time. But the tale

of nicotine is different; there is no doubt in their minds. In this story, they aren't lying in hopes things will get better, they are just lying.

There is no subject that has more documentary proof in the "tobacco papers" than that about the effects of nicotine, and about the knowledge of company executives.

To choose one example: the American Tobacco Company. It has not been the target of many news stories and has so far yielded up fewer internal documents than any of the larger companies. (American has recently been absorbed by Brown and Williamson; perhaps now we can expect more leaks.)

In the spring of 1994, Donald Johnston, chief executive of American, went to testify before Congress with the other six chiefs of tobacco companies. He said, as the others did, that the companies do not set nicotine levels, but set tar levels only, so that nicotine levels simply fall wherever they fall, in some kind of industrial accident.

He made this even more explicit in a formal reply to the committee chairman, Henry Waxman, after the hearings: "At no point in the manufacturing process is nicotine content controlled, adjusted, or restored to compensate for nicotine lost during the manufacturing process. . . . At no time in the new product development cycle is nicotine delivery considered as a criteria [sic] for product design, basically because nicotine delivery follows 'tar' delivery and the inventory of tobaccos available for use. . . ."

But the papers from within the company make it clear that these statements, whatever they are intended to mean, bear little relation to daily life in the tobacco business.

A single, brief memo from among the several dozen papers we have from American probably tells the story as well as anything. It is from June, 1974, an early date for detailed manipulation of nicotine, and is from R.M. Irby, the chief of research for the new products division. He is writing casually, about three pages, to answer J.B. McCarthy, American's Executive Vice President. McCarthy had called on the phone, and asked "about our knowledge regarding increasing the nicotine content of reconstituted tobacco."

The company should have known nothing about it, especially way back in 1974, if Mr. Johnson's testimony is correct.

The most common and reliable method of raising nicotine

content for the industry up to that point had been simply including tobacco leaves with higher average nicotine content from the field. (As another American Tobacco research report said, "The selection of types and grades of tobacco can control the amount of nicotine present in the blend. . . .")

But the problem was that, as the levels of tar were being dropped by customer demand, the nicotine was going down as well. Something had to be done, and in fact by the time of the memo, June of 1974, was already being done.

Nowadays, and already in 1974, as much as 20 to 40 percent of the cigarette is not really tobacco leaf. The rod is filled with other things, including a large dollop of "reconstituted tobacco sheet."

(To make this sheet, the workers take leftover stems, scraps and dust, add a bit of real leaf, and chop it all into pulp. All the dark juices are extracted and held on the side. Then, the pulp is pressed into huge paper sheets. When the brown juices are added back, the sheet looks about the color and texture of a brown paper bag from the supermarket. This is then chopped up as if it were leaf. Finally, real leaf and this pulped junk is mixed to make the cigarette. This mixture saves a good deal of money, because this way a large proportion of what's in the cigarette today used to be garbage. It is like getting deeply-discounted tobacco. The problem is that the stems and other debris have low nicotine content, less than half the level of real leaf.)

Natural leaf has plenty of nicotine, more than is used by smokers on average, so there has always been some room to drop tars and allow nicotine to fall as well. But that slack was played out by the 1970s, and the companies were using more and more of the low-nicotine reconstituted sheet. From the early 1960s through the 1980s, the companies developed several ways to maintain enough nicotine so smokers do not feel as if they are sucking stones.

In his summer missive, Mr. Irby replies to the query by saying that the company has the knowledge and technology on hand to bump up the nicotine level of the reconstituted sheet in at least two ways. First, he reports that "compound W" can be added directly. (Compound W was a code for nicotine — In another comic episode from May 14, 1969, company executives had decreed that: "In future our use of nicotine should be referred to as 'Compound w' in our experimental work, reports, and memorandums, either for distribution within the department or for outside distribution.")

Irby wrote that in Lucky Strike and Pall Mall, commercial nicotine had already been added directly to the product to goose it. But the experiment didn't work well; the method appeared too crude and the smoke was too harsh.

(Years of study had already been devoted to the issue. After one study, it was noted, "An increase in the nicotine content of RC tobacco by the direct addition of commercial nicotine does not improve the smoking and taste properties of the product. The principal effect of the added nicotine was an increase in harshness of the RC tobacco without any improvement in the taste or aromatic properties." If nicotine is to be increased, they wrote, then other things must be put in to mask it. In 1968, "Our smoke panel showed an overwhelming preference for the regular blend" over the nicotine-boosted blend. In 1969: added nicotine "has been found to be detrimental to taste and to make a harsher smoking product." It was not the preferred method, but it could be worked.)

So, Dr. Irby, when asked, knew exactly the quantity needed to boost nicotine in cigarettes for just the right effect on smokers: "about 1170 pounds per million pounds of product" to produce a cigarette with "a nicotine content of 1.8% to 1.9%," he wrote. And because of the issue of harshness, some consumer testing and adjustment would be necessary.

The second method he suggested for boosting nicotine in the sheets was "formula modification." He listed the current formula used for making sheet: about half stems, another third or more tobacco scraps, and a bit of real leaf. He said that some scrap components which have low nicotine content can be replaced with scraps that have very high nicotine content — 2–3 times the level of regular leaf — would be all that was necessary. "If the lower-nicotine-containing leaf components such as Turkish can be replaced with high nicotine tobacco such as Malawi sun-cured scrap (5% nicotine), the nicotine content of the resulting RC would be of the order of 1.6% to 1.7%." He further itemized the number of pounds needed, and specified the amount of nicotine that would result in each cigarette from adding different levels of Malawi sun-cured, and was able to note the amount of nicotine *per puff* that would be delivered to a smoker from the change.

As an aside, Mr. Irby noted that after all this maneuvering, another boost of nicotine could be made available to the smoker by adding an additional small amount of one chemical [probably ammonia] to the blend, if the vice president felt this was desirable.

Altogether, this is a remarkable level of knowledge to have on hand for response to a telephone request. There are not dissimilar memos in hand from at least four companies, showing an extraordinary depth of knowledge about nicotine and its fate at various moments from the field to the smoking parlor.

The knowledge was not confined to those in the lower dungeons of the giant tobacco castle, either. There appear in the record occasional talks and other briefings, as top executives come down to the labs, or as lab chiefs visit the executive offices to pass on the latest finds.

One memo in July of 1965, labeled STRICTLY CONFI-DENTIAL, was a report by R.B. Griffith, research chief for Brown and Williamson, to the top executives of his company, and it appears, to chief executives of all the U.S. tobacco giants.

The memo reports that news would soon break in England: the tobacco industry's research there had demonstrated that ciga-rette smoke was carcinogenic, and that its toxicity could be substantially reduced by such things as carbon filters. The industry-supported scientists in England were hot on the trail, and had asked for more money to build new facilities and pursue the dangerous investigation.

To the executives, this meant, as Dr. Griffith said, "the sponsoring companies may be losing control of the operation of this facility" and that the work of their own lab might bring government regulation down on them.

The memo also informed the committee that the biggest push was to "find ways of obtaining maximum nicotine for mini-mum tar." The methods being tried at that moment were adding nicotine powders to tobacco, soaking cigarette paper in nicotine, using chemical additives to boost nicotine release, and finally, altering leaf blends.

The studies of nicotine among the companies were extensive — far beyond anything outside their walls — and were also sometimes a bit wild.

They studied the levels at which nicotine might become

toxic or fatal (in animals), the rate nicotine escapes tobacco to go into smoke, the absorption in the mouth, the lungs and the blood, effect of acidity, the length of time it stays in body, and the full array of physical responses to different doses — from heart rate and skin temperature to alpha brain waves. They studied what happens when smokers withdraw. They ran students through risk-taking experiments to see if nicotine affected their decisions about when to take risks. They conducted scores of tests of mental and physical performance to see whether nicotine could improve any of it.

Among the crazier studies were those begun in Virginia elementary schools, monitoring hyperactive children. These, they said, were anxious and slightly anti-social and so on — just like the profile of a smoker. Perhaps, they speculated, these *are* the smokers of tomorrow, or at least a profile of them. The schools cooperated by turning over students and records for study, though they eventually backed out. In other work, they delivered electric shocks to college students to test their responses on and off nicotine. They collected thousands of butts from dirty ashtrays in public buildings to see how much nicotine ended up in filters. They also swooped down on one small midwestern town where the whole population quit on one day. The study, called by the Philip Morris researchers Project Bird (for cold turkey), had squads of interviewers going house to house to get a mass of data on withdrawal and quitting.

Among the most productive and telling of all the work was called Project Wheat (because it was intended to be the harvest, I think, after years of study of nicotine in the laboratories, both in Louisville and at the parent company's labs in England and Europe). In it, more than a thousand smokers were interviewed in detail about their habits and needs, focusing in particular on what the study termed "inner need" for smoking. The study was "a first step toward testing the hypothesis that a smoker's Inner Need level is related to his preferred nicotine delivery level."

The researchers were looking for that classic marketplace commodity which launches products — the unmet need of the consumer. They first sounded out their customers, then in the second phase of the study designed experimental cigarettes with very different levels of tar and nicotine, to test them on the same customers.

The inner need was defined as smoking to achieve certain

benefits, such as to relieve stress or aid concentration. They looked for substantial correlation between these expressed desires and the actual behavior of their thousand guinea pigs, including the number of cigarettes smoked, the depth of inhaling, and the difficulty smokers have when they try to give up the habit.

"As predicted by the hypothesis, High Need clusters tend to prefer relatively high nicotine cigarettes, their optimum nicotine delivery being higher than that of the Low Need clusters," the report commented.

The researchers had suggested that two of the primary concerns among smokers were at odds with one another — the need for nicotine and the fear of disease. They said that some people had specially high needs for nicotine, and some had specially high worry about disease. But they said it was quite possible that there were some smokers with both high need and high worry, as well as low need and low worry, and each other combination in between. But the cigarettes on the market did not cater to all these groups. "Three of the cigarette types . . . in the model are not currently available . . . but are technically feasible . . . consumers in these three categories account for some 40 percent of those who took part in the first product test. This figure is quoted in order to give some idea of the possible potential for cigarettes of the three types" if they could be put on the market. Each of the categories not available were essentially ones in which nicotine need had been underestimated — for example, those who wanted low tar because of fear but needed at least medium levels of nicotine, and those who wanted only medium tar but had very high needs for nicotine.

Among all the figures who emerge from behind the simple black type of the memos, I felt that one of the most interesting, and probably the most knowledgeable of all on the subject of nicotine, was William Dunn, Jr. of Philip Morris. He sounds like an artisan, and probably has in his memory, not to mention his files, more illicit information on nicotine than anyone else alive. (He *is* alive, in retirement and unwilling to talk to writers.) He was until relatively recently the chief of research for PM, and although we have little idea of the volume and flavor of his full oeuvre, as all but a handful of pages is still secret, there is one memo that will undoubtedly remain a classic no matter how much of his other work emerges in the future.

"Motives and Incentives in Cigarette Smoking," he called it. It was his summary of what went on at a conference (though much of it is his own thought, as we can tell from earlier bits which have nearly identical remarks and reasoning) that was held in 1971 in St. Maarten in the Caribbean. There were 25 scientists or so and experts on nicotine and cigarettes, including psychologists, pharmacologists, and sociologists present, addressing the question, "Why do people smoke?" not long after the companies had carried out a decade or so of intensive work on that and similar topics.

Dunn begins the argument noting (and this is not casual, but comes from actual data) that "If one asks the smoker himself why he smokes, he is most likely to say, 'it's a habit.' If he is intelligent enough, he might be more to the point and say, 'it stimulates me,' or 'it relaxes me.' "

In fact, this hand-waving by smokers only highlights the fact that people have very little access to the inside of their brains and bodies, little ability to observe inner processes. They are guessing from how they behave, not reading from an inner record.

Dunn says that research can elaborate what smokers cannot know at first hand. "Most of the conferees would agree with this proposition: the primary incentive to cigarette smoking is the immediate salutary effect of inhaled smoke upon body function. This is not to suggest that this effect is the only incentive. Smoking is so pervasive of life style that it is inevitable that other secondary incentives should become operative. The conference summarizer, Prof. Seymour Kety of Harvard, used eating as an analogy. Elaborate behavioral rituals, taste preferences, and social institutions have been built around the elemental act of eating, to such an extent that we find pleasure in eating even when not hungry. It would be difficult for us to imagine the fate of eating, were there not ever any nutritive gain involved. It would be even more provocative to speculate about the fate of sex without orgasm. I'd rather not think about it. As with eating and copulating, so it is with smoking. The physiological effect serves as the primary incentive; all other incentives are secondary."

Reflect a moment on this: tobacco executives have testified frequently that nicotine is a mere taste in cigarettes, one of many important features. But there is no evidence in the companies' papers that nicotine was ever handled by the taste departments of the companies. Here, Dr. Dunn—and each company had scientists elaborating the same principle — points out that the core of the behavior of smoking is nicotine pharmacology. The associations and secondary pleasures all come from their link to that main pleasure.

He went on to say that most of those present at the meeting were clear about the central role of nicotine. "The majority of conferees would go even further and accept the proposition that nicotine is the active constituent of cigarette smoke. Without nicotine, the argument goes, there would be no smoking. Some strong evidence can be marshalled to support this argument:

1) No one has ever become a cigarette smoker by smoking cigarettes without nicotine. [Philip Morris tried making a nicotine-free cigarette once, called Next. It proved the point.]

2) Most of the psychological responses to inhaled smoke have been shown to be nicotine-related.

Despite many low-nicotine brand entries into the marketplace, none of them have captured a substantial segment of the market. . . . 94 percent of the cigarettes sold in the U.S. deliver more than 1 mg. of nicotine. 98.5 percent deliver more than .9 mg. . . ."

"Why then is there not a market for nicotine per se, to be eaten, sucked, drunk, injected, inserted or inhaled as a pure aerosol? The answer, and I feel quite strongly about this, is that the cigarette is in fact among the most awe-inspiring examples of the ingenuity of man. Let me explain my conviction.

"The cigarette should be conceived not as a product but as a package. The product is nicotine. The cigarette is but one of many package layers. There is the carton, which contains the pack, which contains the cigarette, which contains the smoke. The smoke is the final package. The smoker must strip off all these package layers to get that which he seeks.

"But consider for a moment what 200 years of trial and error designing has brought in the way of nicotine packaging. Think of the cigarette pack as a storage container for a day's supply of nicotine:

1) It is unobtrusively portable.

2) Its contents are instantly accessible.

3) Dispensing is unobtrusive to most ongoing behavior.

Think of the cigarette as a dispenser for a dose unit of nicotine:

Think of a puff of smoke as the vehicle of nicotine:

4) A convenient 35 cc mouthful contains approximately the right amount of nicotine.

5) The smoker has wide latitude in further calibration: puff volume, puff interval, depth and duration of inhalation. We have recorded wide variability in intake among smokers. Among a group of pack-a-day smokers, some will take in less than the average half-pack smoker, some will take in more than the average two-pack-a-day smoker.

6) Highly absorbable: 97% nicotine retention.

7) Rapid transfer: nicotine delivered to blood stream in 1 to 3 minutes. [This is a considerable underestimate, as a large bolus goes directly from the lungs to the brain in about 8 seconds, then nicotine levels in the blood rise over 1 to 3 minutes.]

8) Non-noxious administration.

"Smoke is beyond question the most optimized vehicle of nicotine and the cigarette the most optimized dispenser of smoke.

"Lest anyone be made unduly apprehensive about this drug-like conceptualization of the cigarette, let me hasten to point out that there are many other vehicles of sought-after agents which dispense in dose units: wine is the vehicle and dispenser of alcohol, tea and coffee are the vehicles and dispensers of caffeine, matches dispense dose units of heat, and money is the storage container, vehicle and dose-dispenser of many things."

Dunn goes on to say that this discussion takes us only the first step; why do people take nicotine into their systems in the first place? Not everyone does, and so the next question is, who is it that seeks nicotine? Drawing on scores of studies of consumers and their personalities as measured by psychological tests — all done by the companies to know their customers in intimate detail — Dunn describes the traits which are different or exaggerated in smokers. He lists many: Smokers are more independent, more anti-social, more extroverted, have poorer mental health, are more impulsive, are more chance-oriented, more emotional, less agreeable, have less strength of character and have a generally higher level of anxiety. They have poorer school performance, use more alcohol, coffee and tea, have more divorces and job changes, and have more car accidents.

The question about who smokes and who does not is more a question about who is unable to resist the quick gain of nicotine now versus the later catastrophic consequences. In simplified form, this means those who have many other small and large pleasures in their lives are likely to be better at resisting nicotine's lure. So it is that artists and writers are over-represented among smokers: they are also depressives and seek all sorts of counter-pleasures to their mental moods.

As Dunn says, the list, and it is a very long list, of things which happen to the body and brain when nicotine is taken in, is strikingly like the list of things which happen to the body when there is emotional arousal, such as joy, fear, or anger. "Is this perhaps the goal of the smoker, to achieve a body state which mimics emotional arousal?" asks Dr. Dunn. It is a fact that smoking occurs at a much greater rate and more intensely, that is, more nicotine is taken in, during times of great stress.

Because the tobacco battles are economic war, a reporter cannot simply call the companies and get answers to questions. The companies have master strategists who are paid fantastic sums to put out media fires. It is like hiring a professional killer, adept at all the arts of fighting to take on each farmer who comes by with a challenge. (From my childhood, I recall the Seven Samurai, turned into the Magnificent Seven, the tale of farmers helpless against a small army of well-equipped professional bandits. The farmers got together and hired seven professionals of their own to preserve their fields and families. Something like this has happened in tobacco: the hotshot lawyers and consultants have joined the anti-tobacco side. There are now professionals, though perhaps not the same level of weaponry and supplies, on both sides. Fair enough. If one were to cast them, the seven heroes of the anti-tobacco campaigners might be: Henry Waxman, David Kessler, Cliff Douglas, Greg Connolly, Richard Daynard, Stan Glantz, Alan Blum.)

To get a sense of just what sort of tactics are used, one may take a routine example of charge and countercharge from a *Wall Street Journal* piece on nicotine and ammonia during the fall of 1995.

First, the major companies have learned through exhaustive and detailed research that smokers have different nicotine "need" levels. Smokers *must* be able to get the amount they desire, or they'll quit your brand quickly. So there is a lower limit of nicotine which the companies must not drop below ... and this is the amount that smokers have *available* to them. Note that this is not the same as the total amount in the cigarette, nor is it the amount measured as delivered by the FTC machine smoking tests, nor is it even the amount absorbed by the smoker. It is what the cigarette offers to the smoker, whether he takes it or not, from this cigarette or from every other one. This minimum availability is crucial.

The trouble is, as companies continue to lower the amount of tar delivered by a cigarette, most of the methods used to lower tar also lower the nicotine offered to smokers. So, the companies must compensate. Early on, they tried just squirting nicotine on the tobacco leaf to keep the levels up. That didn't work well, so they fell back on other methods. They used leaf that has higher nicotine levels to start with, and this remains the chief tool for selecting nicotine levels in cigarettes.

Once there in the mouth, acidity matters: acid environs tend to deter absorption, but less acidic, or base environs, tend to aid the transport of nicotine across the boundaries of the cells. Thus "free basing," a practice we know from cocaine use, is precisely what the companies offer smokers when they change the acidity of the smoke.

They also found that much of the nicotine in a burning cigarette is not actually released. It is bound up chemically to other chemicals inside the cells of the leaf. To get to a smoker, it needs to be free of other chemical bonds.

Ammonia, in various forms, when added to the tobacco provides the key. It frees up about twice as much of the nicotine. Thus, if the cigarette has little nicotine, but ammonia is added, then more of what is there is being offered to the smoker.

Keep the nicotine up by blending, then make sure that the chemistry of the smoke is right to deliver all that's there. Waste not, want not.

So when the *Wall Street Journal* asked about whether the companies use ammonia to deliver more nicotine to smokers, the honest answer from the companies would have been, yes, of course. But they couldn't say this, because it suggests that they are carefully *dosing* smokers, which puts them in the pharmaceutical business.

So instead they answer, as did Philip Morris, the company "does not use ammonia in the cigarette manufacturing process to increase the amount of nicotine inhaled by the smoker or to affect the rate of absorption of nicotine in the bloodstream of the smoker." In a quick reading, this is simply a lie. However, and remember that it is lawyers making up this language, on closer reading what they are saying is this: they are only making *available* a certain basic amount of nicotine, not trying to make smokers take in more, or absorb more. This is what they will argue in court, if they are pressed to the wall by effective plaintiffs' lawyers. Of course, it has not come up before now, because the plaintiffs' lawyers have not had the documents to show what the companies are doing, nor have they been up to speed on cigarette manufacturing strategies.

In some ways, the whole matter of nicotine seems both serious and silly at the same time. One of the more surprising conversations I have had was in interviewing Jeffrey Wigand, former chief of research at Brown and Williamson, some months before he was made famous as CBS's anonymous source. He described to me two odd debates within the company: One when business planners were thinking of buying a nicotine patch company; they decided against it because it would embarrass them too much to own both ends of the nicotine trade—hooking and unhooking smokers. A second odd moment was when the company contemplated but decided against manufacturing cigarette papers. Virtually all cigarette papers sold these days are used to roll marijuana. Brown and Williamson employees, apparently without self-consciousness, expressed some anger that top management would consider putting them in the "drug" business.

These debates were internal. Externally, on the subject of nicotine, we have testimony at great length from chief executive Thomas Sandefur. He testified before Congress that he did not believe nicotine was addictive, but that it was in cigarettes just for the taste.

Rep. Henry Waxman, chairman of the committee at the time, had asked for all the company's documents, over its entire history, on the subject of nicotine. The company turned over some boxes full of paper and said it was everything.

Mr. Waxman asked why in all those documents nicotine is referred to as addictive, and as a drug, repeatedly. He asked if Mr. Sandefur disagreed with what the company scientists were saying in the documents.

"Yes, sir, I would. I absolutely would," Mr. Sandefur said. A short and slightly pudgy fellow, Mr. Sandefur on that day was confident and feisty.

He was one of the "post-crisis" executives in the tobacco industry. The Surgeon General's report to the nation, confirming officially the hazards of smoking in 1964, was a turning point both within and without the industry. The company executives who had fought for a decade to hide the effects of smoking had begun their work in a different world, one where smoking was more than acceptable, it was fashionable and proud. They had wanted to believe that smoking really couldn't be as bad as the doctors were saying. They had wanted to remove whatever hazards they could find in cigarettes, albeit secretly. They had some hope that things could be different for the industry and for smokers. But the next generation of executives came into the business in a different land. After 1964, they began careers in a trade that was known to be hazardous, companies that were suspected of widespread deceit, and a smoking habit that was fast losing its glamour. These executives came in with no illusions; they learned from the beginning in their careers that tobacco executives did not say certain things in public, and were required to say others, whether those statements were true or not. It was simply part of the business. One lawyer who worked for tobacco companies put it this way: It's like being a defense lawyer. Your job is to go to court and say anything to help your client. Most of the time you know he's guilty. But you have to carry on. It's the same with tobacco. The lying about health hazards is a necessary part of the defense.

Among those who entered the industry after the Surgeon General's report of 1964, was Sandefur.

On the day when Sandefur was testifying about nicotine in Congress, June 23, 1994, after trying to press Sandefur for some time, Mr. Waxman piled the stack of nicotine research papers from Sandefur's company up on the dais.

"And these documents," Waxman said, "let me put them right down here — these documents are research projects undertaken by Brown and Williamson, or BAT, and here is one called 'The Fate of Nicotine in the Body.' Another one is called 'Nicotine in Smoke and Human Physiological Response.' Or, 'The Effect of Puff Volume on Extractable Nicotine.' . . . Here's one called 'Human Smoking Studies — Acute Effect of Cigarette

Smoke on Brain Wave Alpha Rhythm.' What does alpha brain wave rhythm have to do with taste?" Waxman asked.

SANDEFUR: I'm not familiar with that study, Mr. Chairman.

WAXMAN: This is from Louisville, Kentucky, and it was submitted to us by your company.

SANDEFUR: Mr. Chairman, those documents were asked for by the committee, and it is my understanding that we were asked for any documents that we had in our files. Our scientists are responsible for staying abreast of any work done in the area of smoking and health worldwide, no matter who does the work. And they have an opportunity to read those reports and take a . . .

WAXMAN: Mr. Sandefur?

SANDEFUR: Yes, sir?

WAXMAN: Excuse me for interrupting you, but these were research activities in which Brown and Williamson scientists joined with BATCo scientists in conferences. There is never an indication in any of these that the Brown and Williamson scientists disagreed with the research conclusions or even the research premises. But what all this shows is that Brown and Williamson has had an intense interest for many decades about the pharmacological impacts of nicotine. Not a single one of these documents talks about studying the taste of nicotine, only the drug-like impact of nicotine in cigarettes in the brain, in the brain waves, in the central nervous system. Do you imagine that you taste something in your central nervous system?

SANDEFUR: Mr. Chairman, I would beg to differ with you. If you had asked for documents about taste, we'd have sent you documents about taste. If you'd have asked about documents about nicotine, we'd — I mean, about tar, we'd have sent you that.

WAXMAN: We asked you for documents about nicotine, so if you have documents about nicotine and taste, they should be in this pile.

SANDEFUR: Well, I'm sure our lawyers — I hadn't gone through those documents, Mr. Chairman. I'm sure our lawyers complied with the request of the subcommittee.

WAXMAN: I think they did.

SANDEFUR: Yes.

5

DEATH OF THE CIGARETTE

You can fool too many of the people too much of the time.
—James Thurber, *Fables for Our Time*, 1940

One of the other casualties of the tobacco wars and the campaign of disinformation has been the much-loved cigarette itself. The packs of smokes now sold in stores are not genuine cigarettes, but have become devices with half the tobacco leaf that are stuffed with filters, riddled with holes and soaked in additives. And they cost more.

The death of the real cigarette was spurred by the same events as the tobacco-and-health crisis. There was an urgent need to know in industry about the elements of their product, and an urgent wish to apply some kind of new technology to cigarettes to relieve the burden of fear that smokers had. The research on hazards and nicotine, once begun, changed the cigarette radically. The companies learned that, although they could not make a much safer cigarette for legal reasons, they *could* make a much cheaper, half-artificial cigarette and get away with it.

The integrity of the cigarette—just tobacco rolled in paper—was violated for the first time with the addition of a filter, out of concern for health, in 1950. It is odd to speculate about, but it appears that if the companies had told the truth from the 1950s on, they would have been able to continue to market genuine, good cigarettes at the same time they sold "healthier" varieties.

The cigarette of the past—amber shreds of tobacco leaf, julienned, and wrapped in white paper—no longer exists in modern commerce. An artful product, it depended to begin with on the aroma of tobacco, which is one among relatively few flavors of greatness. (The number is limited by the human taste and smell boundaries. Other animals do better — rats can take in and recognize many times the odors a human can. Oh to be a rat in a perfumery in the south of France!) Among the more famous and moving scents are those of brewing coffee, fresh bread, shaved cocoa, and lit tobacco. And maybe lemon, vanilla, and licorice. Perhaps garlic and fried onion in a moment of hunger?

Creating a cigarette began with the blending of tobaccos, which partakes of both science and the senses, and it was not unlike the art of making fine wine, brewing a flavorful beer, or concocting a heady perfume. As in other sensual arts, the first variable is the plant in its locale — different soils and different species of plant produce widely differing tobacco taste. Temperate to warm climes are best. The flavors and colors of tobacco range from the black, strong flavors of some Oriental (in the old sense, it actually refers to Turkish and similar kinds) to the light, yellow and mild tobaccos that are fire-cured in Virginia and North Carolina, and which go by the name of "bright". Until recently it was only the large middle leaves of the tall plants that were counted as suitable for cigarettes. After they are picked, they are cured (warmed) and aged to increase their sugar and maintain the moisture in the leaf.

Blenders of tobacco, like the craftsmen who make wine, must work toward a balanced flavor and content. We cannot contemplate a wine with a balanced flavor but no alcohol, which imparts a lovely warmth and sense of well-being in the brain. It is no different with tobacco (except perhaps that the tobacco blenders have disowned their key ingredient). The art of tobacco might be better appreciated were it not for this.

The art of tobacco began with native Americans who worked generation by generation to refine its properties. The species they finally settled on was what we now call the *Nicotiana rustica*, a leaf with a very high level of nicotine, twice or more the amount in standard American tobaccos of today, and several times more than that of the Oriental types. It also had the full, strong flavor of the sweet, smoked leaves. These people knew what they were doing; they liked the high-nicotine variety and they used it. Europeans, though, on first tasting the stuff, found it had a high "impact" — the jolt of bitter, acid-like sensation of nicotine at the back of the mouth. It was hard to take at first, as today's children find it hard to take the high-nicotine brands of cigarette or of chewing tobacco and so opt for the conveniently provided low-nicotine varieties. In chewing tobacco, they can get from U.S. Tobacco (Skoal Bandits) a low-nicotine brand, and cherry-flavored to boot, until their bodies and brains have become accustomed to regular doses of these highly toxic substances. Smokers develop, so to speak, calluses of their physical and emotional systems. Native Americans had this accommodation built into their culture, were introduced early to the importance of tobacco, and so could handle the rustic tobaccos.

History suggests that it was John Rolfe, and perhaps more likely Pocahontas and her family, who realized that a milder species of tobacco from the Caribbean, *Nicotiana tabacum*, might serve the uneducated European tastes better. This variety contained enough nicotine to be effective in social use (it would not have been useful for the intoxicating, hallucinogenic sessions which native Americans needed for their religious ceremonies), and still had the aroma much desired by smokers.

Rolfe's discovery, combined with another in the nineteenth century when a fellow fell asleep when he was supposed to be warming the fresh tobacco and discovered a new kind of curing, has determined the taste of much of the world since then — the mild and sweet Bright tobacco, yellow-gold leaf cured over heat, was the result.

In addition to the type of plant and the region from which it comes, the central concern of the blender is the "stalk position" of the leaves. In modern handbooks on cigarette making this is the most prominent feature, for a number of reasons. The leaves near the dirt are smaller, often yellow, and contain less flavor and much less nicotine. The middle to upper leaves — large, green and nicotine-rich — are the desirable ones.

When choosing tobacco, some plant-types are chosen for their full flavor or rich aroma. As it happens, these are not the ones with high nicotine, so a blender must balance features. Further, while relatively high nicotine is essential, it is important to defeat its "taste." Despite the public pronouncements of the companies, the testimony of their experts is that nicotine is not a taste at all, but a harsh impact. Smokers come to recognize it, and expect that this hit at the back of the throat will indicate the presence of their most desired ingredient, but neither smokers in company surveys nor blenders mistake this signal for real taste, which comes from the aroma.

(In fact, in company organizational sheets, the nicotine work is handled entirely outside the flavor departments; nicotine research and flavor research are separate.)

So the different elements of the cigarettes are played against one another: Nicotine's harshness is lessened by adding sugar or moisturizers. But many elements are important here: the size of the tobacco or its substitute, the shreds of reconstituted sheet, affect aroma (bigger shreds are better) but add more tar. A cigarette without enough moisturizers will taste harsh, and also burn too fast for what smokers are used to. According to cigarette design expert Colin Browne of the University of North Carolina, it is even said among blenders that an oval cigarette gives more aroma and flavor than a round one. The current mix of tobaccos in the American-style cigarette is burley (20 percent), Virginia (30), Maryland (2), and Oriental (10). This is only the real leaf, and does not count all the trash (literally) used as "fillers" in the cigarette. For the cigarette as a whole, the general proportions are: 60 percent genuine cut leaf, 20 percent "reconstituted" tobacco, 10 percent small chopped stems, and 10 percent flavoring and humectants.

In recent years, the industry has gone to even more exotic forms of tobacco manipulation, including "tobacco expansion" in which volatile materials are pumped into cells and then rapidly removed. The tobacco bloats like puffed rice, expanding the volume so less may be used per cigarette.

The largest percent of smoke in the modern cigarette comes from Bright Yellow, Virginia, flue-cured tobacco which has an acidic smoke of light aroma with medium nicotine content.

Next level down are burley and Maryland types which are alkaline, with a fuller aroma, and higher nicotine content. These air-cured tobaccos are also highly absorbent, an important feature because you can add many flavorings or "casings," usually sugar solutions. Maryland tobacco is heavy in fiber, so gives good burning characteristics to the blend. Oriental tobacco, low in nicotine, is added because of its strong aroma but relatively mild flavor.

Flavors have been added to tobacco for hundreds of years,

beginning for Europeans at least with the Spanish sailors who sprinkled licorice water on cigarettes to preserve them; they also altered the flavor, and licorice has been there ever since. After sugar, the most common flavorings are cocoa and licorice "casings."

After tobacco leaf is shredded to make cigarettes, perfume is added, that is, alcohol with scents from natural ingredients are sprayed on. These supply aroma to the package as well as the smoke from the cigarette. Sometimes, flavoring is also added to the filter, so it comes out with the smoke.

Paper contains the rolled tobacco, but also helps control the amount of smoke that comes out by the amount of air it admits through its porosity, and thus also controls the number of puffs available because of its faster or slower rate of burning.

The filter, as it has developed, gives a neat appearance to the cigarette, keeping tobacco off the tongue and lips, and keeping the end from collapsing with saliva, as it used to do even to smokers like Bogart and Dietrich.

After all this, the amount of smoke taken into the body is not directly related to the amount of material in the cigarette. It is related, instead, to the way the smoker puffs — how many puffs per cigarette, how much volume of smoke is taken in at each puff, the length of time the smoke is held in the mouth, and finally the depth of the inhalation into the lungs.

This means that "low tar" cigarettes simply don't work as a health concept. Puffing less or differently on a high tar cigarette might well be more effective. For example, Dr. Lynn Kozlowski at the University of Pennsylvania has done research which shows that a large proportion of smokers block the holes, and many of them do it intentionally. One extreme example he noted was the Players Ultra Mild, normally a 0.8 mg tar cigarette, which with the holes blocked is transformed into a cigarette delivering 28.5 mg of tar. As David Krogh, author of Smoking, the Artificial Passion, comments, "This is nearly as much of the carcinogenic sludge you would have gotten smoking a straight Camel about 1955."

But as an advertising concept, "low tar" does very well, because it appeals to smokers' fears. Those most concerned about getting less tar may not get less tar, but they feel better about it.

Though the modern cigarette is much altered and degraded

from the real thing, the disguises have been artful, so that the dust (actually swept off the floor) and wasted stems added back to the blend are colored to look like leaf, and re-flavored to give them backbone. The cigarette of today is in fact only about 60 percent shredded tobacco leaves. The rest is disguised, flavorful junk added to lower the cost of making the cigarette while maintaining its aromatic pretense.

Altogether, this is getting to be a rather bad deal for smokers, farmers, and the government tax collectors.

Because of the creation of filters, expanded and recon-stituted tobacco, among other things, the total amount of tobacco it takes to make a cigarette has dropped drastically — by agri-cultural statistics, from 2.6 pounds per thousand cigarettes in 1955, to 1.7 pounds per thousand cigarettes in 1982.

Agriculture Department tobacco analyst, and perhaps the top man on economic statistics of tobacco in the world, Vernor Grise, says that despite the appearance on the market of cheap, "generic" brands (actually made by the same companies), "the price of cigarettes on average has continued to go up, and the percentage of income spent on them has continued to rise."

In other words, fewer cigarettes are being sold for more money. (There were a total of 640 billion cigarettes produced in 1981 at the peak of production. Now even with increasing popula-tion, the total volume is down to 510 billion, as of 1991. The companies must make up the difference by increasing price or decreasing the cost of components.)

The companies are crowding out both farmers and the government in getting their share of those dollars as well. Between 1980 and 1991, for example, Grise notes that the farmers' take on each cigarette is down from 7 cents to 3 cents per dollar. The government's take is down from 34 cents to 25 cents per dollar. At the same time, the companies' take is rising rapidly, from 37 to 50 cents per dollar. And this is after an already-steep price rise: wholesale cigarette prices went up 135 percent from 1950 to 1980, then rose 267 percent between 1980 and 1991.

C H A P T E R

6

FOR STARTERS

Yes, this world is flat and boring; as for the other, bullshit! I myself go resigned to my fate, without hope, and to kill time while awaiting death, I smoke slender cigarettes thumbing my nose at the gods.
— Jules LaForgue, 1880, France, "La Cigarette" quoted from
Cigarettes Are Sublime

When I first began to write about tobacco as a regular beat at the *New York Times*, I noticed something which puzzled me: the industry answers to routine questions were predictable on every subject, except children. When this topic arose I noted a slight change in tone. I had already learned that tobacco men and women these days don't mind being rather frank in private conversation about the diseases and addiction associated with smoking. After all, the companies are still profitable, have political potency equal to that of any other group in society, and have a strong record of defending themselves against claims by injured smokers. There should be a sense of confidence. But that confidence flags when the topic turns to children. The company people become uneasy; they bristle defensively, or else fall into silence. It would be a while before I discovered the reason for this little oddity.

It is commonly said that the great attraction of the cigarette for children is that it is forbidden. "Cigarette smoking begins under the sign of the illicit," as Richard Klein puts it. "Since moralists, no less than doctors, have disapproved of tobacco from its introduction, its use constitutes a form of defiance of authority, of the laws of man and God."

There is defiance, an experiment with disobedience, but in real life it is not just the adolescent and his God at odds. Lurking behind the tree, in the background of the tableau is the agent of the tobacco trade. Unlike the tempter in Eden, the tobacco agents come to their role reluctantly. If the companies could choose, they would not intentionally lure children into smoking. Matters would be simpler if they could keep the whole business between adults and not worry about the young ones.

Unfortunately, and this is still unappreciated, it is not possible to run a cigarette business without actively working the sidewalks where the children are. This is the source of the tobacco industry's discomfort.

The trouble arises from two facts peculiar to the industry. The first is obvious enough, and in private documents beginning in the early 1960s, executives have spoken plainly about their awareness of it: the reason that tobacco is ingested steadily, over many years — not just occasionally, not just tried out — is that the nicotine in tobacco is fiercely addictive. In unguarded moments, even tobacco executives, not to appear as fools who don't understand what they are doing, acknowledge this fact of business.

To bracket the period with acknowledgments:

From 1963, Sir Charles Ellis of the British American Tobacco Company spoke of smoking as "a habit of addiction," and his American colleague Addison Yeaman wrote that nicotine "is addictive. We are, then, in the business of selling nicotine, an addictive drug effective in the release of stress mechanisms."

A more recent example, from the fall of 1994, is the commentary of Ross Johnson, at one time the chief executive officer of R.J. Reynolds Tobacco. While he held that job, he did his duty and denied the hazards of smoking and the addictive nature of it. But after he left, he was interviewed for a profile in the *Wall Street Journal*. His business acumen was noted. He was asked about whether nicotine is addictive. Outside the closed circle of the tobacco industry, he could be plain: "Of course it's addictive. That's why you smoke the stuff."

The exercise of trying to corner executives into admitting what is obvious to others has limited value, of course. But here is the second peculiar fact about the tobacco trade, which, when combined with the first, makes the companies vulnerable in both politics and law:

This addiction, fundamental to the trade, does not develop among adults. Among those over the age of 21 who take up smoking for the first time, more than 90 percent soon drop it completely. It takes more than a year, and sometimes up to three years, to establish a nicotine addiction; adults simply don't stick with it. If it were true that the companies steer clear of children, as they say, the entire industry would collapse within a single generation.

Put in market terms, the most important datum of the tobacco trade is that, among those who will be their customers for life, 89 percent have already become their customers by age 19. In fact three-quarters had already joined the ranks of users by age 17.

This knowledge appears in documents from inside certain tobacco companies. The secret of how and when nicotine addiction develops, why it does not develop in adults, and even how companies might make use of these facts, has been learned only gradually over the years by the companies, but most clearly and intensively in the wave of research that came after the scares of 1954.

Thus, the reason this topic is different from all other topics is that it is both the most crucial of all issues to the continued business, and the issue of greatest exposure for the industry. What an awful conjunction of bright and dark planets!

Because of the companies' fears, over the years the tobacco folks have become less and less candid even in private about the fact that they cannot run their businesses without the children.

If you look into their files, to try to find out what they had in mind when they sent advertising messages sailing on the pages of colored magazines, or across the air to receivers, you can see that the concern about children has always been there. Just how young starting smokers are, and just why and how they started, may not have been entirely clear until after 1960. But the trial-and-error efforts which gradually homed in on the young are there in the record beginning just after World War I. Richard Pollay, a soft-spoken marketing professor at the University of British Columbia in Vancouver, has delved into this history and retold some of the tales of cigarettes from those years. He said that in 1929, Lucky Strikes showed a young man in short pants "breaking the chains of the past" as the ad said, and referred to an "ancient prejudice removed" as the boy reached for a cigarette from an open pack.

J. Walter Thompson advertising agency worked on Old Golds, and in their marketing archives Pollay found campaigns among college students in 1941 and a research plan to find out more about "Youth interest in radio programs . . . a survey of radio listening for 'boys and girls' and radio preferences among 'teenage boys and girls.' "

In 1950, a *U.S. Tobacco Journal* article noted that even though the industry had been extraordinarily successful in making cigarettes glamorous, and had introduced them to nearly half the adult population, "A massive potential market still exists among women and young adults, cigarette industry leaders agreed, acknowledging that recruitment of these millions of prospective smokers comprises the major objective for the immediate future and on a long term basis as well."

The comics were a popular medium for tobacco advertising, and animated and other cartoon characters were used long before Joe Camel appeared in 1988. Lucky Strike had an animated character on television in the 1950s, Philip Morris used cartoons to advertise cigarettes on the *I Love Lucy* show; animated versions of the *Honeymooners'* Jackie Gleason and Art Carney sold Old Gold.

Chesterfield for some time printed up high school football programs for the game, free in return for a two-page centerfold Chesterfield ad which also contained the game score card. Old Gold gave textbook covers with school names and logos on the front, and an Old Gold ad on the back; they provided this service for 1,800 colleges, and more than 8,000 of the nation's 25,000 high schools.

By 1955, the grim health-related advertising (Philip Morris, "The cigarette that takes the fear out of smoking.") about doctors, sore throats, and cancer scares had begun to pass, and the industry was ready with the beginning of what is probably the most successful and long-running ad campaign in tobacco history. It began with a cigarette that had a classy but effeminate name, Marlboro, which had been advertised as a woman's product ("Mild as May").

The early images used to move the cigarette from female to male psyches around the country were images of a man with a tattoo. George Weissman and Jack Landry of Philip Morris in the late 1950s then found with extensive research that young male adolescents picked up smoking because they wanted something which showed independence from their parents. They needed a badge that would not fail to tell others that this was not a kid under his parents' control. Landry, working with Leo Burnett advertising agency, came up with, as they told one writer, "commercials that would turn rookie smokers on to Marlboro . . . the right image to capture the youth market's fancy . . . a perfect symbol of independence and individualistic rebellion." With this in mind, they made some unusual choices. Even though there appeared to be higher readership scores for the tattooed man, they felt that he was a little too sophisticated an image, and appealed to slightly older men. But images of a cowboy caught the attention of those a little younger, and they went with it.

They were trying to portray a rugged, vigorous and self-contained man, alone and not under the supervision of anyone. This is precisely who the target audience of smokers-to-be were *not*. It was a campaign about aspirations, not reality. The campaign was backed up with massive research by Elmo Roper, including a survey sampling 10,000 smokers, the largest done to that time. They went back to the field again and again, pre-testing each message.

As one executive who worked on Marlboro said, "When you see teenage boys — people the cigarette companies aren't supposed to be targeting in the first place — going crazy for this guy, you know they're hitting their target."

After the Second World War, there was a gradual decline in smoking among men, until this campaign helped turn the figures around in the middle to late 1960s. Analysis shows that the increases in smoking during that time came mostly in those between ages 16 and 18, while those both older and younger did not increase.

The Marlboro Man soon began to capture the biggest percentage of starters every year, and that meant, as the starters aged, that the company had the best selling cigarette in the world. The campaign hit the modern starters just right, psychologically, as Camels are just now beginning to do.

The surge of smoking among the young, and campaigns rather openly targeted at young people, came at the same time as the Surgeon General's Report of 1964 in which cigarettes were officially declared to be the cause of disease and death. The industry felt the need to appear as if it were doing something about the "smoking controversy," and so they launched a voluntary code of marketing and advertising. It promised the industry would never advertise or market to children. And in fact, they appointed a public watchdog over the industry, one who could levy large fines if the companies violated their own voluntary rules.

The *New York Times* reported at the time that "The nation's major cigarette companies have agreed on a cigarette advertising code that would be enforced by an independent administrator. The administrator . . . would have 'complete and final authority' over cigarette advertising, including the power to impose fines of up to $100,000 on violators."

The code banned advertising and marketing directed mainly at those under 21 years old. (By that definition, much of the current promotion of Camels and Marlboro, even according to their own documents and public admissions, would be improper and would draw a fine.)

In fact, no violations and fines were ever levied, and the two administrators who tried the job quit because the companies were not serious. Finally, the companies themselves scuttled the gesture. From that point on, the companies simply published a voluntary code and *claimed* that they were observing it; this was much less trouble.

The marketing to youth went on, largely undisturbed. In post-1960 targeting of youth, Philip Morris had the edge with, among other things, 166 "campus representatives" at college — students paid $50 a month to spread good will and free cigarettes among their fellow students. By 1963, just before the companies swore never to target young people again, among 850 college newspapers, cigarette ads accounted for 40 percent of the papers' entire ad revenues.

The Luckies campaign which pitched "Luckies separate the men from the boys, but not from the girls" was an early example of an appeal to the youngest males. Created by Batten, Barton, Durstin and Osborn advertising agency, it was attacked even by advertising trade journals such as *Printers Ink* and *Advertising Age* as callous, cynical and exploitative.

The 1960 marketing goals for Pall Mall noted in an American Tobacco Company document were "to increase the percentage of smokers who think of the brand as being 'for someone just starting to smoke' " and "to increase the proportion of beginning smokers who smoke Pall Mall." (Sullivan Stauffer Cowell and Bayles, marketing report 1964.)

After the huge success of Marlboro with its "positioning" as a cigarette of masculine independence, the company tried to duplicate the success with young girls, and created Virginia Slims. Other companies quickly followed with Eve and Silva Thins.

Beginning in 1967, the ads targeting women began in large numbers. The famous theme, "You've come a long way baby" was used. And, abruptly in 1967, the number of girls under 18 who started smoking shot up. This initiation peaked around 1973, at about the same time as the sales of these brands peaked.

In data collected by Dr. John Pierce of the University of California at San Diego, this period shows an interesting anomaly. Among girls over 18, the figures for starting smoking were stable, with only a slight increase between 1944 and 1960. Then the curve dives downward: as Pierce says, these older youths were listening to the news of cigarette hazards, and fewer started. But for girls 14 to 17 years old, the pattern is different: There was a steadily, slowly increasing number of starters from 1944 to 1967. Then, from 1967, coinciding with the new ad campaigns targeting young girls, the girls 11 to 17 years old showed a sudden, large rise.

The jump was 110 percent in 12-year-olds; 55 percent among 13-year-olds; 70 percent among 14-year-olds; 75 percent among 15-year-olds; 55 percent among 16-year-olds; and 35 percent among 17-year-olds.

Those over age 17 showed no increase, but instead the steady decline continued. So the ad blitz targeting girls either was fantastically successful, if the companies were aiming at girls 17 and under, or the campaign was a complete disaster, missing altogether the company's stated target of young adults over 21.

During this period, 1967 to 1975, billions of dollars of sales accumulated for Virginia Slims, Silva, and Eve. These were all new brands, which went from nothing in 1967 to $16 billion in 1976 sales. After that, the start of smoking among girls began to decline again, and the sales of these brands slackened. By 1974, a decline hit all age groups, even the younger ones, as the anti-smoking movement began and anti-tobacco ads had just become familiar.

Dr. Pierce notes that similar large jumps in initiation of

smoking among the young coincide with large bursts of advertising at many times throughout the century.

Camels, the first great successful brand in American cigarettes, which later declined into a brand for older people with a very small market segment, turned this decline around with young targeting, as R.J. Reynolds documents say without equivocation. The Reynolds' company advertising approach to the cigarette was essentially the same from 1913 to 1988, and was a masculine pitch: "Camel, where a man belongs." Work to reposition the cigarette began in ad campaigns of 1985. (Note that with cigarettes, there is really nothing new in the product; they are all the same, always, so the "newness" of a campaign is only its "position.")

Then, in February, 1988, the company introduced the cartoon Camel, the "smooth character." And the decrepit brand suddenly rose out of its coffin, as in the Irish ballad of Tim Finnegan. The brand jumped from 3 percent to more than 13 percent of the market in just three years, and among the youngest groups, the jump was even larger.

The blitz was essentially an attack on Marlboro, the home of the masculine, youth-oriented cigarette since the 1960s. The shoot-out between the cowboy and the camel continues, with the camel gaining each year.

In Canada, a similar shoot-out over the youth market took place between parallel brands. There, it was Export A that held the youth market, and Players seeking it. Export had the lead with a rugged trucker for its image. Players broke in as Camels had in the U.S. with a somewhat softer, but still masculine pitch.

These cigarette wars all took place after the scare of the 1950s and 1960s. After the scare of 1954 and the discoveries of the 1960s, the tobacco companies began the 1970s with a sense of renewed life. They had confronted the worst, and they were still standing. Their markets, although shrinking, had not collapsed. The new generation of executives had a renewed vigor for both defense against health problems, and offense in once again considering not just holding the line, but finding new markets for cigarettes. They began to think of brands designed specifically for children, for women, for blacks, and even for subsets of these groups.

In looking at tobacco documents and how the concerns

change over the years, it appears that the next great wave of internal research in the industry, after the work on disease and on nicotine, was on why people smoke in the first place, and how to keep them doing it. Every company had its agents in the field digging up data, interviewing young people, deciphering the obscure signals of behavior.

Claude Teague, assistant chief in Research and Development at R.J. Reynolds, in the spring of 1972 when the companies were just coming out of the first wave of learning the technical details about smoke and about nicotine, research of a depth never before attempted in the industry, took the opportunity to review the most salient matters to the companies.

On April 14 of that year he set out in a memo what now could be understood of the cigarette business:

"In a sense," Dr. Teague mused, "the tobacco industry may be thought of as being a specialized, highly ritualized and stylized segment of the pharmaceutical industry. Tobacco products, uniquely, contain and deliver nicotine, a potent drug with a variety of physiological effects." He and others in the tobacco business had been made nervous by the advent of new mind and mood altering drugs such as tranquilizers of various kinds. They saw that those drugs, if they had not been under the tight wraps of medical testing and food and drug law, could be direct competitors to the tobacco industry. People needed release, and it was thought that if they could get hold of their drugs directly, without having to fight off the unpleasant features of smoke and the hazards of illness, they might well bypass cigarettes altogether. Dr. Teague wrote of tobacco that "in different situations and at different dose levels, nicotine appears to act as a stimulant, depressant, tranquilizer, psychic energizer, appetite reducer . . . to name but a few of the varied and often contradictory effects attributed to it. Many of these same effects may be achieved with other physiologically active materials such as caffeine, alcohol, tranquilizers, sedatives, euphorics, and the like. Therefore, in addition to competing with products of the tobacco industry, our products may, in a sense, compete with a variety of other products with certain types of drug action. All of these products, tobacco and other, appear to have certain common attributes in that they are used largely to relieve, in one way or another, the fatigues and stresses which arise in the course of existence in a complex society."

Professor Klein, meet Dr. Teague: these white tubes are antidotes in an Age of Anxiety.

The great advantage of tobacco has been that, unlike most drugs in the modern regulated society, tobacco was a grandfather. It was never brought under the new rules in which one had to check for safety hazards before marketing the drug. In addition to this regulatory edge, Teague said, tobacco has another advantage over drugs sold by other companies:

"Happily for the tobacco industry," he wrote, "nicotine is both habituating and unique in its variety of physiological actions, hence no other active material or combination of materials provides equivalent 'satisfaction.' Whether nicotine will, over the long term, maintain its unique position is subject to some reasonable doubt. With increased sophistication of knowledge in the biological and pharmaceutical areas, a superior or at least equivalent product or product mixture may emerge."

In fact, tobacco labs were already looking for those substances. They were looking for nicotine analogs that might give the mild high without producing the faster heartbeat and higher blood pressure that could be contributing to heart disease. They checked many nicotine-like chemicals and some that were unlike nicotine. And in fact, they found a few substances that did produce a high. It is not known how far this work got, as much of it has not yet been published or leaked.

He concluded that "if nicotine is the sine qua non of tobacco products and tobacco products are recognized as being attractive dosage forms of nicotine, then it is logical to design our products — and where possible, our advertising — around nicotine delivery rather than 'tar' delivery or flavor." The current cigarettes were delivering roughly 1.3 milligrams of nicotine, and they appeared to "satisfy" the smoker. Thus, the researchers had a mark to start with, and could vary the amount delivered as well as the way it was delivered. It might be possible to deliver just the right dose of nicotine, he said, and keep down the amount of hazardous tar.

Along with these new and happy thoughts came the cold moment when he realized that the value of nicotine to smokers, which the companies might exploit, also presented a possibility of serious weakness in the companies' approach to tobacco.

If nicotine is so important, what about people who had never tried it? Why did they start in the first place? What are we doing about these starters, who are after all, our future business?

"Before proceeding too far in the direction of design of dosage forms for nicotine," Teague wrote, and he can be imagined holding up his finger for the listener to pause, "it may be well to consider another aspect of our business. . . . Paradoxically, the things which keep a confirmed smoker habituated and 'satisfied,' i.e. nicotine and secondary physical and manipulative gratifications, are unknown and/or largely unexplained to the non-smoker."

People don't start smoking to satisfy a not-yet-realized craving for nicotine. "Rather, he appears to start to smoke for purely psychological reasons — to emulate a valued image, to conform, to experiment, to defy, to be daring, to have something to with his hands, and the like. Only after experiencing smoking for some period of time do the physiological 'satisfactions' and habituation become apparent and needed. Indeed, the first smoking experiences are often unpleasant until a tolerance for nicotine has been developed. This leaves us, then, in the position of attempting to design and promote the same product to two different types of market with two different sets of motivations, needs and expectations."

And, both segments are essential to survival.

He suggested that eventually, the tobacco companies would have to "take a stand" and admit that nicotine was the heart of things, explain its benefits, and market it openly both to smokers and to non-smokers. If they did not do this, sometime down the road, their unwillingness to directly confront the nature of their business would kill it.

For those whose bodies have learned first to tolerate, then to like, and finally to need nicotine, the path for the companies was clear enough.

But, he said, "If we are to attract the non-smoker or the pre-smoker, there is nothing in this type of product that he would currently understand or desire. We have deliberately played down the role of nicotine, hence the non-smoker has little or no knowledge of what satisfactions it may offer him and no desire to try it." For those who haven't started, Teague said, "we must somehow convince him with wholly irrational reasons that he should try smoking, in the hope that he will for himself then discover the real 'satisfactions' obtainable."

"And of course, in the present advertising climate, our opportunities to talk to the pre-smoker are increasingly limited, and therefore, increasingly ineffective. Would it not be better in the long run to identify in our own minds and in the minds of our customers what we are really selling, i.e., nicotine satisfaction? This would enable us to speak directly of the virtues of our product to the confirmed smoker, and would educate the pre-smoker, perhaps indirectly but effectively, in what we have to offer and what it would be expected to do for him."

What he was suggesting was using advertising to adults, speaking directly about nicotine's pleasures, which would at the same time teach children about it.

Less than a year later, Dr. Teague was back at his typewriter — February 2, 1973 — fleshing out his ideas about youth and tobacco. "Some Thoughts About New Brands of Cigarettes for the Youth Market" was the title. It began, "At the outset it should be said that we are presently, and I believe unfairly, constrained from directly promoting cigarettes to the youth market."

Dr. Teague is a bit unclear about what the "youth market" means. Here he suggests it is 21-year-olds. Two paragraphs later he is speaking of considering ways to influence "pre-smokers to try smoking, learn to smoke and become confirmed smokers." As we now understand, 90 percent of smokers start before age 18, I believe he is no longer talking about 21-year-olds. He later slips and notes that "psychologically, at eighteen, one is immortal." A few paragraphs later, he recommends looking for a name for a youth brand by "careful study of the current youth jargon, together with a review of currently used high school American history books and like sources" for hints. Now, we have slipped below 18 to 14 or 15 years old, which is the age at which we know children actually begin.

"Realistically," he said, "if our company is to survive and prosper, over the long term we must get our share of the youth market; I believe it unrealistic to expect that existing brands identified with an over-thirty 'establishment' market can ever become the 'in' products with the young group. Thus we need new brands designed to be particularly attractive to the young smoker, while ideally at the same time being appealing to all smokers."

He went on, "Perhaps these questions may be best approached by consideration of factors influencing pre-smokers to try smoking, learn to smoke and become confirmed smokers. . . . There are sharp, perhaps exploitable differences between pre-smokers, 'learners' and confirmed smokers in terms of what they expect or derive from smoking. Brands tailored for the beginning smoker should emphasize the desirable psychological effects of smoking, also suggesting the desirable physical effects to be expected later. Happily, then, it should be possible to aim a cigarette promotion at the beginning smoker, at the same time making it attractive to the confirmed smoker."

He then outlined the profile of a cigarette for this "beginning smoker," who we know historically has been between ages 13 and 17 or so, as that is the age of beginning. He said such a cigarette should be mild tasting so as not to put them off, and a slightly lower than normal amount of nicotine, because their bodies have not acclimated to it yet.

He writes that the chief gratification sought by the beginning smoker is social, primarily to be part of the group and respected. These pleasures "sustain the beginning smoker during the largely physically awkward and unpleasant 'learning to smoke' phase."

"Thus a new brand aimed at the young smoker must somehow become the 'in' brand and its promotion should emphasize togetherness, belonging and group acceptance, while at the same time emphasizing individuality and 'doing one's own thing.' "

He recommends a broad research program to work on a new youth brand. Four years later, another RJR research department memo, this one looking ahead ten years to project future markets, expresses some alarm that the company hasn't got itself together yet. "Young people will continue to become smokers at or above the present rates during the projection period. The brands which these beginning smokers accept and use will become the dominant brands in future years. Evidence is now available to indicate that the 14- to 18-year-old group is an increasing segment of the smoking population. RJR must soon establish a successful new brand in this market if our position in the industry is to be maintained over the long term."

Eventually, they did, with a style and ferocity unmatched in tobacco marketing history. It was Joe Camel.

*   *   *

The logic of the situation, which may have been realized only partially in earlier years, is this: Smoking appeals to the very young not because of its nicotine, but chiefly for a number of social reasons — they need this product as a badge of daring and independence, and this is at least partly *because* it is dangerous and discouraged by authorities. Adults *do not* start smoking because that social motivation is not present; adults have already formed up their image of themselves, and found the necessary badges of independence and contrariness elsewhere. Adults most especially do not take up cigarette smoking, which is the least pleasant form of tobacco use. The cigarette aroma is not as good, and the cigarette invites deep inhaling, which leads to awful trouble with breathing and coughing that does not occur as much when pipes or cigars are used.

Once this is clear, then one may ask about the details of the young starting smoker's habit. The young smoker experiments early with a few puffs or a few cigarettes very early between ages 5 and 13, then moves on to smoke a few cigarettes daily in the next stage, between 14 and 17. The habit reaches the full usual addiction by 18 to 21 years old, at a little more than a pack a day — the average lifetime level.

In dollars, this profile means that between ages 5 and 18, the children are spending far less money and buying fewer cigarettes than their older counterparts. A child starting may spend only $100 per year on cigarettes. A confirmed smoker of a major brand might typically spend more like $800 per year.

If the product were video cameras, this annual purchase would suggest marketing to the older, more regular customer and leaving the kids alone.

But with cigarettes, it turns out that because cigarette smoking begins in a psychological need, a brand can become bound up in the very self-image of the new smoker. That creates a very high likelihood that a smoker will stay with their first regular brand for years or even for life. Brand loyalty, it is called, and it is far higher among the young and among cigarette smokers than just about anyplace else in business.

In 1950, a *U.S. Tobacco Journal* article noted that even though the industry had been extraordinarily successful in making cigarettes glamorous, and had introduced them to nearly half the adult population, "A massive potential market still exists among women and young adults, cigarette industry leaders agreed, acknowledging that recruitment of these millions of prospective smokers comprises the major objective for the immediate future and on a long term basis as well." A Philip Morris executive was quoted by the journal: "Students are tremendously loyal. If you catch them, they'll stick with you like glue."

In addition, it turns out that advertising to new smokers often does not reach directly to the candidate smoker, but is filtered through the perceptions and tastes of slightly older, model smokers. So those who take up the habit are carriers: they infect their younger peers. The most needy and insecure kids, who cannot manage their independence without props, but instead find a commercial product to use, draw in others by showing that cigarettes can work. Howard Beals, a tobacco-company-supported researcher, says that "same-sex peers" are the single strongest influence: a boy is eight times as likely to smoke if his best friend does, and a girl is six times as likely if her best friend does.

Taking the long view, investing a larger percentage of your marketing dollars in children will pay off in the future as they remain loyal and their habit grows in dollar value and becomes stable. Further, buying the most loyal smokers, those who start young, helps prevent the dangerous problem of brand-switching which occurs among adult starters more often than among young starters. Though companies have often said they advertise cigarettes to get people to switch brands, this is illogical: those who switch are the least stable, and are likely to keep switching right past your brand.

In 1957, E. Gilbert, a Philip Morris executive, wrote, "hitting the youth can be more efficient even though the cost to reach them is higher, because they are willing to experiment, they have more influence over others in their age group than they will later in life, and they are far more loyal to their starting brand."

U.S. Tobacco, a company which virtually invented a market for chewing tobacco beginning in 1970, explicitly outlined their strategy based on similar principles, creating "starter" brands that don't sell all that well in the market as a whole, but get a user started with sweet tastes and relatively low nicotine.

This situation explains the odd statistical fact that U.S. Tobacco spends half its entire advertising and promotion budget on young people who are only 2 percent of the market: They come in

2 percent at a time, year by year, and both accumulate in numbers and increase their habit later. But without the entry portal which the company punched through, the habit would not exist (and did not exist before about 1970) as a feature in young American culture.

And so it is that we see in the tobacco documents that when getting ready to target a young audience, the data that marketers prepare includes not only which brands are smoked by which sex and age group, but there is more: what percent of this brand is smoked by starters? What percent by switchers? What was the chief factor in getting this smoker started? Peer influence? Package design? Brand image?

So it is that tobacco advertising to children is misunderstood. The difficulty is that anti-smoking groups seem to have blamed advertising for people's smoking habits, whereas no rational soul believes advertising is enough to get people started smoking, or to keep them smoking. It is not to be imagined that children see Joe Camel and think, that's cool, I better start smoking. Not at all.

The role is more indirect and subtle, though still powerful enough to have a major effect on behavior. That is, powerful enough that companies spend $6 billion per year advertising. They would not do it if it did not work in some way, to some degree.

The way in which it works is this: children are just beginning to shape their image of themselves, elbowing out a niche in the world, and must somehow differentiate themselves from parents and other adults, and get out from under what the authorities in life want from them. They dress differently, sometimes shockingly. They listen to different, sometimes shocking, music. In this quest, the children are worried, insecure, seeking to make choices and have them supported by their friends or others they respect. Most obviously, their choices are supported by each other. They have learned to lean on each other for aid and assent. Sometimes older siblings lend support. But because the insecurity is great, as many supports as possible are needed.

Here is the role of advertising for children. It is not that they are messages that argue with and convince children to smoke. Rather, they exploit a natural event of human development. It is natural to rebel and separate oneself from parents and family for a time. What is so troublesome about this approach is that it exploits this natural need, offering a destructive manner of rebellion as an alternative to the more constructive varieties, such as outrageous fashion, music, and politics.

The leading companies insert themselves in the family as it develops, and lend support to a choice the children have made or are about to make. They back it up with images, and sly ads; what is already attractive for one or another reason. It gives an extra push. It helps support the idea, learned elsewhere, that smoking is a pleasurable adult activity.

And we should add, it does so without regard to the consequences, and does so for profit.

Lest you doubt the reach of the tobacco company programs, more than half the teenage smokers in America own gifts, such as lighters, knives, or tee shirts, from cigarette companies.

While much of the documentary evidence on tobacco is about plans and theories, on the subject of children we also have a sheaf of papers giving concrete detail from the industry's direct work with children, and what has come of it.

The most complete set of papers has come from the Canadian sister companies of the U.S. giants Reynolds, Philip Morris, and Brown and Williamson.

In 1976, Imperial Tobacco of Canada, sister company to Brown and Williamson in the U.S. (Imperial sells mostly in Canada, Britain and France, but does sell to the U.S. as well, in small quantities), wanted to establish a substantial base of data on young people, after flying by the seat of their pants for too many years. A series of projects were started, which would extend over the next decade.

The reports were written, for the most part, by advertising and marketing specialists, young to middle-aged men working at outside advertising agencies or in the marketing departments of the companies themselves.

Sharp tobacco executives had learned decades before that tobacco brands have a generational cycle to them; brands that are extraordinarily popular for many years eventually fall from grace with consumers. Camel was the first great cigarette brand. It was followed by Lucky Strike and Chesterfields. Each was leader in its time, then each collapsed. Among these, only Camel was revived by pitching it to an entirely new audience — swinging it away from its usual smokers, over 50 years old, and bringing it to those under

20 years old. The tobacco market has this difficulty: it must be re-created in each generation. Each crop of young people must be addressed anew. The children must choose to smoke and they must choose brands.

The first study in the decade-long project by Imperial was code-named Project Sixteen, for the age of those who were to be studied. It is of course technically illegal for them to be smoking, and it is said publicly by the companies that these children are of no commercial concern. In the documents on Project Sixteen, there is no discussion of illegal sales, or the dangers which the children they were interviewing were hazarding day to day. If the work were real science, ethical considerations would require that those interviewing the children try to help them stop smoking, perhaps by offering them treatment. These subjects didn't come up. The focus of concern was on information that could be of use in advertising.

"Since how the beginning smoker feels today has implications for the future of the industry," the report said, "it follows that a study of this area would be of much interest. Project 16 was designed to do exactly that — to learn everything there was to learn about how smoking begins, how high school students feel about being smokers, and how they foresee their use of tobacco in the future."

The marketing company commissioned to do the work was Kwechansky Marketing Research, Inc. During one fall they paid teenagers to come to hotels in downtown Toronto and somewhat rural Peterborough, for a total of four "observation sessions" with hidden cameras.

The requirements were that the children be 16 or 17 years old, in high school, and professed smokers of 5 or more cigarettes per day. "Recruiting was carried out in such a manner that the respondents had no idea that the subject was to be smoking," the authors noted.

These were their customers; in the next 30 years, each would deposit $30,000 dollars in their accounts. The children were brought into a hotel room, the Sutton Place in Toronto, the Holiday Inn in Peterborough, and asked to watch some advertising. This was not merely an exercise in Q and A, but was intended to develop a psychological understanding of their customers, and the urge to start this often lifetime habit.

They showed them advertising of different types and studied their reactions, looking for the messages that penetrated the teenage skepticism and distance. The children are referred to as "starters."

The children thought many of the ads were suspect. "It's always the perfect person using the perfect product and you're supposed to buy the product and become that perfect person," said one girl. ". . . And they run down women. Car ads do, always a gorgeous woman in it." On smoking, one boy said, "They make it look glamorous. Always some swell chick standing there with a sharp guy looking at her. It's supposed to be glamorous."

The interviewer stopped him. "Supposed to be? Shall I assume you don't think it really is?"

"No. How could it be?" He muttered about seeing "some old bum puff on one."

Wrigley's gum, Hires root beer, and of course cigarette ads from magazines were shown. The sure, skeptical front of the children held up through most of the ads. But sometimes the images caught their imaginations: one in particular, an ad for Players cigarettes which showed someone on horseback in a mountain meadow. Freedom, they thought. "You're free and everything's going all right. . . . You're not being hassled. You can take your time, do what you want."

The children were asked about the ages of the actors, but they couldn't tell. "Respondents could not be sure of their ages, they were young even if not teens themselves, and they might even have been that."

Later in the text, when some conclusions were drawn, the report noted that what was found most appealing to the children were ads showing young people (they guessed their ages from 14 to 25) riding horses. The agency noted models for ads in the future should be over 25 "but should appear to be younger than 25."

As they looked at an ad for Winston and Export Canadian cigarettes, the interviewer turned to one girl: "Janet, compare these two."

"I'm in love with the Winston guy!"

"I know you are! That's why I want you to compare them."

"He looks so rugged," Janet said. "The other guy looks like he doesn't even smoke! A shrimp."

The issues of sexuality bobbed to the surface, again and

again. Smoking is perceived by these children as not only adult, but vaguely masculine, independent, bold, forbidden.

The report said that at these young ages, it is not so much the taste and nicotine boost of a cigarette that are important. They "play a secondary role to the social requirements. Therefore, taste, until a certain nicotine dependence has been developed, is somewhat less important than other things."

For this, the center of their market, it is the image, not the taste, that is crucial to selling cigarettes and establishing that "certain nicotine dependence" in those who may be their lifetime smokers.

This information is what they were after in the Project Sixteen study; this is the secret of the trade. It is not precisely the forbidden nature of smoking which makes it attractive to adolescents, but rather, it is how the teenagers can use the forbidden for their own needs that is crucial. They are insecure, especially sexually — the two topics twine about each other in line upon line of the words that come from the children. They need to appear confident, because they are not. They need to ward off fear and childishness, by adopting poses that appear certifiably adult.

These needs do not usually last past age eighteen or twenty for most people.

Thus, the companies must appeal to children successfully between 12 and 18, so the habit may become an integral part of the image of themselves. It must become part of their emerging adulthood, attached like a limpet to the person emerging from the teenage years. The temptation must be pressed just as the sense of self is forming, just as the child is facing the world at large for the first time, or it will not take hold. What becomes part of the self-image at this age may carry on for many years, to a point at which the addiction has taken hold not only physiologically, but psychologically, and what is not established during these years may never be.

For this reason, of greatest concern to the men who led the interviews, on page after page of Project Sixteen, were the questions about why and how the children start smoking. What would encourage them? What would deter them?

"If the last ten years have taught us anything," the papers noted, "it is that the industry is dominated by the companies who respond most effectively to the needs of the younger smokers. Our efforts on these brands will remain on maintaining their relevance to smokers in these younger groups in spite of the share performance they may develop among older smokers."

The strategists worried about the profile of their smokers. Their chief trademark brands are "aging slightly," they said, and they must do something about it. There is great brand loyalty in tobacco, and smokers who settle on a brand often die with it.

Project Sixteen, dated October 18, 1977, concludes with a brief summary for busy tobacco executives: "There is no doubt that peer group influence is the single most important factor in the decision by an adolescent to smoke. Around the age of 11 to 13, there is peer pressure exerted by smokers on non-smokers that amounts to taunting and goading of the latter to get them to smoke."

Among the details the companies discovered in their research was that tobacco experimentation begins, fairly often, around age five, in imitation of older siblings. More often, though, it starts about age 7 or 8, while serious efforts to learn to smoke occur at 12 or 13 years old. "Part of the thrill of adolescent smoking is the thrill of hiding it from parental wrath."

"In some cases, the beginning smoker is not just emulating the peer group in general, but copying a specific member of it that is respected and admired. . . ."

"More important reasons for this attraction are the 'forbidden fruits' aspect of cigarettes. The adolescent seeks to display his new urge for independence with a symbol, and cigarettes are such a symbol since they are associated with adulthood and at the same time the adults seek to deny them to the young."

The company thus must ally itself with the children, against "adults" and aid the child in proclaiming "his break with childhood, at least to his peers."

There is nausea, sometimes even vomiting on the first try, of course, but "this perceived failure spurs them on to try again, and not fail."

The complexities of adolescent life and parental control are reflected here. When to hide it, when to announce it ("If successfully hidden, the young smoker will announce his smoking around the age of 15 or 16"). Parents nag children to stop; this nagging leads to spiteful attempts to continue secretly. Schools do not offer a significant barrier, and "reactions to formal school

lectures and films about smoking are mainly anger over a perceived intrusion on the right of the smoker to do as he wishes. . . ."

Now, Project Sixteen said, in order to revivify their brands
to appeal more strongly to the young, the most crucial objective
is to "re-establish clear, distinct images for Imperial Tobacco
Limited brands with particular emphasis on relevance to younger
smokers."

They reported that one of their brands, called Players Filter,
already had a significant appeal to those under 20. So they recommended pushing this brand with children. In a media planning
paper they wrote that they intended to "position Players Filter as
the brand with the greatest relevant appeal to younger, modern
smokers, by being part of a desirable, natural lifestyle."

The appeal is to generate "natural social acceptability of the
brand in the peer group environment" and a "strength of taste,
provided that the fullness of taste is perceived as slightly milder
than Export A," another of the company's brands. The paper notes
that in Western Canada, particularly in British Columbia, "the
brand has a special role for young people starting the smoking
habit. . . ."

In March of 1977, the strategists for Imperial noted that, in
case it should be unclear to anyone reading the papers, "By
younger modern smokers, we mean those people ranging from
starters of the smoking habit up to and through those seeking and
setting of their independent lifestyle. Relevant lifestyle is the key
to the brand's positioning, and the youthful emphasis is a psychological not chronological one."

In reading the papers, there is always, between the lines, a
certain odd sense of incompleteness, of lack of full sympathy with
the children, almost a desire to stop the narration so as to ask the
kids how they feel about all this, about the interviewers, about the
consumer life and whether they feel exploited. But there is one
section in the report in which the sense of personal qualities of the
kids breaks through the professional report language.

It is a sad note, struck in the midst of factual lists of likes and
dislikes, jokes about teenage behavior and interest in sex.

One interviewer mentioned quitting. At age twelve the kids
said they were taunted, even lured into smoking by friends, and
they turned to do the same to their uninitiated friends. Why not,
are you chicken? But by age sixteen, when these teenagers sat in

hotel rooms with strangers interviewing them, reality had begun to intrude. Remorse had set in. With a note of puzzlement, the writer notes, "However intriguing smoking was at 11, 12 or 13, by the age of 16 or 17 many regretted their use of cigarettes for health reasons, and because they feel unable to stop smoking."

"Those who had tried quitting were not successful," he wrote.

The regret broke out as one girl observed, "I don't like seeing 10-year-old kids hanging around the plaza smoking cigarette after cigarette. And that's what I used to do. . . ."

Another commented on the false sense of confidence they felt from their smoking, their foolishness to have believed in the weed as a vehicle to status. "I teach some grade 5's . . . and I've known these kids since kindergarten. And now they smoke. Oh God, it looks so stupid. I wish I'd have known how stupid it looked when I started . . . I'd never have done it.

One of the boys said, "I started because it was the thing to do, but now it doesn't matter. . . . Now it's just a habit."

In fact, now, they acknowledged quietly that they have some extra respect for the kids who refused to smoke in the beginning. They knew it was insecurity, a kind of needless social desperation which had betrayed them.

They wished they were among the resistors. "They resisted . . . I wasn't strong enough. . . ." One boy thought of the mornings, day after day, "you wake up and start choking and hacking your guts out."

The light tone of most of these papers, including wry remarks and jokes about the teenagers' interest in sex, gives the documents an unreal quality. There is a certain feel of fantasy to them that comes from not dealing with the lives of the children whom they are interviewing. There emerges like a ghost from beneath the lines, a lack of concern.

This attitude, like male barroom talk, is not only typical of documents from the inside of tobacco companies, but is an essential feature of them. It does not arise out of evil, but out of self-protection. Those who work in these companies must work hard to rationalize what they do for a living, must explain to themselves over and over. It is for this reason that the companies have become an isolated society, which in turn produces uninformed, unrealistic thinking on political and social issues. It prevents change.

Those who are writing these papers, after all, are human. They have families. They must not be too explicit with themselves or with those to whom their missives are directed. This is their living; these products are only something that people want.

Five years after the success of Project Sixteen, the interviewers went back again to interview children in-depth to get more information on specific attitudes which had become important—were the children worried about health? About dying? Would they consider quitting? Would they use light cigarettes to keep smoking even though they were worried?

On probing, they found that the children had first tried cigarettes, for the most part, between nine and twelve years old. Those who started were not unusual; they, too, had nagged their parents and older siblings to quit smoking. They disliked the idea of it: it was strange to see smoke coming out of the inside of a person; the smoke smelled bad; the ashes and butts were nauseating.

But eventually, curiosity drew them. If adults found pleasure enough to overcome all these negative features, it must be interesting, indeed. And as life began to impinge, and frustrations increased as they learned just what the shape of the world really is, they had also become bold. In a landscape of little interest, what stood out? The forbidden pleasures.

As one boy described it, "I started smoking up at the cottage when I was thirteen. There was nothing around and we were out fishing. My uncle opened up a pack of cigarettes and left them in the boat. So we tried it, it's something new, right? At first it didn't taste too good, it made me dizzy, and hey, this is fun. After that we got kind of bold and we'd do it with friends."

The interviewers did ask the children to reflect on the habit:

"How do you feel today when you see a twelve-year-old smoking?"

"I want to go up and punch him in the head. You think you're cool, but you're such an asshole."

"What would you tell him?"

"Well, nothing, I guess. Nobody could have told me anything then either."

The real smoking begins, as the interviewers found, between 14 and 16 when smoking moved from an occasional hit to a more regular pattern. They found that while the children were smoking to seem cool, and perhaps even more, not to be rejected by those who were smoking, this projection was mostly false. Among those who said no to smoking when offered a cigarette, it turned out that no rejection took place. And in other research, R.J. Reynolds and others have found that if there is any feature which helps single out smokers from others, it is insecurity. Those who turn to smoking are actively looking for ways to join, ways to be seen as confident.

They have studied the behavior microscopically, so that the small details become large. They have found that smokers imbue their smoking behavior with meaning, or find a score of little advantages that can be gained by the use of cigarettes. For example, they say that when they are idle they would prefer not to be seen doing nothing. When at a party, it is an occupation so as not to seem unoccupied. And in groups, or in one-on-one conversation, which is always difficult for children, the necessities of smoking allow one another very useful social tool: handling a cigarette allows a smoker to break eye contact without seeming to do so out of nervousness. These and other items are all signals of insecurity.

And so it was that the companies found that smoking begins out of fear as much as anything else. And for fear, they realized, there could be antidotes provided through advertising — images of freedom, acceptance, one's own world. Fleeting impressions of groups and smiles and smokes can reinforce their idea that smoking can work. And here too, is a crucial piece of information for those who want to curtail smoking: If sophisticated ads showing how cool smoking is were replaced with ads about rejection and disgusting behavior, and even more, replaced by ads showing how insecure smokers are, some substantial effect might be had.

The companies, in their studies of children, have also worked to find out just what children think about the hazards of smoking. The Canadian interviewers found that the children were quite aware of the risks of smoking, and believed them. "Why then," they asked in their paper, "would anyone wish to start smoking in the fact of such loud, consistent and clear warnings? Oddly enough, such hazards are literally ignored by starters."

The subject just doesn't come up, really. The researchers suggest that there is no real appreciation in children of the possibility of addiction.

"Didn't you think first about all the things you'd heard about smoking?"

"Aw, no, I didn't. I never thought it'd become a habit."

They are right about this for many substances. When casual users imbibe various substances — including cocaine, heroin and alcohol — relatively few do slip into heavy use. Not so with cigarettes — in this respect, tobacco is the most addicting of all known substances. This is because the high is mild and does not interfere with life, the cigarettes are easy to obtain, the consequences seem quite remote, and the active substance is one which affects neurons widely across the brain, and so has more of a general toning effect on mood than other drugs.

"Thus we have a pattern," says the paper, "that shows how and why the health hazards do not really enter into the decision to start. It is no longer because they [the hazards] are sincerely disbelieved (shows of rebellious bravado aside), but because they are assumed as not applicable to the person who won't become addicted. But addicted they do indeed become . . . what then?"

The paper moves on to quitting: once they realize they have a habit, and this comes by age 16 or 17, they often try to quit. They begin to reflect on what they had heard about smoking but had forgotten to include in their impulses to try it.

When in this bind, the teenagers break out in rationalizations. Everything is harmful, after all; you can't be a hermit. I could just as easily get hit by a truck crossing the street. If I quit, I'd gain 30 pounds immediately — that's worse than knowing you are going to get cancer when you're sixty. I don't worry about it anyway because I know I am going to quit; I have no doubts about that.

Through all of this, the teenagers have acquired, among other things, some mistaken beliefs. When asked how many adults smoke, they say more than half, even three quarters. It is actually one quarter of the population and has been dropping. But this is opinion formed to comfort.

The paper then noted that with smoking, the worm turns very soon. "Once the image enhancement benefit is done with (usually after high school), the smoker realizes he or she ought to at least consider doing something about this habit that they didn't think they'd get, but did."

This information was repeated and emphasized in the study

highlights; for the companies it is crucial to know just how much time they have to reach the children. "The desire to quit seems to come earlier now than before, even prior to the end of high school. In fact, it often seems to take hold as soon as the recent starter admits to himself that he is hooked on smoking. However, the desire to quit, and actually carrying it out, are two quite different things, as the would-be quitter soon learns."

"The age span when smoking provides a positive self-image boost is constricting: it now does not even seem to extend to the later years of high school with very much force, whereas, a few years ago, it did."

In an effort to forestall the quitting, the companies were considering pitching "light" cigarettes to the young people who had just discovered they were hooked. But at this age, there was little appeal for the idea. There was already a certain realism, cynicism, apparent: "The use of truly light brands as a way to compromise with the desire to quit was mostly ridiculed. Some, even in the 16-17 segment, had actually tried this and rejected it. Young smokers see smoking in black and white terms only—enjoy it or quit; no middle ground."

After these thoughts, the paper moved on to the most important calculations—brand choice. It has nothing to do with tar, or mildness versus strength of a cigarette. There were only a few brands that seemed to appeal to children in Canada—Players Light, duMaurier, and Export A. Export was the "macho" brand, perceived as strong and as a 'truck driver's cigarette.' Players, somewhat more mild but still masculine, and duMaurier, sophisticated and cool, were for both sexes.

The dominant brand in Canada, comparable to Marlboro in the U.S., was Players Light—mostly among boys, but relatively strong among girls as well. "That this brand went from introduction to this incredibly lofty posture in so relatively few years is truly a marketing success story."

This "incredibly lofty posture" is success among starting smokers. It is attributed in the paper to several factors, including the package—an appealing blue and white, with the image of independence attached to it.

We have documents which carry on to the next step—the advertising plans which resulted from the insights in the work with children. The advertising plans of course must be more concrete and plain than the theory and discussion elsewhere in the company. So it is here we find the specific mention of ages and "target groups."

For example, in fiscal 1981, the advertising plan noted that the "target group" for the "Players Family" of cigarettes included ages from 12 years old to 24 years old, divided according to their importance, where a weight of 1.0 was the most dominant:

WEIGHT:
     Males, 12–24 years, 1.0
     Females, 12–17, 0.5
     Females, 18–24, 0.4

For Players Light, the favorite of youth, the charts read:

MALES 12–17 YEARS. WEIGHT, 1.0′
     Females, 12–17, 0.7
     Males, 18–24, 1.0
     Females, 18–24, weight,0.5

These charts, and we have scores of them, are used to determine what magazines and other advertising outlets will be used — the idea is to reach the target groups as often as possible in just the right proportions. The weights make it clear that the Players Light is targeted specifically at an illegal audience, the 12–17-year-old males and females. The pattern is similar for Export and for duMaurier, over several years.

Here there can be no doubt: it is not just that children will take up smoking, and the companies supply them with the raw material inadvertently. In most tobacco documents these raw facts can be obscured by discussions of just what a "young" person is. But in the hundreds of pages of advertising documents from two companies, Imperial and RJR-MacDonald, the targeting has not been hidden. They specifically target children above all other groups.

In more recent years, those who write papers for tobacco companies have learned not to be so frank.

After all, targeting 18-year-olds effectively reaches those several years younger than that. There is some data which suggests targeting 18-year-olds reaches the younger set better than it reaches 18-year-olds, according to Pierce. So in most company documents now, the phrases used will be "18–24," and "under 24" or the like. In any case, the tip-off that they are still working the same sidewalk is that the companies keep careful track of smoking among those under 18 by interviewing those over 18 about their childhood experiences.

So far, most of the best documents on youth targeting have come from Canada, because the lawsuits there matured more quickly than those in the U.S., and thus produced the detailed advertising records which we do not yet have from the U.S. companies.

It is on this subject of children smoking that their protestations of innocence are loudest and most explicit. During 1994, when the companies were under the most intense attack in history, several of them ran ads in major newspapers. Though the issue of addicting youth had not come up directly, they addressed it anyway. R.J. Reynolds noted in an ad entitled "Smoking in a Free Society," that "We do not under any circumstances want kids to smoke and we actively sponsor programs to enforce age restrictions."

Philip Morris ran an ad noting, "No one should be allowed to sell cigarettes to minors. Minors should not smoke. Period. That is why Philip Morris developed a comprehensive program to prevent sales of cigarettes to minors."

The protestations are too vehement, somehow.

One newspaper series, in the *Louisville Courier-Journal*, looking into the gap between the companies' public statements and their day-to-day behavior, noted that in the places where strict licensing and strict enforcement have been used against store owners, they have been very effective. But the industry has fought fiercely against giving state health departments the power to carry out effective enforcement. The stories noted that lobbyists in the state legislature had pressed for fines so small they would have no deterrent value, fought against licensing vendors, worked to direct fines and other punishments against clerks rather than store owners, acted to insert language that would require extensive proof of a violation before fines could be levied, and tried to ensure that it is not, in any case, the health departments that do the enforcing of the law, because those are the departments with the motivation to succeed. Perhaps their most successful ploy has been to work to get statewide laws that prevent local governments from enforcing laws, again because local governments often care about the issue and will work to enforce rules, while state governments are both too burdened to act or are more subject to the influence of money and pressure from industry lobbyists. In a quick survey using four volunteers who were 15 and 16 years old, they visited 50 stores, and found that the children were able to buy cigarettes in 31 of them.

In Massachusetts, Dr. Greg Connolly, chief of the state health department's tobacco control program, reported that in their first "sting operation," 70 percent of the time children were able to buy cigarettes; after a year of well-publicized operations, the rate of illegal sales in their tests dropped to 28 percent.

These are all significant hints of what the companies are doing, and the impact of their professed policies. Having worked with tobacco company officials for a couple of years, and listened to how they approach problems and solutions, I believe that if they were even moderately interested in curtailing sales to children, it would have happened in a very short time after they decided to be serious. These are competent people who can measure effectiveness and dump ineffective programs quickly.

Apart from the memos already cited, which show what groups the companies target, there is other, more direct evidence of their intentions.

One example is the RJR program which was established to sell Camel cigarettes, using Joe the Camel and other inducements. The Camel campaign was not a single shot, but was one example of broader strategies outlined in RJR memos. These plans were referred to in company documents as YAS, for targeting of "young adult smokers," and as FUBYAS, for programs that worked to be the "First Usual Brand of Young Adult Smokers." These titles are somewhat deceptive, as they refer to "adults," when, for example, the first usual brand is smoked as a child, historical evidence over decades demonstrates. The appearance of the word "adult" suggests that the company, when it began these programs, was aware that internal documents should be careful not to suggest the targeting of children.

One document written in preparation for changing Camel from an older person's cigarette to the cigarette of "starters" noted, "Camel's flat to declining performance is due primarily to the share losses posted by its non-filter parent . . . it has little to offer FUBYAS."

In public, the company has said Camel promotions and advertising were aimed at those 18 to 34 years old. In the crucial graphs and charts of the confidential Camel business plans, however, the target is much narrower: 18–20-year-olds. The company's charts of the share of smokers they have succeeded in attracting reports that the huge growth among 18–20-year-olds is replacing older, quitting smokers. There is also a chart which states directly that it is not the older groups that matter for Camel, but the "Young Adult Smokers growth, driven by 18–20-year-old group."

Historical data, like that from John Pierce in San Diego, shows that, whatever group they claim to approach in documents so far exposed, they have in fact had the greatest effect on those under 18 years old.

Also, in search of objective data to supply an underpinning for the outrage of health departments, the California Department of Health carried out an extensive survey, reviewing the tobacco advertising and promotions in 5,773 stores around the state. This is the ultimate court of intention — what is actually out in the stores. This is where companies put their money. If convenience stores do not show any evidence that young people are being targeted, then we would have to begin to believe the company protestations.

All things being equal, promotions should end up evenly distributed in stores. But they are not. More promotions are placed in stores within 1,000 feet of a school than are placed in other stores. Promotions are near the candy counters more often than elsewhere. Displays are set at a height of 3 feet or lower more often than higher. In stores near schools, and in neighborhoods with a large number of children under 17, there is a distinctly greater number of signs on the outside of the store and in the windows than is the case in stores not near schools.

These disproportions do not happen by accident, as these ad placements are not only intentional, but carefully governed.

The companies deny marketing to children, of course, and offer various programs of their own — chiefly advertising which says it's illegal to smoke — to prove they are against youth smoking.

But their lobbying pattern is quite different. In 1993, riding on the tide of anti-smoking laws enacted in more than 700 towns and counties around the U.S., Congress passed an amendment to the bill re-authorizing funds for the Alcohol, Drug Abuse and Mental Health Administration, requiring each of the states to pass a law that would make cigarette sales illegal to those under the age of 18, and more importantly, requiring each state to establish a program that would actually work. In the language of the bill, the states would have to establish programs "in a manner that can reasonably be expected to reduce the extent to which tobacco products are available to individuals under the age of 18." If the states fail, in the judgment of the Secretary of Health and Human Services, then federal monies for drug abuse programs to the states could be reduced. States depend on those funds, and so it is a serious threat.

The tobacco companies and their strongest supporters in Congress have worked to delay the day when the "Synar Amendment," as it is called after its chief sponsor, the late Rep. Mike Synar of Oklahoma, takes effect. Rep. Tom Bliley, of Richmond, Virginia, now the chairman of the House Commerce Committee, threatened to challenge the law on constitutional grounds if the HHS ever tried to put an effective version of it into effect.

In a draft of the rule, HHS would require that states demonstrate their programs are effective by showing that children who try to buy cigarettes fail more than half the time. Then, over the next three years, the states must show their stores sell to minors less often than 40, 30 and 20 percent of the time.

The Tobacco Institute in comments to the federal government said this kind of regulation is outrageous, and suggested that the Synar Amendment was never intended to reduce sales to minors significantly. It suggested making sales to those under age 18 illegal, but without any rules to ensure enforcement.

The companies are on record as against most methods of enforcement, including inspections, sting operations, surveys, and holding merchants responsible for illegal sales. Instead they suggest punitive measures which would be certain not only to backfire, but to cast the enforcers in the worst possible light. They suggest targeting for arrest children who buy cigarettes rather than retailers who sell them. They also suggest arresting or fining the clerks in the stores, not the managers or owners.

What the industry is against is quite logical — anything that has been shown to be effective in any studies or in any actual town or state enforcement actions. The situation is similar to that of the CTR — maintain a public posture that appears honorable and in line with public opinion, and in practice prevent anything that would reduce sales in any way. It would be difficult to believe an industry could be so dishonest as to carry out such a two-faced program, but having seen the documents from 1954 to the present, and looking at one example after another when the companies' intentions have been tested, it is impossible to escape the conclusion that the industry is doing just that, again.

To complete the cycle, I pursued the matter to those who were actually responsible for carrying out the targeting of children.

I began with a memorandum first mentioned in passing by the *Wall Street Journal* in 1991. As the Joe Camel and YAS campaigns got underway in 1989, RJR executives held regional meetings with salesmen to explain just who was being targeted, and how they were to be targeted. To the executives' discomfort, they had to be rather explicit with the salesmen.

Company officials realized that making RJR products the first brands of young people would require a completely different kind of marketing than that used with regular smokers. They would be heavy on gimmicks and gifts, tee shirts, cartoon figures, fancy cigarette lighters and knives. The campaigns turned out to be some of the most successful marketing campaigns in the history of the tobacco industry, taking brands from virtually nothing to a major share of the youth market in only a few years.

One key component of the program, company officials said, was the decision to pick out convenience stores near high schools and colleges to hit with a barrage of extra premiums and promotions — from discount prices to free cigarette lighters, tee shirts and caps, as well as access to more expensive items like jackets that could be discounted with coupons from cigarette packages.

(The industry has for many years maintained that it will not advertise to anyone under 21, will not provide samples to them, will not mail samples to anyone under 21, or advertise on any billboards near schools.

The industry's code of behavior, signed by RJR, also states

that "There shall be no other distribution of non-tobacco premium items bearing cigarette brand names, logos, etc. without written, signed certification that the addressee is 21 years of age or older.")

One memo, written after regional sales directors arrived back in their regions, came from J.P. McMahon, division manager in Florida. It was written on January 10, 1990, and was addressed to sales representatives in his area. "VERY IMPORTANT, PLEASE READ CAREFULLY!!!," it read, in underline and capital letters at the top.

"I need all of you to study the attached . . . list of monthly accounts in your [area] that are presently doing more than 100 Cartons Per Week, for purposes of denoting stores that are heavily frequented by young adult shoppers. These stores can be in close proximity to colleges, high schools or areas where there are a large number of young adults frequent the store." (Weird grammar in the original.)

As high schools and junior high schools have students from ages 11 to 18, this amounts to an explicit order to target children. The company at the time denied that was the intent, and said Mr. McMahon misunderstood orders.

However, when the FDA began to check out this tale, they found that there was another regional manager who had misunderstood. R.G. Warlick, chief in Oklahoma, wrote to his sales reps, "Due to a revision in the definition of what is a Retail Young Adult Smoker Retailer Account, you will be required to resubmit again your list of YAS accounts in your territory. . . ." So, not only had they already targeted stores where young people hang out, but now, the sales reps are to be sure to add some specific stores: "The criteria for you to utilize in identifying these accounts are as follows: All package action calls [stores that sell packs rather than cartons, that is, stores frequented by the young] located across from, adjacent to are [sic] in the general vicinity of the High Schools or College Campus (Under 30 years of age)."

Terence Sullivan, a sales rep in Florida under regional manager McMahon, said that he and others objected to the explicit targeting of junior high school and high school children. He said in an interview that while children might well pick up the habit, he did not want to be party to pitching them directly. "We were targeting kids, and I said at the time it was unethical and maybe illegal, but I was told that it was just company policy," he said.

Sullivan has since been fired by the company, and has filed a suit for wrongful dismissal in reply.

To check the tale further, I tracked down two other salesmen who worked on the campaign in Florida.

Mike Shaw, a salesman with RJR for twenty years, said the program was intended to target kids, including high school students, quite plainly.

"At just about every meeting I ever attended, the question came up, how can we get our share of the convenience store business where Philip Morris was doing so well. The convenience stores are where kids buy their cigarettes, one pack or two at a time."

"We wanted to get into that market, and used the promotional items, tee shirts, baseball caps, and one hot item were lighters, knowing full well the people we were giving these away to was kids half the time."

The YAS program, which started in 1989, he said, was the same as other promotions, only more aggressive — more premiums, more discounts.

"We actually would do exactly what those letters said," referring to the McMahon and Warlick memos. "Kids is what we're talking about; most are not adults. These are kids."

He said the idea was to designate the stores where young people were, and load them up with ads and promotions. "If you got a high school on a block, and at the end of the block you got a Seven-11, that's one YAS outlet. The criteria you would use was simple. The stores were the ones where the kids hang out."

He said the concrete description of who they were targeting was not supposed to make it into print, but was intended to be verbal. "The managers weren't supposed to write it down. These two guys who wrote it in their memos were just a little more stupid than the others. They were told to do something and they did it."

After word of the McMahon memo leaked out, mention of the McMahon memo appeared in the paper, and soon many documents about the program were destroyed. Each division office was issued a shredder, he said.

Gary Velcher, Chain Store Account Manager in South Florida for RJR, said that even though the company now says the memos got the company policy wrong, and misconstrued what was laid out at sales meetings, he was at the same sales meetings, and has read the memos.

"I find nothing inconsistent in the memos with what went on in that meeting" in Ft. Lauderdale that kicked off the YAS campaign. The YAS "campaign took a more aggressive posture than any I had ever seen. It was more overt. The purpose and intent was clearer than ever," he said.

The plan, he said, was to identify stores as "young people's hangouts" and concentrate heavily your promotions in those stores — buy two get one free, a free Camel tee shirt with four packs, and so on. He said that he was told to "make sure you never run out there, make sure there's always a chance to buy a 'deal pack' of some kind there."

He also said that when news of the McMahon memo leaked out, documents were recalled and shredded, the program was renamed, but went on as before.

Terri Sullivan said that the clearest statement he heard from RJR headquarters executives came in a question and answer period at a regional sales meeting. Someone asked exactly who the young people were that were being targeted, junior high school kids, or even younger?

The reply came back, "They got lips? We want 'em."

All of this is more than interesting; it has consequences. There are virtually no subjects on which American voters agree more: in surveys in the Southern tobacco states as well as in the North, West and Midwest, over 90 percent of respondents believe tobacco companies should leave children alone. They should not sell to them, market to them, speak to them, or in any way try to get into their minds.

This is the vulnerability of tobacco companies; it is what makes nightmares for tobacco executives. They imagine some severe program which severely limits children who might think of starting. It would be the end of the tobacco heyday for them.

They are aware that, whatever denials they make, they must worry about which children start smoking, when and why they start, whether they might want to quit, and what they want in a cigarette. Yet they must carry out this most important mission for the future of the industry without public visibility. They must market to children, yet must deny it, under oath if necessary.

Their solution to this conundrum is to bluff.

To see it from their view, you must imagine yourself directing the defenses of a walled city against siege: on three fronts you may be confident and bold in your commands, but not so on the fourth front, where you know there is a breach so wide as to be fatal the moment it is fully tested by the opposing forces. What else can be done? Divert attention, feign confidence.

So they work hard to appear to be out front on the issue — with expensive and well-publicized programs that intentionally don't work, and where a town or state threatens to enact legislation that does work, they march out the lobbyists and the cash.

And so we see the companies with programs designed to prevent young people from smoking. *Prevent* smoking?

The most recent example of such unusual behavior is the program called Action Against Access announced in 1995 and run by Philip Morris.

In a flurry of expensive image advertising, the company trumpeted, "Philip Morris announces a program created to prevent cigarette sales to minors."

Of the ten promises highlighted in boxes with icons — very computer fashionable — nine were useless and silly on their face. For example, number one: "Pack notices. We will place a notice on all of our packs and cartons: 'Underage sales prohibited.'" Or number five: "Vending. We will join with others in seeking state legislation to prevent minors' access to cigarettes in vending machines." Sounds okay, but note that it does not suggest eliminating or reducing the number of vending machines, only offering to support some bills which might prevent access of children to vending machines. They suggest, for example, making sure the clerks in stores "supervise" vending machine sales, as if they did not have enough to do already.

But one of the ten provisions sounds quite serious: Number four, "Retail Payments. We will deny merchandising benefits to retailers who are fined for or convicted of selling cigarettes to minors."

These "merchandising benefits" are paid to store operators for giving good display space and prominence to certain brands. Cigarette sales are already the number one volume item for the stores, so they cannot ignore what the tobacco company salesmen want, but in addition, the payments amount to several thousand dollars a year, over and above regular profit. This is real money, and is very dangerous ground for the companies to be treading.

Of course, Philip Morris folks realized that few, if any, retailers anywhere in the country are convicted of selling cigarettes to minors. Police departments, who have the job or at least share the job of enforcing laws against selling to children, have a hard time coming up with good reasons to pull officers from more vital tasks to get entangled in the awkward and hard-to-enforce cigarette laws. Recently, however, as anti-smoking laws proliferate, some states *are* now willing to spend some time and effort on policing sales.

Philip Morris wasn't paying attention to this trend, but the convenience store operators were. As soon as Philip Morris announced the plan, the retail groups shot back. "It is disappointing that the priorities of the largest tobacco manufacturer in the nation have degenerated to posturing blame," they said, in public. Never mind the bad grammar, they were angry. "Your plan will certainly punish our industry for these events, but it will not solve the problem."

Philip Morris sent out representatives to calm the retailers, letting them know they did not really mean it. Joseph DiFranza, an enemy of big tobacco and a researcher at the University of Massachusetts famous for showing that Joe Camel is as well known among children as Mickey Mouse, said the campaign was "an ineffective program whose sole purpose is to convince the federal government that there's no need to get involved." In his recent research, he said he had sent underage children to 40 stores where Philip Morris had said they were working with retailers to stop underage sales. His study found that stores sell to children just as often — the kids can buy at least one third of the time — in stores under the Philip Morris program called "It's the law" as in stores without it.

The climax of this little tale came in October, 1995, when an anti-tobacco group in Minnesota, the Association for Nonsmokers of Minnesota, sent Philip Morris a list of recent convictions for underage sales in Minnesota. Philip Morris wrote back saying the company could not act because the citations from the anti-smoking group did not come from the proper authorities.

But quickly, Hubert H. Humphrey III, Attorney General of Minnesota, decided to back up the group and put Philip Morris to the test. He had an official list of the 17 prepared and sent it to the company.

Philip Morris replied that, though the notification was official, it was "too early" to actually carry out its threat. "We haven't finalized the actual proposal" to crack down on retailers, said company spokeswoman Ellen Merlo.

Asked whether the company would start enforcement actions after the proposal was finalized and sent out to retailers, she said not necessarily. "First we hope to begin training and raise awareness," she said.

Then, maybe in a store where training had been done, and a violation found, and a warning issued, and another two violations found, she said, possibly enforcement would take place if the program was still underway at that time.

On other subject matters, such as defense or ordinary business, such a major public announcement in which a corporation declared itself ready to do the right thing, followed by such amusing and obvious lies, would have warranted a front page story, or at least a story on the front of the business section. Instead, the *New York Times*, which had the story first, killed it with no explanation. Other papers did better, but the impact overall was muted. As A.M. Rosenthal wrote in his column about the television networks' willingness to back down in their coverage of tobacco, the two worst enemies of journalism are the tobacco companies and the journalists themselves.

CHAPTER

7

THE TOBACCO WARS

A cigarette is the perfect type of a perfect pleasure. It is exquisite,
and it leaves one unsatisfied. What more can one want?
— Oscar Wilde, *The Picture of Dorian Gray*, 1891

The chemistry of public life is mysterious in the way that it can create notable moments from compounds of ordinary characters and usual events.

These moments seem sometimes like little plays that create themselves: The players come together, with or without their consent, for an impromptu scene or two, only to be replaced momentarily by another group of players who also have suddenly found themselves together, blinking, under stage lights.

In national politics, the players never really leave the stage, they just pass in and out of the spotlight. And it is said that the media is the spotlight which creates the central focus and the shadows. But I think that is not quite right; the agenda is set when the players each bring a patch of their script and suddenly find that these fit, just for a moment, in a coherent story. They play it out before a gaggle of scribblers, who do not write the lines, but only listen for interesting stories and try to repeat them. The reporters have a role, but the center of the action remains among the players on stage.

The tale of tobacco became a significant story of action and conflict in 1994, when it rose up from nothing to first-rank policy-making in the White House and in Congress, as three characters came together on stage.

The events might never have happened; there was no historical necessity about them. What mattered was simply the characters and how they improvised. An earnest and health-conscious California Congressman had become chairman of an important subcommittee: Henry Waxman. A highly-focused academic found his chance to try to lead a federal agency: David Kessler. An unemployed drama teacher who had nothing better to do risked what was left of his life to bite the leg of the industry that had fed him: Merrell Williams. There were several others who had significant parts, but if any of these three had not been in place, the events might well not have formed into a tale at all.

And later in the story, by 1995 and 1996, two figures emerged at odds with one another. Thomas Edwin Sandefur, the chief executive of Brown and Williamson, and Dr. Jeffrey Wigand, the top researcher at Brown and Williamson. For with their emergence, the battles inside the company finally broke out in public. With Sandefur's testimony before Congress, the public saw the composed face of the company; and with Dr. Wigand's deposition, the public could see what had been going on behind it.

These two are, in a way, opposites. Mr. Sandefur is at heart a salesman from the country. Dr. Wigand is a technical man, a scientist, and now a city schoolteacher. Sandefur is volatile; Wigand is careful and reserved.

And when the tobacco wars are ended, one of the two may be in jail. One of the two is certainly guilty of perjury, as they have each testified under oath to stories that are completely opposed.

Of all places, the recent and public story of the tobacco wars began at the Environmental Protection Agency. Under William Riley, the EPA chief named by President George Bush, the slow-baking issue of second-hand smoke had finally become a scientific report. It said that after a review of the evidence, tobacco smoke must be ranked as a Class A carcinogen, one at the top of regulatory concern. The report was begun in the Reagan administration, a draft of it was released during the Bush administration, and its final version and the policy made of it were heard in Congressional hearings in 1994.

All this makes ordinary policy sense: within the agency there is an office of indoor air pollution, and as anyone who suffers it knows, the most irritating substance in the air around you is tobacco smoke. Smog is bad; tobacco is more intense and personal.

The job for the EPA was to try to get an assessment of how much of a problem second-hand smoke is for health. How much did non-smokers actually take in as they lived and worked with smokers? And how dangerous is it to inhale second-hand smoke regularly?

One measure of how much smoke gets in the lungs of non-smokers is the amount of smoke components, such as nicotine, that end up in their blood. Virtually all the population has been contaminated by cigarette smoke to some degree — we all have higher than natural amounts of nicotine, carbon monoxide, and so on, in our systems because of smoking.

In studying non-smoking spouses of smokers, the EPA soon found that the amount loaded into their systems varied greatly, not only because each person's situation is different but because of the measuring technique itself. Each chemical in smoke has a certain lifetime in the air before it breaks down into other chemicals. The amount of time in the air determines to a great extent how much those in the area will inhale; if it is available only for seconds, very little will make it to the blood. Depending on which chemical is accounted for, the amount of smoke that appears to be taken in by the spouse of a smoker ranges from the equivalent of a few cigarettes per month, to a high of dozens of cigarettes per day.

As might be expected, the rates of disease associated with "passive" smoking are far less than those associated with smoking itself, simply because the amount of smoke inhaled is less in most cases. The rate of disease in non-smokers is proportional to the amount of smoke taken in, just as it is for smokers. Thus, it is estimated that 40,000 lung cancers per year are due to smoking, but only about 1000 to 4000 are due to second-hand smoke inhaled by exposed partners. It seems logical that other illnesses, such as heart disease, are also caused by second-hand smoke, but the data assessing these other illnesses has not been collected in large enough samples yet. For cancer, when the EPA did its work, some 30 studies were reviewed, most of them too small to give good national statistics, but among them, 24 showed an association between second-hand smoke and additional cancers, and 9 of them showed a statistically significant association.

All of this seems relatively straightforward — government science and statistics groaning slowly forward to quantify the obvious. Spouses and children of smokers inhale significant amounts of smoke, as we are now beginning to realize as the smoke clears in homes and restaurants. It has been a strong presence.

But unfortunately, when cigarette smoke is compared to other toxic substances in the air, it rises to the top of the list. The figures for disease caused by second-hand smoke are comparatively speaking very high. The annual deaths that might be associated with cancer caused by inhalation of asbestos is only about 15 per year. Benzene is half that. Vinyl chloride is estimated to be responsible for perhaps 30 deaths per year. In this context, these numbers seem almost shockingly low: do you mean to say we are making all this fuss over killing only 30 people per year? Yet this is rare — very few substances can be said to kill anyone, and the standards that the most conservative, industry-minded advocates have suggested is one-in-a-million. That is, when the casualties rise above one in a million we should regulate the substance, whatever it is.

So, needless to say, it was not a difficult decision for the EPA to conclude, in January of 1993, that second-hand smoke is a prime carcinogen alongside asbestos and benzene. This classification meant that industries must try to clean up their work places of the hazard, and the various federal agencies had to come up with plans to curtail the hazard.

For the tobacco industry, this seemingly minor matter is not. What's a few thousand cases? The estimate of the total damage caused by smoking is already about 450,000 deaths per year. The extra few would not seem enough to raise multi-million-dollar public relations retorts. But they did, not because the numbers were not important, but because of *who* the victims are. Until 1993, the industry had bent all its public relations power into suggesting that smoking was a choice. In court, they had won 800 suits on that simple premise — if you choose to inhale smoke, you must live with the consequences.

But of course, if you smoke *involuntarily*, the tables are turned. Tobacco smoke becomes simply a major air pollutant that causes illness, and in addition to its other troubles, tobacco would now be in the category of polluter. The sympathy of juries for victims of rapacious polluters is legend. The tobacco executives also realized that smokers take a good deal of grief from their spouses and children already, and the rate of trouble goes up as the number of remaining smokers goes down. The EPA findings would provide a brand new weapon to drub your local smoker with. All of this would, possibly, lead to even more quitting.

So at least two tobacco companies rolled out the guns, including the usual expensive, full-page pleadings. One of the ads which appeared to parody earlier deceits was one from Philip Morris, in July of 1994: "A large U.S. study published in the *American Journal of Public Health,* found no overall statistically significant link between second-hand smoke and lung cancer. Why did the EPA not include this study?"

The study, in fact, supported the EPA conclusion. The paper concluded that "In summary, our study and others conducted during the past decade suggest a small but consistent elevation in the risk of lung cancer in nonsmokers due to passive smoking. The proliferation of federal, state and local regulations that re-strict smoking in public places and work sites is well founded."

It would be difficult to imagine advertising that is more deceitful, short of simply making up statements and attributing them to the scientists.

They paid writers to get stories out attacking the science and the scientists. In one series of ads, a piece by Jacob Sullum, who works for a foundation supported by tobacco money, was run whole. In other ads, it was excerpted with the headline, "If we said it, you might not believe it." But of course, they did say it. Sullum not only works for a tobacco-supported foundation, but was paid directly by the company when they used his story. And, more to the point, his arguments came from industry sources and articles which, as you might surmise, are heavily laden with non-peer-reviewed, non-statistically tested "reviews" from "scientific" meet-ings. These are precisely what the EPA was trying to avoid in its study of the literature. The EPA included only the most rigorous, statistically-careful studies published to that time.

What is more striking is that the whole campaign seems so familiar, almost a motion-by-motion replay of 1953 and 1954 when the industry had to begin its campaign of denying that smoking itself causes disease. As then, full page newspaper ads said some scientists "have concluded that the data do not justify EPA's conclusion." As then, a "research" committee was estab-lished: this time it was the Center for Indoor Air Research. It was created in 1988 by the companies, and they hired a number of "independent" experts on air pollution. And just as the real scientists who were members of the advisory board of TIRC and CTR were found to have no doubts about the hazards of smoking, an informal poll of the board members of the Center for Indoor Air Research by Congressional staff members showed that, of the nine members on the board, seven said they believe second-hand smoke causes cancer in humans, one refused to answer, and only one said it does not.

All of this was a bit out of the ordinary even for the contentious process of federal policy making. But not much more might have happened at that moment but for the decision of some of the other players.

Representative Henry A. Waxman had been elected to Congress for almost two decades from southern California, and had for all those years worked to strap controls on the tobacco industry. He had little success. But in 1994, Mr. Waxman had risen to the level of chairman of one of the more important subcommittees in the House of Representatives, the Subcommittee on Health and the Environment.

In the fall of 1993, and then early in 1994, Rep. Waxman began a blitz of hearings to press home the findings of the EPA on second-hand smoke. He had introduced a bill called the "Smoke Free Environment Act," hoping to make policy of the momentum generated by the EPA reports and by the events across the U.S. as well. There was a tide of anti-smoking ordinances in town councils and county boards that had already eliminated smoking in more than seven hundred jurisdictions. More such bans were coming; his bill would have joined all the smoking bans nationally, at a stroke.

In the first week of February, 1994, he managed to get together in a hearing the Surgeons General of all of the previous six administrations — 25 years and equally Republican and Democratic. Each of the doctors endorsed the bill. As a group they endorsed a statement saying the bill could save more than 38,000 lives per year, and more illness besides. This was followed by a hearing at which chief executives of large corporations, such as Merck & Co., endorsed the smoking bill. The announcements seemed to come in batches rather than one at a time: McDonald's went smoke free, the association that represents chain restaurants declared itself for the bill, and the Defense Department banned smoking in most of its thousands of buildings. The bans now seemed logical — only about a quarter of the population still smoked, and there was some reason to believe the other three-quarters could be harmed by their supposedly weaker-willed compatriots at work.

The next player to poke his head out the door on the issue was Dr. David Kessler, Commissioner of the Food and Drug Administration. He is unusual as federal agency leaders go. He seems at heart an academic, not a politician or a political contributor who was handed a fat job. He wears his trousers loose, bunched up under his belt because he has lost weight. His glasses are thick as green glass. His scruffy red, stubbly beard, though now fashionable, does not save him from the image of the intellectual, the nerd, the man who wears plastic pocket protectors to keep his shirts free of ink. He once did carry an actual slide rule. His professional life has been devoted to an unusual double specialty. He is a doctor (a pediatrician) and also a lawyer who has specialized in federal food and drug law.

His mind is thus a map filled with data from health studies and subsections from federal law. He manages to find these subjects' vitals, to see the sinuous and often obscured connections between the torpid language of policy and the living flesh of the people subject to it. It is perhaps an odd calling — why not just treat the sick? — but however mixed and odd, it is what he does. Because of this, there is little doubt in the minds of those who watch this federal agency, and even of those who have once been commissioner, that Kessler has been the most knowledgeable and effective commissioner in the recent era, and perhaps in the history of the agency. Which also makes him perhaps the biggest target ever to pop up at the arcade.

His mission at the FDA when he arrived, already knowing the agency well from the outside, was simple in concept. The agency regulates about twenty-five cents of each consumer dollar in America, and it had been caught cheating, lying abed with industry. There were more than 50 indictments of FDA and company officials for collusion in allowing generic drugs onto the market without proper safety assurances.

The trouble with the agency, of course, is that the issues often arise explosively. Chilean wine. Breast implants. Tylenol killings. Those upset with the agency tend to be corporations with multi-billion-dollar revenues and well-placed friends in Congress and the White House. Because of this, it is unlikely that any commissioner can take the fast pitches and not miss completely sometimes. In the attacks on the agency there is always anger, and almost always money behind it.

In one interview I asked Kessler about tobacco. Why and how did he take it on?

It was not on his agenda coming into the agency, he said. As it is counted as the single greatest public health problem in the United States, he was conscious of it, and the possibility that FDA might act on it. But in the beginning, he said, his chief mission was to restore the credibility of the agency after the indictments for collusion with drug companies.

His notion was that the agency could be both a strict enforcer of the law, and an advocate for industry in getting drugs to market quickly. Both the industry and the public had suffered from the agency's failures, and he could see no reason why both could not be served effectively.

So the issues for him were enforcement, quick drug approval, reform of the food labels, reform of the blood banking system, better standards for mammographies to detect breast cancer, and so on.

Tobacco was not on his mind at first. He had little personal history with the plant — his parents were not smokers, at least not when he had reached consciousness of the topic. He himself did not smoke much, except a pipe in medical school.

It was about four months into his tenure as commissioner that the subject came up. Jeff Nesbit, the public affairs director when Kessler took over the agency, reminded him that the subject would have to be dealt with in some way or another. Several groups had petitioned the agency to take action on tobacco. One group wanted the agency to declare that the tobacco companies were making health claims by offering ultra-low tar cigarettes with disguised language about "lightness," to be read as healthier. Such a health claim, direct or implied, for such a lethal product, would be illegal under food and drug law.

At a meeting of the top FDA staff in early 1991, the petitions came up, and Kessler sent the question round the table — what should we do about these petitions and this subject in general? There was a strong sense at the meeting that tobacco was probably the number one public health issue, surpassing any other issue before the agency. It would be possible to have more effect on the health of the nation on this issue than any three others, Kessler says. There was also a sense that the topic was large, and full of trouble. "I remember saying that I would get to it, but I would need some time," he said. "I also had the sense that going after the low tar cigarettes for health claims, while leaving the regular cigarettes untouched, didn't make sense to me. I told them that I would welcome some thought on what was the right approach to the issue, but that I didn't think the petitions were it."

A small group of top agency officials, from that meeting on, began to talk about the problem of tobacco and FDA. Over time, the discussions began to shift from regulating cigarettes to regulating nicotine. Nicotine was, after all, the single common element among all kinds of tobacco products from cigarettes to chewing tobacco. And nicotine in patches and chewing gum was already regulated as a drug by the agency. Should nicotine in tobacco be exempted?

In the U.S. Pharmacopoeia, the official government list of drugs, nicotine in tobacco remained on the list until the turn of the century. Then it was removed, and though it appears that the history of how tobacco got this special status is lost, those who have looked into the issue suggest that there was a trade made at the time — the Southern Democrats would help establish the precursor of the FDA if tobacco were knocked off the list of drugs. Periodically, from that time to this, the agency has glanced over the issue again, reviewing whether tobacco really ought to be under agency jurisdiction. But until the administration of Kessler, no commissioner was willing to invest the amount of time and political capital necessary to actually investigate the matter and make a legal determination.

Late in 1992, after some thought, a draft of a letter to the leading petitioner, the Coalition on Smoking or Health, a group run jointly by the American Cancer Society, the American Heart Association and the American Lung Association, was drafted. The chief health officials in the Bush administration, Secretary Louis Sullivan and Assistant Secretary for Health James Mason, were both strongly in favor of some action on tobacco.

As the new Secretary of Health and Human Services, Donna Shalala, was coming into office in 1992, Kessler briefed her by suggesting that the agency was ready for a serious look at what companies were doing with nicotine. Some proposals might emerge from agency discussions, he said, but not for some time.

The information they had at that point was all at the surface. They had no documents from inside the companies, and essentially no understanding of what the company officials were saying in private to one another about their "intent" to use nicotine as a drug. At the time they had very little to go on: A few patents and some information on Next, the nicotine-free cigarette, and the Premier cigarette, the one that heated but didn't burn tobacco.

"One thing intrigued us," Kessler said. "That was that the companies could take out the nicotine. We knew that because we had turned up some patents showing they had the technology, and there was the cigarette that was made — Next — which was nicotine-free. So they could take it out, but they decided to leave it in." It was known to be hazardous and so it seemed that if they left it in, there must be a reason for it.

The agency, having laboratory facilities at hand, later did some work of its own to check nicotine contents. The FDA researchers picked the lowest-tar cigarette to test, the Merit brand, to find out what concentration of nicotine it had. It was a test of what cigarette manufacturers had maintained publicly for some time — that they set levels of tar, and nicotine just followed as a consequence; that in fact they did not set the levels of nicotine in cigarettes. Brands are devised as matters of taste and tar, and nicotine simply follows on its own.

The FDA labs found, however, that Merit, the lowest tar cigarette, contained the highest concentration of nicotine. This suggested that tar and nicotine did not move in tandem, automatically, but instead, that the level of nicotine was being kept up to a certain level, even as tar was being removed.

Agency analysts also looked at all the cigarettes on the market, compared their nicotine and tar levels, and found that tar was coming down among the most popular brands, but the relative levels of nicotine were not dropping with tar, but were rising. From reviewing inside documents, of course, this is obvious. When tar was being removed to meet worries about tar causing disease, it was important not to let nicotine drop to the point that cigarettes were no longer "satisfying." So methods had to be devised to keep nicotine concentrations up in the low and ultra-low tar cigarettes. These were a steadily increasing share of the market, and might well be the future of the industry.

Kessler said, "We found they weren't traveling together. They had started to separate." This suggested that the companies were working to reduce tar to contain worries about disease, but knew they could not simply let nicotine drop as well, and so intended to keep nicotine relatively high for its drug effects.

It was then clear that it would be worthwhile at least to carry on a serious investigation. It appeared from patents and other documents they had, that companies did not simply accept the amount of nicotine that came in the leaves of the plant as the amount that would be passed on to smokers. It appeared that the companies actively intervened to ensure that smokers got, not what the plant promised, but what the companies promised — enough nicotine to "satisfy" smokers.

Thus it was that on February 25, 1994, the FDA entered the tobacco wars: Kessler wrote a letter to the Coalition on Smoking or Health. The letter declared the agency's intent to consider regulating the nicotine in cigarettes as a drug. It was an extraordinary move, because tobacco up to that time had been specifically exempted from one health law after another. As Greg Connolly of the Massachusetts Department of Health noted, "Congress has exempted cigarettes from the Hazardous Substances Act, the Controlled Substances Act, the Toxic Substances Act, Consumer Product Safety Act. . . . Every major piece of health legislation since 1964 has had a specific exemption for cigarettes."

But the Food and Drug Administration is not required to consult Congress before determining what are drugs and what are not. The law establishing the agency gives it the power to regulate as a drug any substance that a company sells with intent to "affect the structure or function of the body." Some products have contaminants or substances that affect the body unintentionally.

Mild though it was, the letter represented a significant reversal for the agency. From leaving the issue to others, and declining to regulate tobacco, the agency had said it would now consider regulating tobacco, and was beginning an investigation of the matter.

This might have been shocking and disturbing to tobacco companies, but as it happened, it wasn't. Instead, they were absorbed in their fears and hopes of revenge for the ABC television program which had said the companies intentionally manipulated nicotine to keep smokers addicted.

The opening shot from journalists in the tobacco wars came from ABC's *Day One* program, on February 28, 1994. John Martin, reporter, and Pulitzer-prize-winner Walt Bogdanich, producer of the piece, had been working for a year on the subject of nicotine. They had already done a show several months before on nicotine poisoning experienced by tobacco field workers.

But the next piece was something much bigger. It began with veteran anti-tobacco campaigner Clifford Douglas, who was then working for the American Cancer Society. (He was also the key behind-the-scenes agitator against tobacco, a factor in events from getting out tobacco documents to briefing White House officials.) He had worked the subject for years, had a confidential source at R.J. Reynolds — he referred to the source as "Deep Cough" — and he had told Bogdanich and Martin something which surprised them greatly. Nicotine is no longer just a natural element in tobacco leaf which rides along until it arrives in the cigarette: The companies carefully control the amount of nicotine in cigarettes, and in fact during one part of the industrial process, the companies take out a substantial part of the nicotine in cigarettes, then add it back later.

Douglas, Bogdanich, and Martin realized that tobacco was largely unregulated by government, especially by the FDA, because of the stated excuse that nicotine was simply a natural part of leaf, not a drug delivered in controlled doses to ensure that smokers got enough to be hooked but not too much to be repelled by its harshness in the throat.

This was a critical realization, and it was one which FDA investigators had also been intrigued by.

As the ABC piece began, John Martin said, "Now, a lengthy *Day One* investigation has uncovered perhaps the tobacco industry's last, best secret: how it artificially adds nicotine to cigarettes to keep people smoking and boost profits. The methods the cigarette companies use to precisely control the levels of nicotine is something that has never before been disclosed to consumers or the government. For years, growing and blending tobacco was an art. But about 30 years ago, it began evolving into something quite different. . . ." Clifford Douglas said on the program, "The public doesn't know that the industry manipulates nicotine, takes it out, puts it back in, uses it as if it were sugar being put in candy."

The story was a bit fuzzy about what "adding nicotine" meant, but the general point was made: nicotine is not an accidental contaminant of cigarettes. It was carefully fixed at a desired level. Philip Morris sued ABC for $10 billion, declaring, somewhat off the point, that the company doesn't "spike" their cigarettes with more nicotine than the cigarette would have if it were all natural leaf. The ABC piece did not say that, but did use the word "spiking" in its introductory promotions, to describe the way nicotine was controlled. That was a mistake that gave Philip Morris an opening.

The difficulty with television and mistakes is that they are all on the front page. In newspapers, whole stories are written to retract a piece only when its core is wrong. And those are rarely run on the front page. But in television there is no convenient place to put corrections, so traditionally, minor mistakes are not acknowledged on the air, and significant mistakes are subject to more or less full story treatment.

So it was with the *Day One* story: it was essentially correct, contained errors, and fell squarely between the two extremes of completely negligible errors and errors demanding apologies.

But with tobacco, the landscape is different. The companies define for themselves what the story said and did not say, and run their own corrections in full page ads around the nation, then go to court.

In this instance, the tale takes an additional one or two turns before it is finished. After a year in court, ABC lawyers were ahead, having won several significant victories in court, including a ruling from the trial judge that the company was simply wrong when it said it did not add or manipulate nicotine in cigarettes.

Then, not long before the trial was to begin, and just after ABC had announced a merger with Walt Disney, ABC chairman Thomas Murphy announced that his company would settle the suit, issue a limited apology, and pay $15 million toward Philip Morris's legal fees. This decision was not a legal decision, but a business judgment. In fact, the odds of winning for ABC were rather good, for reasons not made public at the time. And ABC lawyers had tested their arguments and theories before two mock juries in the South, and had won.

The words of the apology itself were not a confession, and in fact if they had been run briefly at the end of a *Day One* broadcast, they might have defused the issue early, but coming as they did, they represented much more, and the show's reporters and producers refused to endorse the statement.

What is ironic about the case is what has not yet been published in detail: the documents that Philip Morris had to hand over to ABC in court showed a story rather different from the company's public position. They were sealed as was the 50-page motion from ABC lawyers to the court asking that the suit be dismissed at once because the company had admitted adding extraneous nicotine to tobacco in the sealed documents given to the court and to ABC.

Philip Morris's manuals for the engineers and technicians who make reconstituted tobacco describe several points at which nicotine may well be added to the sheet. The addition of nicotine as described by Philip Morris is not as the *Day One* piece suggested precisely — the additional nicotine does not come from "flavor houses" outside the company, but comes from the company's own additional supplies of extract.

The semantics get a little thick here, because the company states at every opportunity that no nicotine is added above and beyond what would have been in the tobacco plant in the first place. That is quite true, and has never been the point. It is not necessary to show that the company is loading huge doses of nicotine into cigarettes to make the all-important point: the final levels of nicotine are not "natural" or "accidental." They are precisely what the company wants and needs, and are *unrelated* to the amounts actually in the leaves or the stems or any combination.

As the Philip Morris documents show, a certain amount of nicotine is expected and maintained, and is tested for *hourly* on the production line, and if not enough is there, they add some. It is simple, and it has nothing to do with the original levels of nicotine in plants. It has to do with their intent — the fact that they do control the level of nicotine precisely and purposefully, whether or not they control it *upward*.

If the Motion for Summary Judgment is correct, as it seems, then it proves both that ABC got one suggestion wrong — that the extra nicotine comes from outside the company — and that Philip

Morris executives also got it wrong in denying that they add or manipulate nicotine. They do both, when and how it suits their factory processes.

The motion for summary judgment written by ABC lawyers and submitted just before the company settled the case cites Philip Morris documents extensively:

"Contrary to assurances Philip Morris made to this Court, the admissions in its documents nail down irrefutably that Philip Morris, by design, adds substantial amounts of what may be characterized as extraneous nicotine to its cigarettes during manufacturing. . . ."

The tale is rather convoluted in detail, but not too difficult in outline. We can imagine one bale of tobacco with leaves and stems coming into the "stemmery" where the leaves and sticks are separated.

The leaves, the real tobacco, are shredded and readied for inclusion in cigarettes.

But the stems and other junk are not yet ready. In a separate factory process, the stems, which in the past were thrown out altogether, are "disassembled" and made into a paper sheet.

The company says that to make this "reconstituted tobacco," after the dry stems are separated, they must be softened with "water." Then, they are put through rollers to press out the soluble materials — sugars and nicotine among other things.

This drawn-out material including nicotine is called the "liquor," while the stems that go on are called "sheet." It appears simple enough — they take the stems, squeeze out the liquid, make the stems into a paper sheet, then reapply the "liquor."

The result, as the companies suggest, is much the same as what they started with, with stems and solubles reunited, and nicotine levels perhaps a bit lower than they started out. In conception, this is correct.

But in fact, and what the ABC lawyers discovered, is that it is technically not true. As the Philip Morris documents seem to prove, the company does not take out liquor and put it back. Actually, the company also adds nicotine that was never part of the original tobacco stems. The reasons for this are engineering reasons. When the stems first come into the factory, they are dry, and so to begin making paper of them, when some water must be added, the company does not add regular water for this first soak.

Instead it adds what is called "weak extracted liquor 3 (WEL3)," that is, water left over from other tobacco that went before it through the process. It is not very strong liquor, but there is some tiny additional amount of nicotine in it, and this additional nicotine comes from other stems, completely different and additional to the ones just coming in to be pulped. The minute amount of nicotine in the weak liquor is therefore, genuinely, "added" nicotine.

Similarly, there is yet a third liquor that is a by-product of the process and is re-used, called by company technicians "rich brown water," because, while it is also weak, it contains enough of the nicotine and other plant materials to turn the water brown.

As the ABC lawyers wrote after reading Philip Morris documents, "Philip Morris blends all these ingredients — the dry raw tobacco materials, the WEL3, and the rich brown water — in the pulper to form a slurry, which proceeds to the next stages. . . ."

As the ABC lawyers wrote to the judge, these additions alone prove that nicotine that was not in the original tobacco plant, leaves, or stems, is technically "added" in manufacturing, though the additional nicotine is very small.

But there is more. When the company is rejoining the sheet and the liquor, it is very important to add just the right amount of liquor to the sheet. There must be just the proper amount of sugar, nicotine and so on.

(And, interestingly, at this point the company removes potassium nitrate from the liquor because it is a carcinogen and the company is worried about the health effects of cigarettes, according to their manuals!)

When the company technicians add the liquor back to ensure the proper amounts of solubles get into the cigarettes, they do not automatically add back just the amount that was there when the stems came in. They have no idea what amount was there originally. Rather, they pour on enough liquor to get the level of nicotine, sugars, and so on, to come up to company specifications, regardless of how much nature might have put or not put in the stems originally.

In fact, just for the emergencies when the sheet falls far below the needed level, the company manufactures its own, separate supplies of liquor to keep on hand. This is dumped in when machinery fails. This, too, is completely extraneous, and might as well come from an outside "flavor house" as the ABC program reported.

So in the end, we cannot imagine the stems going in, having their liquid content extracted and the same liquid content, including the nicotine, reapplied to the same stems. It does not work that way, although from Philip Morris statements it *sounds* like that is what they are saying. They have said that the process is an "entirely closed" one, suggesting that no nicotine not in the original tobacco and stems finds its way into the final cigarette. "No nicotine whatsoever not found in the original tobacco materials is introduced in the production of the reconstituted tobacco sheets," said Philip Morris in its original complaint against ABC. Does the "original tobacco materials" mean just those stems used to make the sheet, and not others? If that's what they meant, it was completely false. Perhaps, in the lawyerly way, they will argue that they did not mean *exactly* those stems, not exactly *those* "tobacco materials," as long as the nicotine comes from some materials brought in that day or another day by Philip Morris rather than some outside company.

As the ABC lawyers would have argued if their company had not settled, "Tobacco extract is a stand-alone, physically separate, manufactured product. It is not just temporarily removed from and then returned to the same natural tobacco from which it came."

It would be industrially ridiculous to try to keep a particular tobacco stem together with its nicotine, as if this were the Red Cross blood bank, so that the stems might get their own nicotine in transfusion later. Probably, the actual stem and its nicotine never see one another again after separation, and probably, the exact level of nicotine that occurs in nature never occurs again after the stems enter the factory.

But what happens, according to company documents, reveals precisely what the company's intent is: to carefully control the amount of nicotine in the cigarette. And in fact, in the Philip Morris documents is evidence that might well convict tobacco company chiefs of perjury. They testified before Waxman's committee that nicotine is measured in tobacco only very early, just after the plants are harvested, and very late, after the cigarettes are made. As Philip Morris CEO William Campbell testified before Waxman's committee, "Nicotine levels in tobacco are measured at only two points in the manufacturing process — at the stem-mery, where tobacco leaves are prepared for processing, and then 18 months later after those leaves have been manufactured into finished cigarettes." This gives the impression that they really don't worry about the nicotine levels along the way.

But the Philip Morris documents show that the company *does* measure "solubles" and measure them *hourly*, during parts of the process. The documents say that "solubles," which they define as "nitrates, nicotine, sugars, etc.," are measured frequently. As one paper instructs employees: "Finished Sheet Solubles: Percentage of dissolved solute in finished sheet sample, checked once per/hour to ensure that they are within specified ranges."

What this whole process amounts to is technically silly, but historically important. Tobacco was an agricultural product with natural levels of various elements, and this argument has long been used by the industry to say that cigarettes cannot be seen as drugs or drug-delivery devices. But the modern cigarette, with its reconstituted tobacco and its clever and efficient industrial stream, is no longer an agricultural product.

As the ABC lawyers wrote, "It does not have the texture, size or shape of any tobacco found in nature. It contains significant quantities of chemicals — diammonium phosphate, urea, and paraben to name only a few — that are entirely foreign to to-bacco.... Philip Morris's pre-determined specifications, not Mother Nature, govern the width, thickness, chemical composi-tion, and moisture content of this tobacco sheet."

It will be debated for some time into the future what made ABC cave in to the tobacco company. Some executives and lawyers feared the trial, and also feared the consequences to the company of a bitter public fight just as Disney was taking them over. Whatever the internal dynamics, it is clear that the ABC lawyers had little interest in the issues of press freedom and fighting the intimidation of tobacco companies in this case. Their concern was about corporate "exposure" rather than news or truth in the long run. This seems a congenital failure of television news, which is a mere appendage of a giant entertainment operation. Newspapers, anachronistic as they are, still have little of this corporate corruption.

It seems likely that the ABC episode is over, and so it ends in this odd state in which ABC officially accepts the blame for saying the company adds nicotine; while the documents themselves show they do just that, in their own convoluted way.

One ABC executive who worked on the long investigation said that for all the frustration with the company about the suit and how it was settled, with a forced apology, that the final result was not the worst part of the episode. At least the story got on the air, he said, and it had an important impact on the developing issue.

But the worst moment, he said, came after the suit was filed and the news people were under the gun. At that moment, a batch of never-before-seen tobacco documents were handed to the reporters. They were from a different company, and had nothing to do with the suit. Though it wasn't certain at the time, they would turn out to be the first few memos in the biggest and best of all caches of internal tobacco documents — the Brown and Williamson papers.

But, because of the Philip Morris suit, fear ruled. The executive said that Alan Braverman, in-house counsel for ABC, said not only that ABC should not report on the papers, but in an action that stunned those in the business, the papers were confiscated from news staff. They were ordered to erase their computer notes about the papers.

All this *sturm und drang* occurred about a program that aired on February 28, 1994, a Monday. The previous Friday, the Food and Drug Administration had also made its first important statement on the subject.

With the two striking events, the center of gravity of the issue shifted in Washington. It moved from second-hand smoke to nicotine. Rep. Waxman maintained the beat of the hearings through the change of focus, and brought in Kessler to testify about his reasoning and some of the evidence for the agency's belief that nicotine was deliberately used by the companies to keep smokers addicted.

Kessler knew he could not make any mistakes at the hearing, and asked his staff and investigators to go over every detail of his testimony. In an interview he described what he said to his staff: "This, you cannot get wrong. You cannot make a mistake. They are extremely aggressive." The key piece of information in the hearing was a single chart, one which flatly contradicted the company assertions that tar and nicotine are set with a single decision of the company — the decision to set the tar level. The chart showed that while that had been true historically for decades, after the 1970s it was no longer true. The "lighter" tar cigarettes could not have their nicotine levels continue to drop; they had to be shored up, and so gradually the relative rate of nicotine to tar in these cigarettes went up. And, because they were selling more and more low tar cigarettes, in that group the relative amount of nicotine was rising.

These numbers simply could not be argued with, at least rationally. They were either right or wrong. Something appeared to have happened to separate the levels of nicotine and tar; an old, solid line of defense for the companies seemed to be demolished.

On the same day, company scientist Dr. Alexander W. Spears, from Lorillard, testified that the FDA was wrong. He said under oath, "We do not set nicotine levels for particular brands of cigarettes. Nicotine levels follow the tar level." He went further: "The correlation is an essentially perfect correlation between tar and nicotine and shows there is no manipulation of nicotine."

This sort of flat contradiction is what is normally expected from company executives when they testify.

But this time, something seemed to go wrong. The congressmen and reporters were asking unusually detailed questions. The companies tried to recoup after the hearings by reanalyzing the data, but they could not make the numbers come out right, and reporters didn't go for the bait.

Then, it got worse. The chief executive officers of the seven giant tobacco companies were due to testify before Waxman's subcommittee on April 14, a Thursday.

It seemed incredible that they agreed to appear before Congress, to be sworn in, and to be questioned by hostile House members. But the momentum was with Waxman. If the companies refused, he could hold "an empty chair" hearing, in which the committee is called to order, the chairman begins, and he points to the empty chairs in front of him, and asks what exactly the witnesses who failed to show up were trying to hide.

C H A P T E R

8

IN CAMERA

The political arena leaves one no alternative, one must either be a
dunce or a rogue.
                    — Emma Goldman, 1910

So they appeared, in a large wood-paneled hearing room, with
red, white and blue carpet; the room was crowded wall to wall and
dais to doors. People gathered in the hallways, where banks of
television and radio equipment half-filled the corridors coming
and going.

The best remembered image from the hearings is the one
that may remain the best known image of tobacco companies
permanently. It is of the seven chief executives standing in a line
with their right hands raised, under the headline "Tobacco Chiefs
Say Cigarettes Aren't Addictive."

I wrote in the *New York Times*, "The chief executives of the
top seven U.S. tobacco companies appeared in Congress today for
the first time together, and each of them under oath said he does
not believe that nicotine or cigarettes are addicting, but they
agreed to give Congress virtually all the research on humans and
animals they have done on nicotine and addiction."

They jousted for more than six hours with Democratic
committee members, and were gentled and stroked by Republican members. They suggested that smoking cigarettes is no more
harmful than eating Twinkies or drinking coffee.

Rep. Waxman began a long series of questions about what
the executives were willing to say about smoking and disease and
smoking and addiction.

WAXMAN: Mr. Tisch . . . In a deposition last year you were asked whether cigarette smoking causes cancer. Your answer was "I don't believe so." Do you stand by that answer today?
TISCH: I do, sir.
WAXMAN: Do you understand how isolated you are in that belief from the entire scientific community?
TISCH: I do, sir. . . . We have looked at the data and the data that we have been able to see has all been statistical data that has not convinced me that smoking causes death.

Rep. Ron Wyden of Oregon asked each of the executives about nicotine and addiction.

WYDEN: Let me ask you first, and I'd like to just go down the row, whether each of you believes that nicotine is not addictive?
CAMPBELL: I believe nicotine is not addictive, yes.
JOHNSTON: Congressman, cigarettes and nicotine clearly do not meet the classic definitions of addiction. There is no intoxication.

[No one, not even tobacco company scientists, are usually willing to make the assertion that there is no intoxication; cigarettes are in fact intoxicating, mildly in the doses achieved through cigarette smoking, very heavily in greater doses like those achieved by Native American shamans. As for the classical definition, it was classical in 1950; as the phenomenon has been studied the classical definition — that used by the medical and psychological societies and in diagnosis — has been revised and has not emphasized intoxication for some years.]

TADDEO: I don't believe that nicotine or our products are addicting.
HORRIGAN: I believe nicotine is not addictive.
SANDEFUR: I believe nicotine is not addictive.
JOHNSON: And I too believe that nicotine is not addictive.

There were numerous issues raised in the hours of testimony, and numerous interesting answers; from a lawyer's point of view there were probably several statements which could be chargeable as perjury if a prosecutor ever takes it to court, as the Justice Department appears ready to do.

One illustration, one thread from the charge and counter-charge, gives some sense of the ferocity of the contest. The day before the executives were to appear before a packed hearing room, Waxman's staff called reporters to release a new piece of paper they had just found. It was a paper written by Alexander Spears, who had just vehemently defended the nicotine-follows-tar argument. In it, he outlined in clear detail just how the companies were working to separate the nicotine and tar levels. The article was a bit obscure — it was presented to the 35th Tobacco Research Chemists Conference in 1981 — and it is unlikely that Spears expected to be confronted with it. But there it was. The paper, copies of which Waxman's staff distributed, pointed out that, just as FDA had said, low tar cigarettes have 20 percent more nicotine than other brands. He said these higher nicotine levels were apparently achieved at least partly by using blends of tobacco with higher concentrations of nicotine in their leaves.

"Higher nicotine levels can be achieved by decreasing Oriental, and the stem and tobacco sheet, and increasing the Burley and upper stalk positions of both flue-cured and the Burley tobacco," the paper said. It was as clear a statement of how the companies work as has ever been put to paper.

What could be his defense? His paper clearly contradicted his own testimony, unless you could imagine him saying something like, well, it's true that the companies raise nicotine levels in some cigarettes, but overall the nicotine still sticks closely to tar levels.

But no, he addressed that issue as well in the paper. He wrote that the company's attempts to reduce tar ran into trouble at first because the nicotine levels had also dropped. As a result, he wrote, "current research is directed toward increasing the nicotine levels while maintaining or marginally reducing the tar levels."

He had written about intentionally separating tar and nicotine levels, but then boldly testified that it was not being done.

Waxman was angry. As he released the copy of Spears' paper of 15 years before, he said, "the tobacco companies have lied to us" and said "it is a criminal offense to try to mislead Congress."

The little by-play, only one of the games of tug and pull between the charging anti-tobacco partisans and the tobacco companies, did not end there.

The next day, Dr. Spears appeared alongside the chief executives of the companies. Andrew Tisch, the chairman of Lorillard, again took the boldest approach. In his opening statement, he abandoned prepared remarks and attacked Waxman and the committee for statements about Mr. Spears. "You have made a number of very serious claims and assertions during the press conference you called yesterday; claims and assertions that question the integrity of our company and Dr. Alexander Spears, who is with me today." Tisch demanded time for Spears at the hearing to defend himself. The committee had told him that Spears could not be added to the day's list of witnesses just for that purpose. So Tisch said, "I am left with no choice but to cede the balance of my time to Dr. Spears, to ensure that he will have the adequate opportunity to correct the very serious misstatements and misconceptions that were conveyed in yesterday's press conference."

Waxman balked, and said Spears would have his chance, but not at that moment.

Tisch pushed on. "I want to reaffirm and emphasize what Dr. Spears said during his appearance on March 25th, and to make absolutely clear to the Congress and to the public that the level of nicotine in the products manufactured and sold by Lorillard is solely determined by . . ." and here you would expect him to say, loud and clear for the cameras, "tar levels."

But he didn't. He said just the opposite: "the level of nicotine is solely determined by the tobacco we buy and the blending of the different tobaccos used. . . ."

That is precisely what Spears had said in his paper, and denied in his testimony. If you were not paying attention, the tone of anger and defiance made sense. But if you were following the technical point, it was a bizarre statement, and got worse: "Nicotine levels follow tar levels and are not raised or reduced for particular brands." Again, the opposite of the comment just before it.

Later, Rep. Kreidler of Wisconsin showed Spears a copy of the chart Spears had produced at the earlier hearing, which he had said was a copy of a chart from the 1989 Surgeon General's report which showed nicotine levels decreasing from 1950 to 1990.

Kreidler brought out a copy of the actual chart from the Surgeon General's report, and compared it to the one that Spears had produced. "Now that we have had time to look more closely at your chart, and the data upon which it was based . . . we see some problems. At least over the most recent decade, the chart does not appear to reflect either the FTC data or the 1989 Surgeon General's chart, upon which it is supposedly based. . . . Your chart shows a continuing decrease in nicotine levels after '82, but the Surgeon General's chart shows . . . an increase in nicotine levels. For instance, the Surgeon General's chart shows a significant increase in nicotine yields in '85. This is not reflected in your chart at all. In fact, your chart shows a decrease from 1984 to 1985. . . ."

Asked whether he made mistakes in preparing his chart, Dr. Spears said, "I'd like to say a few things about this. Obviously there's a lot of confusion. And let me say, number one, what I represented to you was not the very minute detail that you're now talking about, but the fact that tar and nicotine decreased through the period 1950s to the present in a parallel fashion."

Spears then dodged and weaved through another 26 questions and answers, avoiding acknowledging any error or even that his chart showed the opposite of what the original chart showed.

SPEARS: Sir, I did not make that as a profound statement. . . .

KREIDLER: You submitted data that would lead us to that conclusion.

SPEARS: The statement was that nicotine follows tar from the period 1950s to 1990. I stick with that statement, and I believe it is accurate. I've gone back and rechecked the calculations. Now, if you want to debate me for a second—

KREIDLER: Excuse me, Mr. Spears, but you submitted this as a Surgeon General's chart. Is it or is it not a Surgeon General's chart?

SPEARS: This chart came from the Surgeon General's report that was identified, yes.

KREIDLER: Was it presented accurately? Why does it—for the last ten-year period why does your chart show that the levels are decreasing when, in fact, the data shows us they were increasing?

SPEARS: . . . It looks to me like my chart might show a ten percent decrease, but the data you put up there might show a zero, or certainly much less than a ten percent increase. . . .

Just as he reached that point, the time expired.

The original chart shows just what the FDA data showed, and just what he had written in his paper that the companies were trying to do: the nicotine and tar had separated, and nicotine was rising relative to tar.

I was covering the hearing, and recall a rush of adrenaline when I saw the chart. It was clearly wrong. Amid the frustrating tangle of verbiage, here was a clear lie. The data showed a change, and nicotine proportions began to rise; the companies were trying to use the data over forty years as a whole to mask the recent change. But they seemed to have gone too far. Could he possibly have presented a fraudulent chart, under oath, to the committee? After Rep. Kreidler's questioning, I waited until the break in the testimony, walked over to the witness table, and introduced myself to Dr. Spears. I told him I noticed that the chart was not actually a copy of the Surgeon General's chart, that the companies' chart showed nicotine levels continuing to drop relative to tar after 1982. I asked, "That's wrong, isn't it?"

He looked a bit startled. "It goes down overall."

"Right. But at the end there, 1982 to 1990. That's wrong, isn't it?" The company chart showed a ten percent *drop* in nicotine from 1982 on, where the Surgeon General's actual data shows just less than a ten percent *increase* in nicotine.

"Yes. It's wrong," Spears said.

"That seems important. How did that get wrong?"

"I don't know."

Whether the Republicans from Virginia and North Carolina, Bliley and McMillan, were aware of all the distinctions is unclear. I suspect they were, but in any case they kept repeating the obfuscating line, that the nicotine was down overall from 1950. So what was the problem? Why do people keep talking about increases?

CHAPTER

9

DR. WILLIAMS

Ultimately a hero is a man who would argue with the Gods, and so awakens devils to contest his vision.
— Norman Mailer, *The Presidential Papers*

As all these shenanigans went on, Merrell Williams was slouching toward Washington to be born.

Late one afternoon after the April 14 hearings I got a call at the Washington Bureau of the *Times* from a government official with whom I had never talked before. He identified himself, but spoke in a whisper; he seemed to be in an office where others might easily overhear. He said he had documents, unbelievable documents. He didn't want me to come to his office, and he didn't want to come to the *Times*. How about his house in the evening? Okay.

When I arrived he led me to the dining room table, which was bare except for a pile of papers maybe six inches high. He was nervous. He said I couldn't take them with me, but I could look at them, make notes, tell him which ones I wanted, and maybe he could get me copies.

They were all from the files of Brown and Williamson Company, though some of them originated in other companies. I had no idea what I was looking at, and didn't really know enough about tobacco to choose, but I didn't argue. I asked where they came from, and he said that he didn't actually know their origin, though they had come into his office "over the transom," though he said he thought he knew who the intermediary was. I asked, Any way of telling if they are genuine?

He didn't know. After ten minutes of reading there was no doubt in my mind, but checks of internal facts such as names, dates and events should easily give us the answer. The pages were fully marked with officers' names and titles. Not hard to find out.

From those first papers I wrote a story which appeared May 7, 1994, "Tobacco Company Was Silent on Hazards." The heart of it was the memo from Addison Yeaman and documents from research on nicotine that showed how nicotine exerted its addictive effect. It began, "Internal documents from a major tobacco company show that executives struggled with whether to disclose to the Surgeon General what they knew in 1963 about the hazards of cigarettes, at a time when the Surgeon General was preparing a report saying for the first time that cigarettes are a major health hazard. The executives of the company, Brown and Williamson Tobacco Company, chose to remain silent, to keep their research results secret, to stop work on a safer cigarette and to pursue a legal and public relations strategy of admitting nothing. In more than one hundred documents, letters and cables from the 1960s and 1970s that provide a rare look at the internal discussions among tobacco executives, the officials spoke of the hazards of cigarettes and stated plainly to one another that nicotine is addictive."

Within a short time, I got another call from an anti-tobacco group asking if I was interested in more documents: essentially, the larger set from which the first 100 documents or so had come. When I got it — it came in a box, in the mail — it was about 4,000 to 5,000 pages, again all from the Brown and Williamson files. Because this set was so much larger, and there were minutes of so many meetings, it was much easier to write a clear bit of history about what the company executives were thinking and doing on the subject of smoking and health. I wrote a three-part series for the *Times* on the papers, beginning June 15, after much internal debate and editing.

Soon, I located the original source of the papers, Merrell Williams, and I flew down to visit him.

On a rainy night in Mississippi, Williams sat alone in a bar on old highway 90. He was fleeing from Kentucky back to the country of his childhood, the Gulf Coast where what he really wanted to do was to sail.

He waited with a dark beer and a drawn face, for a reporter, myself, to walk through the door so he could unravel the story. He was not, he felt, a criminal. It was true that he had come down here rather than face contempt of court and jail in Louisville.

He had taken documents from a tobacco company, and had begun a shock wave of stories, dispute, subpoenas and the scurrying of lawyers. One lawyer even said that, while plaintiffs had sued tobacco companies for decades, now, with the papers Merrell had carried out of the company, the smokers might actually win a case.

Williams was — well, actually he was Dr. Merrell Williams — a professor of drama. He was 53 years old, wore a work shirt and jeans, and looked troubled and unsure of himself in the bar.

He had committed what he knew were acts that might be illegal, and he wasn't sure exactly why he had done it, either.

He wanted assurance from the reporter first that he was actually a reporter and not an agent of the tobacco companies. At first, when the reporter appeared with a white shirt, dark suit and tie from his Northern business, Merrell said he would not admit having any documents. "You could be anybody," he said. "Do you have identification?" The reporter showed his blue-and-white *New York Times* building pass.

"I had not read *The Firm*," he said. "First, I lived it, then I read it."

Like the central figure in that novel, he was working for a law firm, and found himself staring at documents he thought were plainly evidence of criminal acts, a decades-long conspiracy of tobacco companies and lawyers to hide what they knew about the dangers of smoking and what might be done about it.

Day after day, his job as a paralegal sitting in the research department of Brown and Williamson Tobacco Company was to read private company papers, most of them boring, but a few of which raised the hair on the back of his neck.

He was himself a smoker, having inhaled Kools for more than 25 years. The company he was now working for, through a law firm, was the company that made his cigarettes. He had tried to quit, of course, and he had switched to the low tar brands.

His life had not gone as he imagined it, and so when he took the job as a paralegal in a large Kentucky firm in 1987 (Wyatt, Tarrant and Combs), he was pleased to be making $9 per hour, though he was the oldest of the paralegals, nearing 50 years old.

He had begun as a promising writer, a playwright who had

written some modestly successful scripts that were put on stage at La Mama in New York and some bits of his work made it to television, he said, not long after college. He went to Baylor University, then University of Denver, and got a full scholarship to University of Mississippi for a Ph.D. in 1971.

He glided into the job of teaching drama and writing part-time at Jackson State University in Mississippi.

One marriage failed, and after ten years of teaching and the beginning of another marriage, he moved where his wife wanted to be, with her family up in Louisville, Kentucky. They had two children, and moved to Louisville though he had no job lined up.

That was 1981. "I couldn't find a job teaching," he said as he watched me eat a chopped steak, onions, fries and gravy. "The food's good here. It'll kill you, but it's good."

He said he went back to school at the University of Louisville, and took courses on the law — criminal justice, constitutional law, labor law. "But inside three years my wife was in preparation for divorce. What I had when it was over was a bicycle with one brake left, the front brake, and an old Renault. I was on the street. I took jobs as a car salesman, a waiter, and I cut roses at one job."

He went to the Bar Association and asked about jobs. They said he was qualified to be a paralegal and get a decent job. Williams was not concerned with just what the job would be. It paid almost as much as his teaching, he said.

It was 1987. He found himself assigned to the task of reading through memos and reports, heaps of them, from the files of Brown and Williamson, among the biggest tobacco firms and the maker of Kool and Viceroy cigarettes.

His job was to find the "sensitive" and "significant" documents that might get the company in trouble. He found them.

He felt a bit old to be sharing his surprise with the youngsters he was working with. He began to feel isolated, unable to talk to anyone about the astonishing admissions he was reading day to day.

"You get these moral pangs, you get bottled up with these strong feelings, and there is nobody you can talk to," he said. He was told he could never divulge anything he saw or read or learned while at work.

After the beginning of an interview over beer, he and I

repaired to his hideout, a small modern apartment in a little maze of modern apartments that seemed a little out of place in the trees and among the semi-rural town strung out along the old highway, which had been long since bypassed by the interstate.

The refrigerator had little food, but plenty of beer and wine. Boxes were not yet unpacked, the room was dark, and there were no lamps set up yet. Mr. Williams and I sat in the dark, with a weak light coming in from the kitchen. He had been there for six weeks; his two daughters, he fretted, were still in Louisville, vulnerable to impulses of his former wife and to anything his imagination could conjure up about angry tobacco company employees who wanted revenge on him. "No, I don't really think they're in danger," he said. "No, not really."

He took a sip of pink wine and said, "It took some time, but I realized I had signed a compact with the devil."

The papers he worked on were electric. He couldn't help feeling stirred and upset at the same time. "It was almost as if I had walked into a job and been told 'You'll be reading some stuff.' Okay, fine, and I went to the filing cabinet, opened it up, and said to myself, well, it looks like these people are engaged in, ahhhh, murder," he said.

He gestured in the dark as if he were looking through files. "Here is a list of the crimes. And you go to your supervisor, and say: Well, it looks like you killed 12 people, is that what you did?

" 'Yes,' the supervisor says, 'but that's why we are here. We are going through these to defend ourselves. . . .' Then I went back to the file drawer, looked at more papers, and found out they planned to kill 12 more. I had a job that was not just protecting, but perpetuating some kind of method of dealing with, if not murder, certainly a kind of deviousness that would cause people great damage."

It was near midnight. He put down his wine glass and pulled up the leg of his jeans, the right leg. "I have the proof of the damage right here. That's where they take your veins to do the bypass," he said.

He had smoked cigarettes for a long time. He is thin, has low cholesterol, and has always been fond of seafood, so he thought of all things he would not have heart trouble. But there it was, major heart disease in the blockage of arteries to the heart, and in 1993 he had quintuple bypass surgery to route the blood around five choked arteries.

According to the federal government, the greatest death toll from cigarettes is not from lung cancer, but from heart disease, says Merrell Williams, and he is convinced that's where his disease came from. Not that that conviction has anything to do with his motivation, he says, because he took the documents first, and found out about the disease later.

He began to call his mother, a middle-class woman from Mississippi, who sells real estate. He didn't know whom else to turn to. There were guards around the rooms in which he worked, and he was told that the people who keyed documents and their sensitivity into the computers could not speak English; this so they could not be called in a court case.

"I don't know if it's true," he said. But he was reading code names, Hippo, Mad Hatter, Rio, Ship, and he says he saw that some of the documents were not included in the coded lists that might be produced when a plaintiff demanded documents in court. These items were handled separately.

Williams said, "I quit smoking on September 27, 1989." He was smoking Richland and Merit low tar cigarettes at the time. "I knew what they did, what they were still doing, knew they were aware of the disease, not the cardiovascular like I had, but other things."

He paused and gestured in the air noncommittally. "I know this is strange, but I was up in the mountains in Kentucky. I am a Catholic but don't go to church. I am not a good role model for my children," he said, rambling in the way that he does habitually as he tells stories.

"But I do believe in some kind of higher order than human beings," he said. He told of a lawyer he met who changed his life very late. "I really felt the Lord meant for him to do something in the last part of his life. I had the same experience. I really did."

As he stood in the mountains, he said, he was frustrated with life in general. "Just tell me what the hell I need to do," he said, speaking to the air or God. "I was stricken by an attack of Gandhism. I was freezing cold, my dumb girlfriend was still smoking, and I am not going to say that God said, 'steal documents,' but after that, I did."

The motive is still unclear to him, he says. "Because I had to do something," he says now. "And because otherwise there is no proof. There just is no proof." He felt that for many years the companies had made great profits on tobacco but had known what kind of damage was being created. But after all the years, still no one had the proof that the tobacco company executive knew. "There was just no proof: that was what bothered me most."

"I became captivated by the idea — have you read Jean Genet?" He had "kind of a spiritual thief inside him. It's an absurdity, I know. I just had to do it."

He knew there was a high risk. "I was paying $400 in child support, and I'd not missed a day of visitation with my kids. And I knew I could be caught. And still I was doing it," he said, with his voice registering surprise.

The "it" he was doing, he said, was looking over documents for the ones that seemed particularly damaging to the company. He would slip papers into the wide band of the back brace he wore under his shirt. He walked out with them against his belly, copied them, and brought the papers back.

"The ones I picked were always the kind of things that there was just no way of denying it. They had denied to a magistrate in California that they had done any biological studies on the hazards of smoking. They said they just never did them, had nothing to do with it. But all of a sudden I had the biological studies," he said.

By this time, he was making a project of it. He was reading about litigation and tobacco matters. He knew who were the figures who had set themselves up against the companies. He had also refined his method.

"I would go in at 5:30 in the morning, or on Saturdays. I would pick the times, or I would hear of documents that sounded very interesting to me. I would go by the person's desk and eye it, get the number of the box, and come back," he said.

He said that it made him feel half crazy. "It was very stressful," he said. He was frightened, and stimulated. "I was a thief and knew I was a thief," he said. But his big problem was that he had no idea what he was going to do next. "I didn't know what to do with this stuff. I knew I had to do something. I knew there was something wrong, especially the lawyers directing and hiding the science," he said.

But the documents piled up in his apartment. He eventually called an anti-tobacco activist, met with him, and asked what to do next. He spoke to a writer and began to work over what he had. But it was clear that for himself and the writer, any publication would mean jail for stealing and disclosing confidential documents.

He stopped working on them, but realized that "I had them, and they were sitting there. This was very dangerous. I was walking around with somebody's hot documents," he said. Finally, he worked out a way to turn them over to a lawyer, who would in turn get them in the mail to those who might use them. From there, they were sent without any provenance to a member of Congress, among others.

The issue of tobacco was hot again, after Dr. David Kessler, the Commissioner of the Food and Drug Administration, had said he was ready to regulate cigarettes for the first time. The papers made their way to me; I wrote half a dozen stories from them, and then flew down to Mississippi to meet Mr. Williams and ask *why* he had done all this.

"You know, whatever I say, I don't know," he replied. But he recalls sitting on a boat, stilled by a storm in the gulf and tied up, going nowhere for many hours. He picked up *The Firm*, and began reading. "Oh My God!" he whispered to himself.

Now reclining amid the scent of mildew at midnight, telling his tale to someone he really did not know, he seemed to sink into the foam of the chair. His life was being improvised moment to moment. All he could think of at that hour of night, he said, was to get his children out of Louisville. He wanted to be with them, to start thinking of their lives as the center of his.

In some sense, Mr. Williams was a creation of the tobacco companies themselves. It would be impossible for so many people inside the companies to know what had developed over the years, and where the evidence was, but for none of them ever to try to breach the security and bring some evidence out beyond the walls. There were after all many bitter people and many people with failed dreams and lives that needed some large act to redeem them.

The company tried to prevent such behavior by regular lectures to their employees about prosecution and jail to those who spoke of their work on the outside. They also successfully kept most of their employees compartmentalized, so that none had a broad understanding of what they were doing and what it might mean.

Nevertheless, the appearance of a curious and persistent

character like Mr. Williams was inevitable in principle, if not in this precise person. He appeared, he took out documents, and so changed the history of the industry and its position in society permanently.

So it was that thirty-four years after the tobacco executives met at the Plaza Hotel in New York, long after their strategy had proved a success, an odd series of events in Louisville, Kentucky, began to shift the earth beneath the companies.

In Louisville, Williams, who is a bright and tousle-haired man with a soft, slurring speech, and a habit of abrupt jumps from subject to subject, went to work for Brown and Williamson. He and his closeted compatriots first got lectures about the tobacco business and about the sensitive nature of the documents they were working with.

One of the supervising lawyers, Merrell said, told the group, "I want you all to know that our client is very sensitive about press coverage. I ask that, we ask that, that is, Wyatt asks that you be especially careful in mentioning the client in any way, shape or form. You have probably been aware that our client is Brown and Williamson Tobacco Company. Brown and Williamson makes, well, cigarettes, chewing tobacco, snuff, all that. We believe in B & W and have been hired as their hometown counsel to help them do their best to fight the alleged charges that tobacco — used in any product — is dangerous or causes any kind of human disease."

One woman asked whether she could tell her boyfriend Mike who she worked for.

"No. You work for Wyatt, Tarrant and Combs. That's what you tell Mike. That's what you tell your mother, your brother, your uncle. Wyatt signs your checks. You work for Wyatt. Beyond that — and I emphasize this because we don't want 60 *Minutes* hauling in cameras . . . We want to keep it clean and respect the client's wishes."

Another of the potential employees ventured that it was a little odd that secrecy was required even though Brown and Williamson didn't have anything to hide.

Merrell and the others were to sign elaborate confidentiality agreements, saying they would not disclose what they learned on the job. Merrell says he does not remember the signing.

He and the other 20 or so paralegals worked on fold-out

tables, in an uncarpeted room, amid hundreds of cardboard boxes. They worked heads down, reading documents, most of them boring and largely meaningless pieces of paper from transactions that no one understood now, and few had reason to understand years ago. This was archeology, and most of the time was spent brushing dirt aside gently, looking for the unusual features. It was done mostly by paralegals, though there was the occasional entrance by a supervising lawyer, all attached to one of three different firms: Vincent and Elkins in Texas, Wyatt in Louisville, and King and Spaulding in Atlanta.

Merrell soon understood that the great secret paper project had been under way for some time, months at least, and the day to day activity was run by "box checkers," and carried out by the "box reviewers."

The job was to "screen" documents; literally, to find documents that would either help or hurt the tobacco company in court. The records were jumbled, the papers were bits in a mosaic whose outline was unknown to all those working through the papers except the supervising lawyers.

Preliminary work, Merrell learned, had been going on for at least two years. Copying and sorting, mostly, but not reviewing, which was the more important task. That had just begun, and he was part of it.

The work was essentially scrubbing the company's files — trying to cope with the company's past, to get a clear sense of what was in the mountain of boxed material, to hide the documents that could do the worst damage, Merrell said, and to be ready to try to explain the others.

Curiously, though they tried to keep documents from plaintiffs and out of court, it appears that they did not destroy documents. For years, Jeffrey Wigand, chief of research for Brown and Williamson, told me, executives had become practiced in not writing down damaging things, or "editing" documents before they went into the files.

Though at first Merrell knew little about tobacco companies, the documents seemed unusual. There was one from 1963, called "A Tentative Hypothesis on Nicotine Addiction." Didn't the companies deny that nicotine was addictive? Yet here was a paper 25 years old giving the details of how nicotine addiction worked. There was another, just before the Surgeon General of the United States issued his crucial report of 1964 declaring that without doubt, cigarettes cause deadly diseases, among them lung cancer. One of the lawyers within the company was suggesting, "Whatever qualifications we may assert to minimize the impact of the (Surgeon General's) Report we must face the fact that a responsible and qualified group of previously non-committed scientists and medical authorities have spoken. . . . One would hope the industry would act affirmatively and not merely react defensively. . . . We are, then, in the business of selling nicotine, an addictive drug effective in the release of stress mechanisms. . . ."

Stunning material, both because it was so frank and because it was so old. The companies apparently had a very good grip on the nature of smoking even in the 1960s. What had happened in the meantime?

After some weeks of work, one day Mark, the associate lawyer, appeared in the documents hall. "I want to tell you new people and I guess I don't have to remind you old people, that there are some things you should be aware of in this room. Nothing leaves this room." He told a story of someone who, a few weeks before, "and this is settled with this person now," had "taken, copied, and took out of the room, this room, against orders, some kind of document."

He said some of those present knew what had happened, and "it won't happen again. Never, never . . . and I mean that. We will press criminal charges. We WILL get the person. . . . No one makes copies of anything. This copy, the one that left this room, was not serious, well, it was serious because it happened, but it wasn't anything that had to do with our archives, just a training sheet. But this is fair warning, and this is the only warning . . . bring in your body to work, leave your coat at the door, leave your books or anything else at the door, and when you go out in the evening, leave as you came. Got me? And we will fire you. And we will prosecute you. Is this understood?"

They were told of the first lawsuit against tobacco companies, one in the 1950s, which was in Kansas City, where the law firm defending the companies was Shook, Hardy and Bacon. From that point on, Shook Hardy had been the leading firm in defending tobacco. They won that case and every one since. Now, the paralegals sifting through documents were the eyes and ears of the companies. "Your job is to look at this from the point of view, as if you — who will become expert in this field — are in fact suing as a plaintiff."

The Texas firm and its paralegals would concentrate on advertising and marketing documents and issues. Those from Atlanta's King and Spaulding would concentrate on "biology," the research on smoking hazards. Those from Louisville, the hometown firm, would work on "corporate issues," including the lawyers, the CEO and other executives.

The woman who led the instruction in the secrets of tobacco history began by explaining the taxonomy, the list of terms and categories that were important to the company. It was a map to what the company was worried about, essentially a list of all the most damaging documents the company had. Relatively few of these have since become public.

There were categories: D was for disease.

"Cancer: When a document states that a certain substance is carcinogenic it should be coded to the general Cancer code (DD). Even if the document does not discuss cancer specifically, if it implies that the substance is capable of causing cancer."

"DA: Addiction/dependency/habituation: Documents which specifically mentioned the alleged condition of physiological dependence, characterized by unpleasant reactions upon withdrawal of the substance . . . Documents will often discuss nicotine, especially in terms of maintaining 'satisfactory doses' or maintaining a 'psychological need.' Key words to look for are dependence and habituation."

DDA was lung cancer; DDB was throat cancer; DDC was other cancer; DDD was cellular or "pre-cancerous" changes found in experiments. DDE was the category for permanent genetic damage. In the instructions alone was the full list of diseases and the states of addiction which scientists were studying.

There was the conspiracy as well. MG was the category code for "failure to warn." These were "documents suggesting that members of the tobacco industry were aware of health risks associated with smoking but did not warn smokers of those risks. . . ."

"MH" was the category for assurances of safety: "Any documents giving express or implied guarantees concerning health consequences of smoking (e.g., public statements by industry executives that cigarettes are 'safe', or marketing strategies designed to 'reassure the smoker,' etc.)."

Category EE was "safer cigarette": Documents suggesting

that Brown and Williamson, BAT, or other tobacco companies conducted experiments or had the knowledge and capability to manufacture safer cigarettes, but did not put such cigarettes on the market. Key phrases or names to look for include "low CO," "Gio Gori," and "Project Rio."

Category ABEG was work that targeted youth: "Documents concerning advertising, marketing strategies, or market research (i.e. studies of brand awareness, message recall, or usage behavior) focusing on smokers 18 years of age or younger."

The next category was ABEH, and was called "starters." It was for advertising and marketing to "persons who have not yet started smoking."

Merrell and his cohorts in the bare rooms in Louisville were to find all these references in memos between staff members of the tobacco company, planning documents, invoices, and whatever other papers existed; they were to mark them, and pass them on to the supervising lawyers with notations about their importance. There were even memos about how to bury the evidence contained in these documents.

The woman giving the seminar went on; Merrell was interested. Then, she began to describe something called "Special Account Number 4." He says now that he remembers the words she used, almost exactly: "Special Account Number 4. This is one thing that Plaintiff doesn't know about, but would love to know about."

She said nothing more then. In reflecting on the moment, Merrell believes that moment was the one in which his interest was suddenly engaged in a new way. What was this? Special Account 4? It was a secret project account, obviously a deception of some kind.

From this moment on, Merrell's job began to develop an extra, furtive dimension. When he heard the conspiratorial undertone of the woman who had come over from Shook, Hardy and Bacon, he could feel the weight of his loyalties shifting. He felt a little like a spy, but in reflecting on his life up to that moment, it was exciting. He imagined that he was part of something rather important, and for the first time, he began to dwell on the fate of poor sons of bitches who died of smoking.

That night, he opened a beer, sat down, and began to write out notes after work.

From the cache that Merrell Williams had brought out, and from other sources inspired by Dr. Williams, the papers would continue to come in over the next year and a half. (I wrote about 80 tobacco stories during that period. A few others were written, but were spiked by editors who opposed giving the tobacco companies "a hard time.") The impact of the papers appeared significant. They were reported on television and in all the major newspapers, and quickly led to another set of hearings before Henry Waxman.

At the FDA, David Kessler has said that the agency was still working hard to get individual documents that shed light on the case, and very few were forthcoming. Suddenly we were writing about documents by the score, most of them containing extraordinary admissions. In fact, perhaps some of the most enlightening of all the material were the indexes and company-written research histories.

The publication of the Brown and Williamson papers, Dr. Kessler has said, "was a major moment, beyond which all went in one direction. It was the first time we had anyone saying, 'We are in the business of selling nicotine, which is an addictive drug.' Before that, all was indirect evidence. When I woke up on Saturday morning and read that, it was personally a very important moment, a moment beyond which there was no turning back, it seemed. Of course there was a lot more to do, more to look at, but this was no longer a hypothesis, that the companies intended to use nicotine like a drug."

Not long afterward, on a hot, shirt-saturating afternoon in Washington, D.C. in the summer of 1994, a bill was slipped into the hopper in the U.S. House of Representatives.

In roman type, House Joint Resolution #367 suggested that the Congress award a medal of valor to one unnamed man, a hero, it said, who had risked everything to take from a tobacco company thousands of pages of damning documents about what they really knew and when they knew it.

"Whereas one or more tobacco companies have known for decades that cigarette smoking is addictive and threatens the health and life of its users; Whereas one or more tobacco companies have continued to market for financial gain in spite of their knowledge . . . ; Whereas someone has made public some of these concealed documents . . . ; Whereas one tobacco company and its law firm are seeking to punish the whistleblower through legal action; and, Whereas anyone with common sense recognizes that the true criminals are those who concealed the evidence . . ."

"Now, therefore, be it resolved by the Senate and the House of Representatives of the United States . . . that the Congress shall bestow a Congressional Medal of Appreciation for Public Spirit to the courageous citizen who made the concealed documents public."

The bill followed by a few weeks another action, one in the marbled federal court building down the street from the Capitol. There, Judge Harold Greene had been asked to summon to court Congressmen and reporters who had taken the stolen tobacco papers from the unnamed man and made them public. The tobacco company was after the man and all those who had used the papers. Judge Greene listened to the arguments, then wrote that it was not the unnamed taker of documents who should be disciplined, it was the tobacco company after him. The company, Judge Greene wrote, said they had come to court "merely attempting to gain control of property that was stolen or obtained in violation of an attorney-client privilege. . . . However," the judge continued, speaking of the stolen papers, "viewed from another perspective, they may be evidence supporting a whistle-blower's claim that the tobacco company concealed from its customers and the American public the truth regarding the health hazards of its tobacco products, and that he was merely bringing them to the attention of those who could deal with this menace. . . . This is a seemingly arcane dispute over subpoenas and motions to quash them. But what is involved at bottom is not arcane at all: it is a dispute over documents which may reveal the Brown and Williamson tobacco company concealed for decades that it knew its products to be both health hazardous and addictive. The subpoenas are the means by which the company is seeking to intimidate, and in a sense to punish the discoverer of evidence of this possible concealment and the national legislators who are seeking to investigate the subject further. . . . There are several rules, even constitutional doctrines, that stand in the way of so high-handed a course of conduct, and one so patently crafted to harass those who would reveal the facts. . . ."

The man to whom the bill and the judge's opinion referred

was, at the time, unnamed and hiding somewhere along the
Mississippi coast between Biloxi and Pascagoula. He had fled
from Louisville, south to the territory where he grew up, among
the swamps and tall pines at the edge of the ocean. Teams of
lawyers from the tobacco company were pursuing him, and
hoped to put him in jail. Public relations officers were vilifying
him, sending out press releases on his thievery and violation of the
law, their equivalent of wanted posters, suggesting he was a crazed
employee who had been fired and wanted to retaliate.

1 0

UNDER OATH

He entered the territory of lies without a passport for return.
— Graham Greene, *The Heart of the Matter*, 1948

The figures in the tobacco companies are shadowy, and that is so intentionally.

They do not give interviews, and have an amazing record of keeping themselves out of the newspapers and magazines. Even in testifying before Congress, when the execs have appeared on hundreds of radio and television stations, and in thousands of newspaper stories on a single day, there are virtually no stories about the executives personally — their lives, interests or personalities.

Among all the tobacco figures to emerge from the past three years of intense press coverage, it is the whistle-blowers who have come to life — Merrell Williams and Jeffrey Wigand — even though neither of them has appeared before Congress or in public for questioning. Both worked for Brown and Williamson, and both had for a nemesis the fierce tobacco boss Thomas Edwin Sandefur, Jr.

Sandefur did appear before Congress, the only one of the top tobacco executives who appeared more than once. He sat before cameras, microphones and reporters for a total of about ten hours. Still, barely a word appeared about who he is and where he came from. He has turned down interviews regularly, and the company offers little data about him.

Although it is difficult to be sure, it appears that only a single news story on Mr. Sandefur's life and manners has appeared in newspapers, wire services and magazines in the past decade. That was a brief story in the *Wall Street Journal,* by Alix Freedman, the *Journal's* leading tobacco writer and likely the number one tobacco reporter in the country. And Mr. Sandefur refused to sit for his portrait in that case as well.

The picture which emerges of Mr. Sandefur from that story, and a few other scraps of information gleaned from co-workers of Mr. Sandefur, is that he is in some ways a terror, with a leadership style more like a mafia figure or a back-alley scrapper than a smooth executive. He can be loud, angry and abusive, and is highly confident of the worth of his own opinions.

He has known no other business outside tobacco, where he began by selling cigars and chewing tobacco in the mountains of northern Georgia in 1964.

He is one of the figures who rose up in the industry after the crisis of 1953, and after the Surgeon General's report of 1964. After that, there was no fear. They had faced the worst, and got away without great damage. So, they soon turned back to aggressive marketing strategies to counter health concerns and dips in sales.

He was born in Cochran, Georgia, went to Georgia Southern College in business accounting and from that straight to R.J. Reynolds as a salesman. He worked his way up until in the 1970s he scored a significant hit with the introduction of the Doral brand for RJR. He worked extensively on low tar brands such as Now and Camel Lights before moving on to Brown and Williamson in 1982, where he led the introduction of the Barclay brand in Europe. All of these were cigarettes in which, because of fast-dropping tar levels, nicotine was a crucial variable that had to be maintained. So it seems likely that throughout his career, Sandefur was deeply familiar with the issues of setting nicotine levels.

He also led the tobacco companies into an aggressive price war among premium brands — Brown and Williamson's Viceroy was the first premium brand to drop its price in what became a bloodletting of huge proportions; the day when the price war took hold is still called Black Friday in the industry.

His best accomplishment over the years apparently was his pushing a trash brand — GPC Approved, the cut-rate knock off that was intended to slip in underneath to erode the sales of the standard and expensive cigarettes such as Marlboro and Winston — until it hit number three in the U.S. with a 5 percent share of the whole American market.

His chief failure at B & W has been the decline of the Kool menthol brand, which once commanded 8 percent of the U.S. market, but slipped, under Mr. Sandefur, to about 3.5 percent.

Mr. Sandefur's ferocity is something remarked on in the industry, and the most common phrase about him used by executives of other companies is that he is a "loose cannon." In one prominent battle, Brown and Williamson was taken to court over its tactics in pushing its low-priced brands. Liggett and Myers sued Brown and Williamson, and Sandefur became a key figure in the trial. Liggett charged that Brown and Williamson used predatory pricing tactics and stole package designs in order to drive the smaller Liggett from the "generic cigarette" business. Internal memos released at the trial suggested that Brown and Williamson wanted to "put a lid on Liggett."

On the issue of package-design copying, Sandefur astonished people in the tobacco industry with what appeared to be an obvious, bold lie. He said he had never seen one of Liggett's generic cigarette packs, the one that was so similar to Brown and Williamson's.

Liggett executives recalled Sandefur berating his own attorneys during a break at the trial for letting him "look like a fool" in front of a jury he called "yokels."

Sandefur and B & W lost the case; but the decision was reversed on appeal.

Another evidence of his strong-arm style was the case of the tobacco called "Y-1," a super-high-nicotine variety that Mr. Sandefur insisted be developed. Company insiders said that Sandefur had been warned that such a project wouldn't be worth the trouble and could bring a strong negative reaction when people found out. Also, it appears that B & W may have broken the law in order to carry out the project in secret in Brazil. But over all objections, Sandefur pressed ahead.

The *Wall Street Journal*, in its story on Mr. Sandefur, noted that one consultant suggested to him that he had so intimidated his co-workers that he should call a meeting to put his subordinates at ease by telling them that it was okay to disagree with him.

"Even after the meeting, few dared," the story said. Former B & W official Brian Stauss said that "People are scared to death of Tommy Sandefur—he comes across as very unpredictable." Another former colleague of Sandefur, marketing executive Doug Keeney, recalled being berated by Mr. Sandefur for a decision he had made. "He is volatile by any standard," Keeney said, "but that's just his way of talking." He was a good chief executive, Keeney said.

In the Justice Department investigation, in which two grand juries are now working through the evidence, Sandefur is probably one of the two leading candidates for a perjury charge among all those in the industry. That is chiefly because his sworn statements before Congress are at odds with the voluminous documentation found in the Brown and Williamson papers, and secondly, the fact that there is a live body, Dr. Jeffrey Wigand, who has testified that Mr. Sandefur personally told him that nicotine was addictive and is the main product of the company.

He quit smoking some years ago, it is said. Because he has aplastic anemia, an illness in which infections can be caught relatively easily, he installed an air-cleaning system in his office and wore a surgical mask when visiting the company's tobacco plants.

He began his solo testimony before Congress, as his reputation suggested he might, with a two-fisted attack on David Kessler and Henry Waxman.

He reiterated testimony given in April: "I repeat, I do not believe that nicotine is addictive." He went on to say that FDA's possible regulation of tobacco is "back-door prohibition . . . that seems to be where we are headed . . . down the road of putting this industry out of business. There's certainly no doubt about it in my mind. That's clear, that's clearly the intent of giving FDA superpower jurisdiction."

Though the bill being considered in Congress at the time prohibited FDA from banning cigarettes, Sandefur said, "they could make it impossible for us to sell cigarettes because of the reach of their regulatory powers. For example, the FDA could say you could sell a cigarette, but it can't have any nicotine. . . . It's like telling a company it's okay to sell a beer as long as it doesn't contain any alcohol. The pathway to regulation is the pathway to prohibition. . . ."

This comment was an interesting admission, in a way. In comparing cigarettes to beer, he may have forgotten that the beer contains a drug, alcohol, which the brewers fully admit. They do not attempt to portray alcohol merely as a taste. Further, the alcoholic beverage industry has submitted to federal and state regulation, the thing Sandefur was arguing the tobacco companies should be exempt from.

He went on, "Mr. Chairman, and members of this committee, if I sound concerned or even alarmed, it's because I am." He said that the attack on tobacco companies and him personally was "saying it's okay to return to the age of McCarthyism, when blacklisting and vilification of honest and respectable people were sanctioned for the sake of advancing a political agenda. I'm concerned about our government regulating the lives and lifestyles of the American citizens. . . ."

The subject of high-nicotine tobacco was one of the first up.

Rep. Synar asked, "Now, the export permit is usually on the condition that the seed or plant would be used only experimentally. There is a limit of half an ounce on how much can be exported. But last Friday, Brown and Williamson informed the FDA . . . that several annual shipments of about a million pounds each were imported to Brown and Williamson. How did you manage to grow and ship millions of pounds of Y-1 if the USDA permits only experimental quantities to leave the country in the first place?"

"That's a good question," said Sandefur. "I don't know." He said he would find out.

Later in the hearing, Mr. Waxman pressed the point on Y-1 tobacco and its purpose. Mr. Sandefur had said again and again that the company did not manipulate nicotine. But it seemed clear to Waxman and to the FDA that the company could not say both that it had a large program to breed super-nicotine tobacco plants *and* that the company was not manipulating nicotine in tobacco.

WAXMAN: You say you wouldn't go out and buy nicotine and add it, but you went out and genetically engineered a new tobacco that had a higher nicotine level. Why'd you do that?
SANDEFUR: Well, Congressman, because I was looking for . . . a steady supply of nicotine leaf, or leaf with high nicotine. As I've

said, we can buy Zimbabwean leaf with the same levels of nicotine . . . but we wanted a steady supply, and we were trying to adhere to what many, many people were saying that you needed to think about doing. To reduce the tar and maintain the nicotine. And this was a blender's tool — potentially a blender's tool that would allow us to do that. That was why we did it. . . .

There, sandwiched in between the fireworks and the fog, was the simple statement which confirmed what the FDA had reported about Y-1, and essentially what ABC had reported about Philip Morris.

The companies do not allow tar to dictate nicotine, Mr. Sandefur admitted, but they blend "to reduce the tar and maintain the nicotine."

Later in the hearing he said the blending allows "us to meet specific tar and nicotine deliveries."

Also in the hearing, Rep. Ron Wyden from Oregon opened the subject of a coincidence which he felt he had detected in the history of one Brown and Williamson cigarette, one that Mr. Sandefur had introduced to Europe, the Barclay.

Wyden quoted from the company documents on Project Wheat. "In considering which product features are important in terms of consumer acceptance, the nicotine delivery is one of the more obvious candidates. The importance of nicotine hardly needs to be stressed as it is so widely recognized."

WYDEN: Do you agree with this quote, Mr. Sandefur, that nicotine delivery is an important product feature for consumers?
SANDEFUR: Nicotine in terms of taste, as a constituent of taste, is important, yes sir.
WYDEN: Now the purpose of this project and I quote, "was to classify smokers into a number of categories showing distinct patterns of motivation, different levels of so-called 'inner need' as a first step towards testing a hypothesis that a smoker's 'inner need' level is related to his preferred nicotine delivery."

The study went on to say that it found about 40 percent of the smokers sampled had average-to-high nicotine needs, and above average concern for health. That is, they wanted a high nicotine cigarette but feared high tar cigarettes. Thus, a potential market was open for a cigarette with above average nicotine and below average tar.

WYDEN: So, my question to you, Mr. Sandefur, is what specific actions did Brown and Williamson take to follow up on Project Wheat?

SANDEFUR: I have absolutely no idea. This is the first time I've ever heard of Project Wheat. . . .

WYDEN: This document, Mr. Sandefur, was submitted by your company to this subcommittee while you were CEO, and you have no knowledge of it?

SANDEFUR: Congressman, we submitted all the documents we had on the subject that you asked for. There is absolutely no way that I could be knowledgeable about all these documents. . . .

Wyden pointed out that just after Project Wheat was carried out, the company created Barclay cigarettes, a high nicotine content, low tar cigarette.

Then, Rep. Waxman turned to the subject of the years of work inside the company that demonstrated that cigarettes cause tumors.

WAXMAN: I have before me a series of over 30 Project Janus studies. These are studies that you have submitted to us, and I want to stack these up. . . . These studies have titles like "Carcinogenicity of Smoke Condensate on Mouse Skin" and "Investigation of the Mutagenic Effect of Inhaled Smoke on Mice." In mouse skin painting experiments, the researchers paint, say, condensed tobacco smoke on the skin of a mouse and then observe whether any tumors form. Well, the Project Janus experiments repeatedly found that tobacco caused tumors when painted on mice skin. In a 1971 survey of the Janus mouse skin painting experiments, over 80 percent of the mice exposed to a flue-cured blend of tobacco developed tumors. And in a 1973 report on "Carcinogenicity of Smoke Condensate to Mouse Skin," over 70 percent of the mice developed permanent tumors, and over 50 percent developed malignant tumors.

Mr. Sandefur . . . how could your company in good faith tell the public that smoking is not dangerous to health when you knew from the Janus studies that tobacco smoke condensate produced tumors in mice, many of them malignant?

SANDEFUR: Congressman, I can't answer that question. I wasn't around in 1971.

WAXMAN: Well, you're the chief executive officer of Brown & Williamson. You're here to represent them. There have been accusations in the press. This is not something new — completely. I think we have more information than had otherwise been known, but it had been written about even in the *New York Times* and probably other publications as well. Wouldn't you expect that, as the chief executive officer, you would be knowledgeable about something which is clearly part of the inquiry today?

SANDEFUR: Mr. Congressman, or Mr. Chairman, I have certainly discussed this with my scientists, and I can tell you that I'm told that you can take concentrated tomato juice and put it on mice — the skin of mice and create the same type tumors. That's what I've been told. I'm also told that fresh whole smoke has never demonstrated anything like this.

WAXMAN: How can that be?

SANDEFUR: Well, I'm telling you what I've been told.

WAXMAN: . . . Now, you claim you don't know about it and you weren't there, but let me ask you this: Do you think that it was a responsible action on the part of Brown & Williamson to, on the one hand, be conducting what was called Project Truth to tell people, "Don't worry about these reports about cancerous tumors in mice because of tobacco, because we don't think it's really happening," and on the other hand, you have your scientists at the same time telling you it is happening and that you have this information, at least as of that time the people in charge had that information? Do you think that was a responsible way to behave?

SANDEFUR: I think — Mr. Chairman, I can see how you would be concerned about that and what — and the quandary that this issue raises. But I can tell you that the research that you are referring to was done by a sister company. Yes, it was in our files.

WAXMAN: Now, wait a second. I'm not going to let you get away with that. You are part and parcel of British American Tobacco. You share the research budget with them. Your company participates in all their research conferences. Your scientists were reporting, I assume, to the whole family, because after all, you sent this to us. We didn't get it from British American Tobacco in London someplace. We got it from you, wherever your headquarters is, wherever it was stored. It was from you to this committee.

SANDEFUR: I understand.

WAXMAN: Now, you evidently didn't read these things, but what do you think about your predecessor, who presumably did read about it, who presumably knew what was going on, because CEOs are supposed to know what goes on in their business, hearing from the scientists that tumors are being caused by this tobacco condensate at the same time that the CEO was managing a campaign called, euphemistically, Project Truth to say none of this is true? What do you think of someone who would do that?

SANDEFUR: I really can't speculate on what the —

WAXMAN: Well, what do you mean speculate? I'm giving you exactly —

SANDEFUR: I can't speculate —

WAXMAN: Would you do something like that?

SANDEFUR: No, sir. If I was — if I were convinced, and if my scientists told me and was convinced that this was, in fact, the case, I would make that publicly known. But, you know, Mr. Chairman, as far as I'm concerned, this is a moot point, because the Congress of the United States has already decided that the way we're going to warn the American smoker, the American public, is through the warning statements on the pack. And the warning statement says smoking causes lung cancer.

WAXMAN: . . . I'm trying to figure out what kind of responsibility the chief executive officers of the tobacco companies have when they know that there are scientific studies that they are sponsoring that give them information about a danger to public health and at the same time they're saying to people that there is no danger. Well, do you believe this information now that cigarette smoking causes these tumors?

SANDEFUR: I would — as I've just testified, I would make that public. I really can't speak for what other CEOs might or might not have done.

WAXMAN: . . . According to the New York Times, your lawyers took extraordinary steps to keep the Janus study out of the hands of the public and plaintiffs suing your company.

Specifically, on January 17th, 1985, a senior lawyer for Brown & Williamson, J. Kendrick Wells, declared that the Janus reports were deadwood and ordered the reports removed from the — removed from the Brown & Williamson files. Wells wrote, and I quote from the New York Times, "I have marked with an X documents which I suggested were deadwood in the behavioral and biological studies area. I said that the B series are Janus series studies and should also be considered deadwood." And then he said, "I suggested the research development engineering department should undertake to remove the deadwood from its files, and I suggested that Earl tell his people that neither he nor anyone else in the department should make any notes, memos, or lists."

Mr. Sandefur, the Janus studies are a significant body of scientific work. You tested many different variations of tobacco for cancer-causing effects. Some of the results showed a striking reduction in the incidence of tumors. Shouldn't you have disclosed these important studies to the public instead of trying to purge the files of deadwood, so-called?

SANDEFUR: Mr. Chairman, I'd like for Judge Bell [Griffin Bell, Sandefur's lawyer] to answer that question.

WAXMAN: Well, I'll be glad to let you consult with him, but what I want to know is don't you think the public should have had this information? . . .

SANDEFUR: Mr. Chairman, I'm advised by Judge Bell I shouldn't answer that question because it's attorney-client privilege.

WAXMAN: Will you provide the subcommittee with copies of all pending discovery requests in product liability cases in January 1985?

SANDEFUR: Yes, sir. We will be more than happy to do that.

WAXMAN: I just want to close my comments by indicating to you that 40 years ago, January 4, 1954, your company published what was called a frank statement to cigarette smokers in the *New York Times* and other leading newspapers. And it said, "We accept an interest in people's health as a basic responsibility paramount to every other consideration in our business," end quote. And the company also pledged to cooperate closely with those whose task it is to safeguard the public health. I have trouble seeing how one can square pledges in the frank statement to the public and actions such as Project Truth and Project Janus . . . your company told the public that smoking is not dangerous, even while it had extensive evidence from animal studies that showed smoking is dangerous. It seems to me that there is an inconsistency, to put it mildly. A minimal standard of corporate responsibility ought to require Brown & Williamson to disclose the results of Janus, not conceal them as deadwood and that apparently is what, in fact, happened, even though your lawyer doesn't want you to comment on it. Any comment you want to make?

SANDEFUR: No, sir, I wasn't there 40 years ago. I don't know.

WAXMAN: By the way, that lawyer who made that recommendation is still your lawyer, isn't he? J. Kendrick Wells?

SANDEFUR: Yes, sir. He works for Brown & Williamson.

WAXMAN: Thank you.

So it went. Mr. Sandefur was smooth and simply out of reach; the sensation was of one boxer chasing the other around the ring, with no referee to force them into a real engagement. It was not that Mr. Sandefur was not prepared; he was perfect. It is difficult to believe that his familiarity with the documents was not much greater than he said. I found them utterly absorbing and I am not in the tobacco business. How could he *not* get interested in them? Seven thousand pages? I read them in a weekend.

This exercise, finally, was completely familiar. This was live, but versions of it have been seen in print and on tape from tobacco people for decades. This is the defense lawyer doing what is necessary for his client.

Not long after that testimony, Jeffrey Wigand, who had been chief of research under Mr. Sandefur for three years, began to testify against his former employer.

He had a rather different approach; he did not bob and weave, he went directly to the point. Although over the years Mr. Wigand had learned how not to address the issue as well — it is required training in tobacco — Mr. Wigand had dropped all that. He had been fired, he had been threatened, and he had no refuge.

Jeffrey Wigand is a careful and fastidious man, not given to excess and not by nature a whistle-blower. He makes lists, keeps his desk neat, and chooses his words with the eye of a technician, not a salesman.

He is unusual in a number of respects, and not a sedentary executive. He has a doctorate in biochemistry and a black belt in judo, serving at one time as a sparring partner for U.S. Olympic teams.

When he went to work for Brown and Williamson, he knew what he was getting into. He had at least six employment interviews and was questioned about his attitude toward tobacco.

During the three years he was at the company, he did not step off the reservation, even after he had been fired, when he was questioned by lawyers for the Justice Department. He had a Brown and Williamson lawyer present and keeping an eye on him during that testimony, and he told the government that he had not observed any illegal activity by B & W executives during his tenure there.

It was only when he and his family received threats to ensure his silence that he decided he could no longer remain an insider and he began to cooperate with the government. He also worked with CBS's *60 Minutes* in what was originally intended to be an interview in which he was not named, and he was willing to speak to other reporters to help them understand the way the business worked, though not for direct quotation.

The company tried another tactic after Wigand became a public figure through the CBS show, its delay and finally its airing. They hired a team of lawyers and private investigators to dig up negative information about Mr. Wigand's personal life, and after amassing 500 pages, they offered the pile of unsubstantiated slurs to reporters to use in writing profiles of Mr. Wigand. They asked that the source of the material not be named.

As the *Wall Street Journal* reported after checking the details in the dossier, "A close look at the file, and independent research by this newspaper into its key claims, indicates that many of the serious allegations against Mr. Wigand are backed by scant or contradictory evidence. Some of the charges — including that he pleaded guilty to shoplifting — are demonstrably untrue."

The title of the dossier was "The Misconduct of Jeffrey S. Wigand Available in the Public Record." The subheads included, "Wigand's Lies about His Residence," "Wigand's Lies under Oath," and "Other Lies by Wigand."

The most serious violations of ethics or law by Mr. Wigand which they were able to find and substantiate were exaggerations by Dr. Wigand. For example, when he was looking for a job after B & W fired him, he made a tape of a mock employment interview to help guide the employment agency he was working with. On the tape he said he was "on" the U.S. Olympic Judo Team. Actually, he was a sparring partner for the team in one Olympics and helped train the athletes for another Olympics. In the end, the attempt to slur him backfired.

*　　*　　*

Dr. Wigand had joined B & W just after R.J. Reynolds had made an abortive but famous attempt to market a safer cigarette called the Premier, which heated but did not burn the tobacco. Dr. Wigand was told that he could work on projects at the company related to safer cigarettes and in establishing an outside medical advisory board that could judge the results of attempts to make cigarettes safer. But in the end, the offer was withdrawn and a continuous tension developed between Dr. Wigand and Mr. Sandefur over safer cigarettes and the industry's attempts to obscure what it knew.

The following is a pared-down transcript of the deposition that Mr. Wigand gave in Mississippi — a sharp contrast to the Sandefur testimony. It is only a sketchy outline of Mr. Wigand's knowledge, of what he said in court against the companies and against Mr. Sandefur. It is sketchy because of the unusual circumstances: the room was jammed with tobacco attorneys, and though I have edited out the objections and arguments from them, the tobacco lawyers objected vehemently to virtually every question, sometimes at length. I have preserved only a few of the objections which seemed to me the more amusing ones. The questioner is Ron Motley, of Charleston, South Carolina, one of the lead lawyers for the "Castano group" in New Orleans, that is, the squad of plaintiff's lawyers pressing the case against the companies on behalf of a now-deceased smoker, Peter Castano.

Q: Sir, during the entire time, or shortly after you became employed by Brown & Williamson, did lawyers for the corporation involve themselves in the type of research you were doing?
A: I would say there was direct lawyer intervention in numerous research projects, review of research documents. I believe the first really direct involvement of lawyers in research matters occurred [in connection with a meeting] in the fall of 1989.
Q: Would you please elaborate on that for us?
A: The meeting involved a meeting of all the research managers of all the BAT companies. There were representatives from Brown & Williamson, where I was. There was Souza Cruz, which is the Brazilian entity, BATCO, which was the U.K. entity, Germany, which is BAT Cigaretten-Fabriken, and from the Canadian, Imperial Tobacco.
Q: And these were all scientists?

A: These were all scientists, the number one scientist of each and every one of the companies mentioned.

Q: At this meeting in Vancouver, British Columbia, sir, was there a discussion of the effort to develop a safer cigarette, as you have previously described that?

A: The meeting encompassed a number of topics such as nicotine analogues, discussed biological assays and biological testing methodologies, it discussed how to reduce selectively the particular noxae that was in tobacco smoke.

Q: What does that mean?

A: Poisonous substance.

Q: Poisonous substance. Anything else, sir?

A: How to find various scientific research group studies.

Q: Subsequent to that conference in Vancouver of scientists, was one of the scientists assigned to memorializing, or putting into writing, minutes or summaries of the discussions?

A: Those minutes of the meeting were memorialized by a gentleman by the name of Dr. Ray Thornton. The meeting, really, was conducted by Alan Heard.

Q: Who is Mr. Thornton?

A: Mr. Thornton was the secretary for the meeting but worked for Mr. Heard in the BAT. That generated, I'd say, roughly a 14 to 15 page, maybe more, document which summarized the minutes and the actions of the meeting. Subsequently, those meeting minutes were sent to me. I circulated the minutes throughout the corporation in terms of upper management.

Q: Including Mr. Sandefur?

A: Mr. Sandefur and Mr. Pritchard and those in upper management. At that time, there was significant objection to the content of the meeting, particularly since the meeting referred to non-addictive nicotine analogues. It talked about a safer cigarette. It talked about biological testing. Subsequent to that, a meeting was called in which Kendrick Wells, one of the attorneys —

Q: Who was there other than Mr. Wells?

A: Mr. Sandefur, Mr. Pritchard.

Q: Mr. Pritchard was the top man in the company. Mr. Sandefur was the second man, and Mr. Kendrick Wells was the top lawyer, correct?

A: No. He was not the top lawyer. He was assistant general counsel. . . .

Q: As a result of this meeting that you have described—I don't want to know what happened at the meeting—but as a result of the meeting that you described, was there any change made in the minutes of the meeting in British Columbia?

A: Yes.

Q: Did they eliminate 12 pages of the minutes?

A: Roughly 12 pages of the minutes.

Q: And what did they eliminate, the stuff that said cigarettes were harmful?

A: They eliminated all reference to anything that could be discovered during any kind of liability action in reference to a safer cigarette. Statements were made that anything that alludes to a safer cigarette clearly indicates that other cigarettes are unsafe, and it, furthermore, would acknowledge that nicotine is addictive.

Q: Let me ask you, sir: how many conversations would you say you had between 1989 and 1993, when you were dismissed by Mr. Sandefur, about cigarette smoking and the addictive nature of nicotine?

A: There have been numerous statements made by a number of officers, particularly Mr. Sandefur, that we're in the nicotine delivery business—

Q: The nicotine delivery business?

A: —and tar is nothing but negative baggage.

Q: Tar is negative baggage. And so, were you in the presence of Mr. Sandefur, the president of the company, when he voiced the opinion and the belief that nicotine was addictive?

A: Yes.

Q: And did he express that view on numerous occasions?

A: Frequently.

Q: I'm going to show you, sir, Mr. Sandefur's testimony under oath before the Congress of the United States when he was sworn to tell the truth. Do you see where I have highlighted where Mr. Sandefur swore to tell the truth under oath under penalty of perjury what he told the Congress of the United States?

A: Yes, I do.

Q: He said, "I do not believe that nicotine is addictive." Do you see that?

A: Yes, I do.

Q: Is that the opposite, contrary to what he has expressed to you a number of times? It is not true, is it?

A: It is not true. . . .

Q: Now, can you tell me, sir, whether Mr. Sandefur at any time sought to keep you, Jeffrey Wigand, from attempting to develop or conduct research that would lead to the development and marketing of what you have described as a safer cigarette?

A: Yes.

Q: Will you describe how he did it as best you can?

A: Shortly after the Vancouver meeting, Sandefur called me to his office and told me there would be no further discussion or efforts on any issues related to a safer cigarette, even though there was research being conducted in both Canada and in the U.K. in removing selectively noxae. . . .

Any activity or allusion to a safer cigarette would be deathly contrary to the company's position relative to liability issues associated with smoking and health issues and that that matter would not be pursued any further and I was not to discuss it any more. He also told me at that time there will be no scientific and medical advisory committee to provide direction or support to the development of a safer cigarette.

Q: Dr. Wigand, were you a designee or representative of Brown & Williamson who was to attend certain industry, tobacco industry-wide trade association meetings?

A: That's correct.

Q: Were you allowed to go to those meetings alone, or were you required to take some kind of person with you?

A: Depends on the type of meeting. A number of times I went to meetings, particularly on ignition propensity, I was accompanied by a lawyer.

Q: Is that sometimes called a fire safe cigarette?

A: A fire safe cigarette, yes.

Q: And they sent a lawyer with you?

A: That's correct.

Q: Was this lawyer a scientist?

A: No, he was not.

Q: In the course of your tenure at Brown & Williamson, did you become interested in whether or not there had been, before you joined the company, research on such things as nicotine, whether it was addictive, or biological activity of cigarettes and things like that?

A: Yes, I did.

Q: Did you inquire as to whether that research was conducted, and, if it was, were the reports of the findings available to you as vice president?

A: I was not told that it existed. I was not made available to those studies. However, in the various meetings with some of the senior folks, not anyone in my group, but folks that had long tenure in the company as well as overseas meetings, I learned that various studies were undertaken, particularly relative to nicotine, nicotine ranges, biological activity, biological studies, looking at contrasting of various biological activity of various types of blends, various types of cigarettes.

Q: So what you just described for the jury and the court under oath was the type of studies you were asking about and learned may have indeed been conducted; is that correct?

A: That's correct. It was totally alien to what I experienced in the pharmaceutical and biomedical industry. If I was an advisor, I would never be precluded from understanding what research transpired over 20 years prior to me taking a position.

Q: Would you say, sir, that company officials suppressed information of a scientific nature that you considered to be important in discharging your mission as vice president of research and development? . . .

A: Yes.

Q: Dr. Wigand, to your personal knowledge, did at any time Mr. J. Kendrick Wells, associate general counsel of Brown & Williamson, alter scientific research?

A: Yes.

Q: He did. On how many occasions?

A: Several.

Q: How do you know that, sir?

A: Well, he changed the minutes of the meeting in Vancouver to delete anything that could be discoverable. Documents of research conducted at BAT, Southampton, to be pre-screened by Kendrick Wells prior to dissemination to the R & D folks . . .

Q: As a scientist, did you take exception to lawyers reading your scientific work?

A: Yes, I did, as well as many of the other scientists at BAT.

Q: They did that in your presence?

A: That's correct.

Q: And as a scientist, sir, did you find it scientifically unethical that a lawyer would edit or suppress information contained in a scientific report?

A: Yes.

Q: Did you complain about that?

A: Yes.

Q: To whom did you complain?

A: To Sandefur, to Kohnhorst, to Wells. The principle behind his editing documents was removing any reference that would be discoverable during any kind of liability action.

Q: And Mr. Sandefur, the former salesman and president of Brown & Williamson, how did he receive your objections to Mr. Wells' suppressing and editing scientific studies?

A: He supported it.

Q: He supported Mr. Wells' efforts in suppression?

A: That's correct.

Q: On more than one occasion?

A: On several occasions.

Q: In fact, sir, did Mr. Sandefur have a position that if science affected sales, then science would take the back door?

A: Yes.

Q: Did he express that to you?

A: Several times.

Q: Indeed, sir, was that the policy of Brown & Williamson while you were there so far as you observed it?

A: Yes.

Q: And, sir, did you make complaints about that particular type of policy, that is, sales over safety?

A: I had a number of discussions with Mr. Sandefur, particularly over safety issues. I felt that the additives as they were reviewed and the policy within B & W did not adequately use what I considered the proper duty of care on a scientific level. It was inconsistent with what was being done overseas in other BAT affiliates as well as what I knew was going on in the other industries.

Q: Sir, at any time did you learn that Brown & Williamson was using a form of rat poison in pipe tobacco?

A: Yes.

Q: What form of rat poison is that, sir?

A: It is a compound called coumarin. It was contained in the pipe tobacco —

MR. BEZANSON: Object on trade secret grounds and instruct not to answer.

MR. MOTLEY: You are objecting that the man is revealing that you used rat poison as a trade secret? You may answer, sir.

Q: If they used rat poison in pipe tobacco that human beings were taking in their bodies, I want to know about it. Will you tell me about it, sir?

A: I was concerned about the continued use of coumarin in pipe tobacco after the coumarin had been removed from cigarettes because of the FDA not allowing the use of coumarin in foods with additives. The reason why it stayed in pipe tobacco is the removal would change the taste of the pipe tobacco and, therefore, affect sales. They continued to use it until the time I left, even after the NT program —

Q: What is that, NT?

A: I'm sorry. The National Toxicology program released evidence that coumarin was a lung-specific carcinogen.

Q: That means a cause of cancer?

A: That's correct.

Q: And you asked that coumarin be removed, and you were told what?

A: Once it had been released in the NTP study, even though it was still being used in Sir Walter Raleigh aromatic tobacco at significantly higher levels, other pipe tobacco manufacturers had removed it. There was clearly a document in B & W's file that the use of coumarin was in direct conflict with existing B & W policy on additives.

Q: Let me see if I understand you correctly, sir. You learned that coumarin had been taken out of cigarettes because it was dangerous, and you learned that coumarin had been taken out of other companies' pipe tobacco because it was dangerous, and you requested that coumarin be taken out of Sir Walter Raleigh pipe tobacco, is that fair? Is that what you said?

A: Yes, I did.

Q: And what did Mr. Sandefur tell you when you asked him to take that rat poison out of that particular pipe tobacco?

A: We got into a very significant debate. I'd probably consider it an argument. And that it could not be removed because it would impact the sales of the STP business particularly since the aromatic pipe tobacco was one of the higher selling products.

Q: And until the day that you were dismissed by this same former salesman, Mr. Sandefur, the president and CEO of Brown & Williamson, did they continue to have coumarin in the pipe tobacco that you described?

A: Yes.

Q: And there was no scientist or researcher with the company higher than you in the structure of the company; is that correct?

A: In terms of experience and education?

Q: No. You were the top management guy in research and development?

A: Yes.

Q: And one of your jobs was to report to and consult with and give advice to Mr. Sandefur, was it not?

A: That is correct.

Q: Would you say generally Mr. Sandefur was receptive to your ideas to try to find a safe cigarette? . . . Was he receptive to your advice and counsel about trying to find a safe cigarette?

A: No.

Q: What did he say to you in general in the various times you recommended a search for a safe cigarette?

A: That there can be no research on a safer cigarette. Any research on a safer cigarette would clearly expose every other product as being unsafe and, therefore, present a liability issue in terms of any type of litigation.

Q: Now, sir, did you maintain a log or a diary, a written log or diary in the laboratory at Brown & Williamson while you were employed there?

A: I maintained two logs.

Q: Would you describe them one after the other?

A: I had a standard research notebook that many scientists in the laboratory generate on a daily basis which reflects their work or comments or their reflections on work, what meetings. I kept a log in a bound scientific notebook, numbered page, that really reflects contemporaneously things that happened. I do not have that. That was sequestered from me when I left Brown & Williamson. However, I also have another diary which is a duplicate.

Q: And where is that diary, sir?

A: In my possession.

Q: And, sir, have you recorded in any fashion your recollections of events — Excuse me — I don't want you to tell me where it is, but just generally, have you recorded somewhere —

A: I have a videotape, and I put it in a secure place, of everything that transpired while I was at Brown & Williamson in which I actually taped myself.

Q: Discussing the events that occurred?

A: Discussing the events that occurred back to when I first joined the company.

Q: And did you discuss in that video the inference of suppression by Mr. Kendrick Wells and Mr. Sandefur of scientific research?

A: Yes.

Q: Did you discuss the other matters in that video that you have in a safe place, the other matters we've discussed so far in a general way?

A: Yes, plus more.

Q: Plus more. And we've not indeed even gotten started good sir, on my questions. Sir, have you been requested to serve in a scientific consulting fashion with the Food & Drug Administration of the United States Government?

A: Yes, I have.

Q: Have you been asked to give testimony by the United States Department of Justice in an antitrust investigation currently being undertaken against Brown & Williamson and others?

A: Yes, I have.

Q: Sir, can you tell me why you felt it necessary to record and store in a safe place by videotape and place in a safe place your recollection of the events that occurred while you were at Brown & Williamson?

A: On April 22nd, 1994, I received a threat on my daughters. On April 28, 1994, I received a second threat warning me further. At that time, I went to the local FBI. I reported it. I was concerned for the welfare of my children. I became concerned for my own welfare. And I thought I'd chronicle and memorialize if something ever happened to me.

Q: Sir, were you recently served with a lawsuit by Brown & Williamson in your hometown of Louisville, Kentucky?

A: It's the second time.

Q: The second time that you were served. Will you describe for the court, for his information, how it was you were served with the papers that let you know they were suing you?

A: This time or the first time?

Q: This time.

A: I was leaving du Pont Manuel High School, and I was proceeding to my car with two other teachers. I don't know who the service officer was, but he drove across the parking lot rather abruptly in a high speed. At that time, he almost hit the other two teachers walking. He pulled his car in front of my car and jumped out and said, Jeff, you are served.

Q: Did you know the gentleman?

A: No. But he was a danger, I think.

Q: Did you feel that this was an invasion of your rights?

A: First of all, it was trespassing on school property. Second of all, he could have done it in a much more professional manner. I would have accepted the lawsuit at my home. He did not have to do it in the school in the manner in which he did it.

Q: Sir—

A: I was just wondering if there was an objection.

Q: No, they don't object to you being served that way, I'm sure.

BEZANSON: Object to the comment on the absence of objection.

Q: I want to make sure that I understood correctly what you told me earlier. When communications between scientists at Brown & Williamson or between scientists at British American Tobacco Company and Brown & Williamson were exchanged in writing, did I understand you to say they had to come through Mr. Wells or his law department first?

A: There are a number of reports that were considered sensitive, before I could receive them they had to be reviewed by Kendrick Wells. Some of the reports were never kept on the premises. They were sent back.

Q: Back where?

A: Back to BAT, Southampton, so they would not be discoverable.

Q: You mean in England? They were sent back across the water?

A: That's correct.

Q: And did they bear any stamp on them that Mr. Wells or one of his underlings may have placed on them?

A: I don't understand.

Q: Have you seen scientific documents that had something like attorney client work product, privileged, confidential, prepare for litigation, on scientific reports? Did you see those stamps on some of them?

A: On a number of reports, yes.

Q: To your knowledge, were these scientific reports prepared for a lawsuit or prepared to try to understand the chemistry of smoke and the biological effect of cigarettes on human beings?

A: They were prepared on scientific research conducted in Southampton, which Brown & Williamson was paying for, partly.

Q: Did any of those documents say, this is a document we are going to use in the lawsuit of Ms. Haynes vs. Liggett & Myers and others in New Jersey or anything like that?

A: No. You surprise me.

Q: To your knowledge, when you were there, 1989 to 1993, what other tobacco companies worldwide did British American Tobacco Company either fully own or have an ownership interest in?

A: They had a 49 percent in Imperial Tobacco, which is the Canadian; they had 100 percent ownership in Souza Cruz, which is their Brazilian; they had 100 percent ownership of BATCO, which is the U.K.; 100 percent ownership in BATCF.

Q: What's that?

A: BAT, Hamburg Cigaretten Fabriken, which is the German subsidiary, Wills in Australia and a host of others . . .

Q: Did the BAT affiliated companies cooperate on research projects on an international basis?

A: Yes, they did.

Q: Did they share research results?

A: Yes, they did.

Q: Did you regularly communicate with scientists involved with BAT or other affiliated companies?

A: Yes, I did.

Q: Did you regularly get scientific reports from England?

A: Both regularly and irregularly.

Q: Did there come a time when you were cut off from certain research projects?

A: There was a process set up where Kendrick Wells would pre-read documents. As a result, a number of people in BAT, Southampton, were sending reports to me at my home via fax machine so I could read them and edit them and send them back.

Q: Let me understand. The regular procedure that was set up was for Kendrick Wells to review scientific writings before you got them; is that correct?

A: Not in all cases. What was considered sensitive issues: biological research, safer cigarette or the noxae.

Q: This process by which Mr. Wells was to review documents,

scientific documents that you described, biological research, addiction — did I hear you say nicotine addiction? — noxae, you were not allowed to directly receive these documents, but they first had to be sent to Mr. Wells, is that correct?

A: That is correct.

Q: Were you ever given access to, while you were with Brown & Williamson, a research project entitled Hippo? H-I-P-P-O?

A: I was not given the documents. However, I learned of a number of projects completed before I was there, particularly with people like Elmo Litzenger, Bob Johnson, also during some of the research policy group meetings or technical reviews. There was always somewhat of sidebar conversations of projects that had been done in the past. I received from one of the scientists in BAT, Southampton, the nicotine study that looked at the boundaries of the nicotine pharmacology effect.

Q: What do you mean by the boundaries of the nicotine pharmacology effect?

A: There was a study done early on, I think sometime in the late 70s, early 80s, that looked at the margin of the pharmacological effects of nicotine. And there was a draft that was presented that had from .4 to 1.2 milligrams of nicotine were required, in that range, to maintain smokers.

Q: What do you mean by that?

A: Keep them using the product.

Q: In other words, keep them purchasing the product in order to maintain the level of satisfaction for nicotine?

A: That's correct.

Q: To your scientific knowledge, did Brown & Williamson ever engage in the manipulation of nicotine levels in tobacco products?

A: Yes.

Q: They did? Brown & Williamson, it is your testimony, manipulated nicotine levels?

A: Yes, they did.

Q: Yes?

A: Yes.

Q: How did Brown & Williamson manipulate levels of nicotine in cigarettes?

A: There are a number of ways you manipulate nicotine levels. One way is to use additives.

Q: Go ahead.

A: Those additives are usually in the form of nitrogenous bases.

Q: I'm going to interrupt you every now and then so you can explain what a scientific term is. What does nitrogenous bases mean?

A: Nicotine as it exists in a plant of tobacco is locked up in an inactive form as a salt. In order to free that salt to be pharmacologically active, you need to change the pH. You need to change the pH of the tobacco. You also need to change the pH of the smoke, such that you convert total nicotine to free nicotine. Free nicotine is pharmacologically active. Nicotine as a salt, as in the tobacco itself, is not pharmacologically active.

Q: What other ways, sir, did you learn Brown & Williamson manipulated the levels of nicotine in cigarettes?

A: Well you can also — They also utilized blending techniques, blending techniques in terms of flue-cured to Burley ratios as a way of assuring the appropriate nicotine level. The other way is by looking at a genetically engineered tobacco called . . .

Q: Go ahead, sir.

A: Y-1 was a breeding project conducted by DNAP in New Jersey. The intent behind Y-1 was to manage the tar-to-nicotine ratio.

Q: Manage the tar-to-nicotine ratio?

A: Manage the tar-to-nicotine ratio. If you could increase the Burley component of nicotine from three and a half, four percent to seven to eight percent, you would substantially change the tar-to-nicotine ratio from twelve to one to five to one and ultimately one to one.

Q: Tell us what happened with Y-1.

A: Y-1 was a project dedicated towards increasing the tar-to-nicotine ratios. If you can have less mass of tobacco at higher nicotine, you'd essentially be reducing the negative character of smoking, as you'd be reducing tar or maintaining the nicotine delivery at a constant level. That was a way of managing the tar-to-nicotine ratios, lowering the tar while maintaining the nicotine.

Q: Did there come a time when someone took seeds to Brazil?

A: Yes, there was.

Q: Would you tell us who and in what way they did that and whether or not that was illegal?

CRIST: Object because it calls for a legal conclusion.

MOTLEY: They have lawyers that practice science, and now they're objecting to a scientist practicing law.

Q: My question simply put, let me start over. Can you tell us whether anyone, to your knowledge, took seeds, tobacco seeds of any kind, to Brazil?

A: Seeds were harvested at Centiments in New Jersey, and they were taken out knowingly when it was illegal to take them out and bring them to Souza Cruz to be grown.

Q: Souza Cruz is in Brazil?

A: Brazil.

Q: How were these seeds taken from the United States to Brazil?

A: Several times it was taken by Mr. Phil Fisher.

Q: Who is he?

A: He was head of the reblending group.

Q: Of who?

A: Of Brown & Williamson.

Q: How did he take them down there?

A: He carried them in a cigarette pack.

Q: He hid them?

A: He hid them.

Q: You mentioned the word "illegal." How do you know hiding seeds in a cigarette pack and taking them from the United States to Brazil is illegal?

A: At the time they were taken out, I knew the law.

Q: And what was that, sir?

A: That you weren't allowed to export seeds without approval.

Q: And to your knowledge, did Brown & Williamson obtain approval to take seed and hide it in a cigarette pack and take it to Brazil?

A: No.

Q: They did not have approval?

A: Did not.

Q: All right, sir. Are there any other ways that Brown & Williamson manipulated nicotine, to your knowledge?

A: You can do it through cigarette design, through filtration, through paper design, through blend.

Q: Reconstituted tobacco paper, too?

A: The primary form of managing or manipulating nicotine delivery—and I told you about nicotine. It is in a free state, which is pharmacologic, versus that which is in the bound state. It is by use of ammonia compounds . . . Any compound that can change pH creates an equilibrium in the rod that frees up nicotine. When the cigarette is combusted, urea and other nitrogenous compounds, protein-containing compounds, also form bases. Those bases change pH of smoke; pH of smoke directly affects the continued conversion and impact associated with nicotine delivery.

Q: Now, sir, are the methods of nicotine manipulation that you have just discussed well known in the cigarette industry, to your knowledge?

A: Yes.

Q: As a Brown & Williamson scientist, did you ever engage in what I believe is called reverse engineering?

A: Yes.

Q: Would you explain what that is, sir?

A: Reverse engineering is basically a process by which you take apart a competitor's product and you analyze it physically and chemically.

Q: And did your research and development department engage in reverse engineering with respect to other competitors' products?

A: Yes.

Q: Did you do that on occasion to determine nicotine delivery procedures that would be reflected in the cigarettes that you analyzed manufactured by other companies?

A: Yes.

Q: Is that how you are able to answer that these common methods of nicotine manipulation were reflected in the products of people other than Brown & Williamson, using reverse engineering?

A: Particularly in the non-menthol segment.

Q: Now, sir, can you tell us what the Leaf Blenders Manual is?

A: The Leaf Blenders Manual is a comprehensive document that deals with the use of ammonia and ammonia compounds to effectively convert, equilibrate and change nicotine from salt into a free base.

Q: Did you, sir, Dr. Wigand, have anything to do with a writing or preparing of the Leaf Blenders Manual?

A: I did some editing.

Q: You helped edit it?

A: I helped edit it.

Q: Does B & W, at least did B & W while you were there, use ammonia technology?

A: Yes.

Q: They did?

A: Yes.

Q: What is ammonia technology?

A: Ammonia technology is the code word for a — for using nitrogenous bases, whether they be proteins when pyrolyzed give rise to changing pH to ammonia in the form of DAP, ammonia in the form of ammonium hydroxide, ammonia in the form of ammonia gas.

Q: Does the ammonia technology have any influence on the levels of nicotine?

A: It doesn't change the total nicotine. What it does primarily is convert bound nicotine to free nicotine.

Q: And the free nicotine, is that what you previously described has a pharmacological effect?

A: That is correct.

Q: In other words, it acts as a drug on the body?

A: Yes.

Q: It acts as a drug on the body?

A: Yes. It is pharmacologically active. There are a number of studies that confirm that.

Q: Studies by whom?

A: By independent scientists, by BAT scientists.

Q: That confirm that free nicotine is pharmacologically active and is a drug?

A: Yes. It produces a physiological response, as the definition of a drug.

Q: Sir, did you learn while you were with Brown & Williamson why nicotine was important to the sale of cigarettes? You were telling us about this graph earlier, and I was wondering why the nicotine, the inclusion of the nicotine, was important to the ability to sell a cigarette.

A: Nicotine is associated with impact satisfaction, arousal, pharmacological effect that goes across the blood brain barrier. It possesses an order of transmitter activities. Below a certain level of .4 milligrams does not sustain satisfaction. Over 1.2 milligrams becomes too harsh and has too much of an impact, impact associated with the physiological effect associated with nicotine.

Q: Okay. Now, sir, what is — and I can't pronounce these scientific terms very well at all — A-C-E-T-A-L-D-E-H-Y-D-E?

A: Acetaldehyde is an impact booster that augments the effect of nicotine.

Q: Does this impact booster and nicotine have synergistic or a combined multiplicative effect on the smoker?

A: Yes.

Q: In what way, sir?

A: It enhances the impact, and, hence, is the transport of nicotine.

Q: And did Brown & Williamson, to your knowledge, use this acetaldehyde knowingly in cigarettes to enhance the effects of nicotine on the smoker?

A: Yes, sir.

Q: They did?

A: Acetaldehyde was an additive that was used.

Q: Additive that was used to boost nicotine effect; is that correct?

A: Acetaldehyde enhances the synergistic effect of nicotine and physiological effect. It was also well documented outside of the tobacco industry.

Q: So if you put that in there with nicotine, you are adding to whatever natural effect nicotine imparts; is that correct?

A: So to speak, yes.

Q: To your knowledge, did Brown & Williamson knowingly add this substance that I can't pronounce to its tobacco products? Did they know what they were putting in there?

A: Yes.

Q: Can you tell me what the Additives Guidance Panel is?

A: B & W had a group which consisted of two scientists and a lawyer that reviewed . . . additives prior to use of the tobacco products or as an ongoing process of reviewing additives in general.

Q: Was this lawyer who sat on the Brown & Williamson Additives Guidance Panel a scientist?

A: No, he was not.

Q: Do you remember his name?

A: Kendrick Wells.

Q: Was one of your jobs at Brown & Williamson to become knowledgeable about the pharmacological properties of nicotine?

A: I came to Brown & Williamson with that knowledge already.

Q: Once you were with Brown & Williamson, though, did you further try to learn as much as you could about the pharmacological properties of nicotine?

A: Yes.

Q: And did you express your opinion within the company to people who were interested?

A: I think it was generally recognized that nicotine was addictive.

Q: Generally recognized by whom?

A: By most of the scientists and management.

Q: Of which company?

A: Of Brown & Williamson.

Q: What is the basis for your opinion, professional scientific opinion, that nicotine is addictive?

A: I think nicotine is addictive in a number of aspects. First of all, nicotine is a pharmacologically active compound. I think it has been clearly demonstrated that nicotine elicits pharmacological effects. Nicotine crosses the blood brain barrier intact. Nicotine also mimics many of the endorphins, which are the body's natural analgesic compound, painkillers.

Q: Go ahead.

A: I think the reinforcing effect of nicotine is one. I think it is clearly documented in the scientific literature outside the tobacco industry that nicotine is an addictive substance and a drug.

Q: Finally, sir, you mentioned to me, sir, that you had received some threats. And I don't want to dwell on this, but I want to ask you, sir, were these threats that were delivered directly to you of a physical nature?

A: Yes.

Q: What was the general nature of these threats delivered to you?

A: I believe up until April 28th of 1994 I religiously reported to Brown & Williamson any time I was contacted. At that time, I was being contacted regularly by people at Waxman's staff to provide input. I reported it as required by the agreement. And I generally fed that through my attorney in Louisville who fed it to Jim Milliman at the local law firm, and then it was reported to B & W.

Q: On one occasion, sir, did you meet with B & W lawyers for a period of up to two weeks prior to your giving testimony to the Department of Justice pursuant to a subpoena from the Antitrust Division?

A: Yes.

Q: And you fully disclosed and discussed your testimony with them at that time?

A: I did.

Q: Did these threats that you have described to your family's well-being occur at any time contemporaneous with your reporting to Brown & Williamson about the matter of the anti-trust investigation?

A: It happened after the anti-trust investigation.

Q: It did?

A: Yes.

Q: How long after?

A: The testimony deposition on the CID I gave on January 24th. The threats came on April 22nd and April 28th of 1994, both directed to my children. And they basically stated, and I'd have to go and read them to you exactly, but one is, we have warned you, don't mess with tobacco. The second time is, how are your kids, you don't want them hurt, do you?

Q: Now, sir, as a result of those threats, did you decide to cooperate with federal officials investigating the tobacco industry?

A: Yes.

Q: You recall seeing this Brown & Williamson document dated 1963?

A: Yes, I did.

Q: And this is an excerpt from it, from Mr. Addison Yeaman?

A: Correct.

Q: Will you read it into the record, sir?

A: "We are then in the business of selling nicotine, an addictive drug effective in the release of stress mechanisms."

Q: Now, sir, did you learn anything as the vice president of research and development at Brown & Williamson, did you learn anything of a scientific nature that Brown & Williamson had in their possession that would dispute the remark their lawyer made that nicotine is an addictive substance?

A: No.

Q: In other words, what you learned was consistent with that statement, correct?

A: From a scientific and from a daily conversation basis, continues to reinforce that statement.

Until now, this kind of direct conflict in testimony between two top executives had never occurred in the tobacco wars. Too often, the battles have been between live tobacco executives and paper rebuttals. Jeffrey Wigand has changed the chemistry between the plaintiff and the jury permanently.

C H A P T E R

11

CASH CROP

Yes! Ready money *is* Aladdin's lamp.
— Lord Byron, *Don Juan*

After the summer of revelations, in which the companies themselves said that the industry had never experienced so broad and deep an attack, came the election of 1994.

Momentum for the anti-tobacco campaigners had been building. Major suits against the companies had been filed, suits that both sides acknowledged were different and more serious than the 800 filed and lost up to 1994. Some came from plaintiffs, but this time, seeking to establish class-actions so they could represent all smokers in the nation. For the first time, states too got into the action, asking the courts to force companies to pay for the illness they had caused by their deceit. At the same time staff attorneys at the Justice Department were musing, for the first time, about the possibility of indicting tobacco company executives for perjury before Congress.

At that moment, the election was held which turned Congress over to the Republicans for the first time in decades. Tobacco was not on the ballot in most states, nor were their issues. Where tobacco was on the ballot, for the most part, the companies lost. The most important and widely publicized attempt was in California, where Philip Morris had crafted a referendum which they called a "tobacco control" measure. It would impose restrictions on smoking all across the state. Of course, they worked through front groups so voters could not easily identify the measure as designed by a tobacco company. The heart of the bill was to take away from cities, towns and counties all power to ban smoking. Instead, the state bill would impose very weak rules in which smoking would be permitted in most places. It was an attempt to stop the local uprising against smoking. Despite attempts to disguise the measure, and all-time-record amounts spent to pass it (at least $12.5 million accounted for), Philip Morris lost by a margin of almost 70 to 30 percent.

But the companies had been working different strategies simultaneously, and so while they lost the election, they won the Congress. Rightish Republicans, absorbed in money issues and unconcerned about voters' attitudes on tobacco, immediately welcomed the tobacco companies to their councils. Thomas Bliley, the representative from Richmond, Virginia, who had been in the minority on Mr. Waxman's committee, now took over as a committee chairman. Among his first comments was to announce that the investigation of tobacco companies by Congress was over. Mr. Bliley is said to be the man in Congress who has taken the most money from the tobacco companies. Although it is impossible to know how much he has taken, about $127,000 had been traced up through 1995, not counting the frequent gifts of travel to warm places that he has taken and jet service for other purposes.

The internal papers that the companies promised to turn over to Congress were never sent in. The companies were home free. By December, 100 members of Congress had even signed a letter recommending that President Clinton name a doctor from Georgia as the first pro-tobacco Surgeon General for the nation.

The tobacco companies do sometimes seem invulnerable. They thrive despite public outrage about their tactics and brazenness; they are the most hated and most disbelieved industry in America, year after year, in the polls. Voters readily express their desire for strong tobacco controls measures.

But political opposition to the tobacco trade has always wilted in Congress and in state houses. In these chambers, tobacco thrives. This inversion of politics, in which the voter's attitudes are opposite to the votes of their representatives, needs to be explained. It pertains not only to tobacco, but to other issues such as anti-abortion politics and opposition to gun control, which are also unpopular across the country but nevertheless are secure within the bounds of the legislative halls of both state government and Congress.

There is a kind of mystery of democracy that emerges when scanning votes on tobacco issues. There are only six tobacco states with a handful of representatives who are devoted to the issue in Congress, but tobacco has nevertheless built an unparalleled record of victory: Until 1983, tobacco never lost a single legislative battle in Congress; the measures that appeared to be anti-tobacco, such as warning labels and advertising bans, were actually bills crafted by tobacco lobbyists to protect the industry from more serious regulation.

Since 1983, tobacco has lost a few battles, but very few. In the 100th Congress (1987–88), 145 anti-tobacco measures were introduced and 144 of them were defeated. The only success was to ban smoking on airline flights of 2 hours or less. In the 102nd Congress (1991–92), 29 anti-tobacco bills and amendments were introduced, 28 died, and only one minor one succeeded — eliminating a federal subsidy for overseas tobacco advertising.

Health and tobacco control groups, in fact, have won only 5 marginally notable legislative victories in the past decade, against hundreds of defeats.

But in popular elections, the record is the reverse. Where voters go to the polls to register their feelings directly, tobacco has lost. In local governments — town and county councils — in 1993, for example, 214 local anti-tobacco ordinances passed and only 26 were defeated. It has become a commonly-understood fact of lobbying life for both sides in the tobacco fight, that the closer the issues are to the voters themselves, the more tobacco loses; and the more issues are handled out of sight and in committees, the more tobacco wins.

How does this happen? The simplest answer is the power and money of the tobacco lobby. But the true answer is more complex. It includes the fact that there is not only a strong lobby working for tobacco, but virtually no organized opposition. It includes the fact that on many bills, representatives do not have to answer for their votes at home, because they helped kill bills at a level that does not get reported at home. Tobacco does well partly because representatives, especially committee chairmen, are susceptible to the effects of lobbying and campaign contributions, while they remain insulated from voters' vengeance because few of the crucial actions are even recorded.

To give a single example, a bill to ban smoking in many public places in the U.S., the Smoke Free Environment Act introduced in the spring of 1994, probably would have passed the House of Representatives if it ever could have reached the floor for a vote. On the floor, votes are recorded and debate is open, so members of Congress can be held accountable to the electorate which, polls show clearly, are strongly in favor of limiting smoking in public places. But the bill died in the Energy and Commerce Committee. Tobacco companies have given members of that committee cash at a level three times higher than they gave other members of Congress — averaging more than $21,000 each. Thirteen of the members got over $25,000 in recorded contributions from tobacco groups in the past five years, not counting soft money or other aid. Five of the committee members got $40,000 and more. (As the level of contributions in political campaigns is low, a gift of $ 1,000 earns a lot in the eyes of the desperate Congressman; the amounts tobacco companies give is more than a lot.)

It was a substantial victory for anti-tobacco forces in this case just to get the Smoke Free Environment Act passed out of a subcommittee and up to the level of committee at all. More than eighty anti-smoking measures in the past ten years were interred in the same subcommittee, and the Smoke Free Environment Act was the first in the past decade to pass out of subcommittee. The vote was a narrow 14–11, and it took weeks of infighting and pressure from the subcommittee chairman of the time, Henry A. Waxman of California, to achieve that vote.

Votes in favor of tobacco can be expected from Congressmen whose districts have tobacco companies and growers. But many of the committee votes came from elsewhere, such as from Rep. Edolphus Towns, an otherwise progressive Democrat from Brooklyn.

On the day before that subcommittee vote, May 11, Congressional finance records show, Mr. Towns received $4,500 from the R.J. Reynolds PAC. Within the five days after the vote, Mr. Towns received another $2,000 from other tobacco PACs. He is a regular tobacco voter, and has received $43,325 from tobacco PACs in reported contributions alone in the past five years.

Asked about his vote, Mr. Towns would not comment for the record, but a member of Mr. Towns' staff, in comments made after asking not to be quoted by name, said, "I know that the perception is that his vote has been bought, but that is not the case." The staff member, when asked why Towns would vote that way said tobacco companies have given large sums of money to inner-city organizations that are desperately short of cash. He called the money "an attempt by the companies to assuage their consciences."

As editor Vicki Kemper wrote in *Common Cause* magazine, "Tobacco remains largely unregulated 31 years, 50,000 studies and more than 10 million smoking-related deaths after the first Surgeon General's report certifying that smoking causes disease, not only because of the fabled 'power' of the tobacco lobby," but also because of the other half of the equation—the lawmakers who take the money.

Money is not the only issue. In another instance, it was the single-mindedness of those pressing tobacco interests that mattered. Congress, like other democratic bodies, is vulnerable not only to the influence of money but to the actions of a few dedicated, one-issue members, "kamikaze" members as they are often called, who will go to extreme lengths to disrupt votes on other issues in order to gain advantages for their issue.

One tale from the tobacco fights of 1994, a fight over whether to put high excise taxes on cigarettes, comparable to those in the rest of the developed world, helps illuminate the political dynamics. It is the tale of two Congressmen faced with similar choices, and how tobacco came out the winner. The House Ways and Means Committee, one of the four most important committees in Congress for both tobacco and health reform measures, has 38 members. On the issue of health care reform, in particular the package proposed by President Clinton, the votes were split about evenly. So then-chairman Rep. Sam Gibbons went in search of his "20th vote" to get a health care reform bill through. The Clinton health proposal was paid for in part by a large increase in the excise tax on tobacco—proposed to be $1.25 per pack, about 15 times larger than any tobacco tax previously enacted in the U.S., but still smaller than those in place in Europe.

Chairman Gibbons went to Rep. Mike Andrews, a Texas Democrat, among others, to find the 20th vote. Andrews says he wanted health reform, but didn't like the Clinton version of it. He wanted more cost control and other features. What he liked best about the health care proposal was the tobacco tax; he had worked for years to pass such a tax. Both Democrats and Republicans, tobacco and anti-tobacco, knew that a very large tobacco tax could probably pass the House of Representatives if it could only get out of committee, and over to the floor for a vote. But when it came to a choice, Rep. Andrews did not want the excise tax enough to make him vote for an unpalatable reform package. Getting the tobacco tax was not his overriding priority; he hesitated.

The chairman also went to Rep. L.F. Payne, a Republican from Danville, Virginia, in search of the 20th vote. Payne didn't much like the Clinton proposal either. But what was more important, he was fiercely opposed to tobacco excise taxes. He was willing to vote for a health package he disliked in order to save tobacco. This was the overriding interest for him.

Mr. Andrews said in an interview, "I guess I might have been the 20th vote. Time was when things were up for grabs. But there was a crucial difference for me and for L.F. For me, there were other issues, it wasn't just tobacco. For L.F., it was just tobacco."

So chairman Gibbons found his 20th vote — Republican Payne — by chopping the tobacco tax down from $1.25 per pack to 15 cents per pack in the first year, rising to no more than 45 cents over five years. It was by far the lowest tobacco tax increase suggested by any committee in the House or Senate during that debate. But once accepted by the Ways and Means committee, and with additional pressure from an aroused and solid bloc of tobacco-state members, both majority leaders in Congress incorporated the low figure into their packages being readied for floor votes. The single-minded tobacco voter from Virginia, who incidentally took more than $15,000 from tobacco PACS between March and July of that year alone, carried the day.

In 1994 a surge of damaging hearings and news stories nationally, combined with a swelling tidal wave of anti-smoking laws locally, put tobacco companies on the defensive. Those working for the companies said it was the worst year they remembered and perhaps the worst year in the history of the tobacco business. But in concrete terms, very little was lost. There have never been many or large successes for the anti-tobacco campaigners. What victories have come occurred when the bills or amendments which failed in committee somehow are permitted to reach the floor for a vote, a rare occurrence.

The best example, and a story told with fervor by anti-tobacco workers, is that of the ban on smoking on airline flights of two hours or less. It was a bill hastily written by Rep. Richard Durbin, D-Ill. He arrived at the airport late one day, and found that all the non-smoking seats were taken. He realized he would be forced to sit in the smoking section. "Isn't there anything I can do?" Mr. Durbin asked the airline clerk. "Yes, Congressman, you can pass a bill banning smoking on board."

Durbin wrote the bill, introduced it, and saw it fail the Appropriations Subcommittee on Transportation. It also lost in full committee. And usually, the Rules Committee would have prevented the bill from being offered as an amendment to some other bill on the floor. But in this case, Chairman Claude Pepper, himself a smoke-irritated traveler, let the amendment be offered. Durbin's staff was told he allowed it on the floor figuring it would be defeated anyway. It wasn't. "All the chiefs said no, but the Indians voted yes," said Tom Faletti, legislative aide to Mr. Durbin. With the support of flight attendants who appeared in droves for the vote, the bill passed 198–193.

The central principles in these tales of tobacco votes are ones well-learned by lobbyists. One such agent of tobacco was Victor L. Crawford, a lobbyist who worked for the Tobacco Institute, and who may be the only man who ever defected from the industry's lobbying army. He did so after he got cancer of the throat from smoking. He worked the Maryland legislature between 1986 and 1991 for tobacco, after he had been a member of the House for many years.

He is a blunt man, and has always spoken plainly on tobacco's behalf; now, he is speaking plainly about what it is like to lobby for tobacco. In an interview recently, just before heading off to the doctor for another exam, he explained that the chief job of a tobacco lobbyist is relatively simple:

"The job of lobbying for tobacco was to kill bills and to amend them, to weaken them. The whole action for tobacco in the United States is a holding action, keeping the status quo here, while the Third World is being flooded with cigarettes," he said. It is easier to kill or cripple legislation than it is to pass it, because it takes fewer people to do the damage, whereas it takes many people cooperating to pass a bill. Also, the tobacco companies don't need new legislation—the companies have very little regulation to govern their behavior now — they just need to be sure nothing bad for them is enacted.

For this purpose, a handful of legislators totally dedicated to a single issue, legislators who believe tobacco is their main job in political life, can be extremely effective.

Next, Mr. Crawford said that if it is not possible to get allegiance from legislators and other figures who become important in tobacco fights, "often you can at least buy their silence or inaction." Thus, in addition to care and feeding for the loyal tobacco Congressmen, it is important to target all those who are on crucial committees or in leadership jobs, not because they will vote with tobacco every time, but because they may not vote, or at the very least, they will listen politely when lobbyists come to call.

Tobacco lobbyists must make sure that the chairmen and members of a few important committees get huge contributions as well as regular personal contact. Matthew L. Myers, a lawyer who works part-time for the Coalition on Smoking or Health, an anti-tobacco group, said that, for example, during the first debates on heath care reform, when Rep. Dan Rostenkowski was still chairman of the House Ways and Means Committee, tobacco lobbyists had numerous meetings in person with staff members for Rostenkowski, while he and other anti-tobacco campaigners "couldn't get two minutes with them, not a single meeting with them." This kind of access in committees is crucial because bills originate in subcommittees, where committee chairmen schedule votes on them, and committee members can cripple them with amendments. From subcommittee the issues may rise up to full committee. Often they must pass muster this way in more than one committee. All of which means numerous opportunities to quietly strangle anti-tobacco bills. And, most often, action in committees and subcommittees is not reported.

Above the committees, if bills ever get that far, are the party leaders. They help determine when and whether bills may come from committee up to the floor for a vote. They also determine whether crippling amendments can or will be offered there.

Thus, as one might expect, tobacco lobbying and money is focused heavily on members of important committees and the party leadership. In a study completed in September, 1994, by the U.S. Public Interest Research Group in Washington, this sort of targeting was clear: On average, tobacco PACs gave about $6,800 to each member of the House of Representatives since 1987, said Edmund Mierzwinski of the research group. But the tobacco contributions to House leaders and members of just two committees — Ways and Means and Energy and Commerce — averaged more than $21,000 each during the same period. Party leaders got much more, no matter what their ideological inclinations. Former Majority Leader Richard Gephardt, a Democrat, took $76,000 up to the end of 1995. Majority whip David Bonior took more than $54,000 and Newt Gingrich took more than $54,000. Senator Tom Daschle, from the well-known tobacco state of South Dakota, who is now the minority leader in the Senate, has taken at least $21,000 in a state with low campaign expenditures, and the contributions are expected to rise rapidly as he has just assumed minority leadership.

These figures, in addition, are only what has been traced so far and do not include gifts and travel, or other kinds of contributions useful to Congressmen. For example, there are the "honoraria," which in the rest of the world are fees for making speeches. Between 1986 and 1990, after which payments were banned, the companies paid out $1.3 million to members of Congress. Rep. Dick Durbin described an incident to *Common Cause* magazine from the time when he was still a green Congressman, being invited to talk to the Tobacco Institute. He said he "obviously didn't know how this process worked" and had spent a lot of time preparing his speech. When he arrived at the Institute's plush headquarters, he said, "I was shocked at what I found. There was no audience. The audience consisted of the lobbyist who gave me the check."

Then there is Newt Gingrich, who has more ways to accept money than even his donors can keep up with. In addition to the $54,000 he received in contributions through 1995, RJR contributed at least $50,000 to GOPAC, his private political committee, and $5,000 to his college course. None of that counts the large sums contributed to his favorite "think tanks" in Washington, contributions for which he gets significant credit with the think tanks, which can act as a second staff for him.

These figures make it clear that resources are no problem for the tobacco companies. In fact, according to internal documents unearthed from Philip Morris's lobbying offices, frequently situations arise in which the companies have money to give, but representatives cannot take it for fear of, as one lobbyist put it, "sticking out like a sore thumb."

Mr. Crawford said his experience was similar. "Our resources were enormous. Money was simply no object. Whatever I wanted in support, I could get."

And so goes the politics in Congress, and in state legislatures: these are facts of political life which have driven many hearty souls from public service, and darkened the days of many who decided to stay. The fact is that for most decisions made on Capitol Hill, the constituents are not their voters at home. Those are the constituents only for the obvious and important votes. Day to day, the constituents who reward or punish Congressmen are the lobbyists, and chief among them, the tobacco lobbyists. It is hard to be shut off from an easy source of campaign cash, that most crucial commodity to the life of Washington politics. And it is even harder to put one's self in line to be a target, knowing that your opponent will get extra cash and help from tobacco companies.

CHAPTER

12

PRESIDENTIAL SEAL

Tobacco, divine, rare, superexcellent tobacco, which goes far beyond all the panaceas, potable gold, and philosopher's stones, a
sovereign remedy to all diseases . . . but as it is commonly abused by
most men, which take it as tinkers do ale, 'tis a plague, a mischief, a
violent purger of goods, lands, health; hellish, devilish and damned
tobacco, the ruin and overthrow of body and soul.
— Richard Burton, *The Anatomy of Melancholy*, 1621

The discussions about tobacco at FDA had begun in 1992, moved
in fits and starts, accelerated in 1994. Now, the FDA was silent in
public for a period. There were, from time to time, mostly among
political editors, rumors that the FDA would fold its tent. The
debate was over. "With that Congress!? There is no way they
could try regulating tobacco . . . ," the pundits would say.

But after all, the FDA is a federal agency which operates
under laws that outline what it should and should not do. Once
the agency has taken action, it is possible that Congress may vote
to stop the agency from carrying out its plans. But generating such
action is harder than it seems, because the public, which after all
does elect Congressmen, is on the other side and because the
President must concur if the Congress is not to face a veto.

So the agency continued its investigation quietly. It went on
over more than two years, with the work of a number of top agency
staff members. One of them, Mitch Zeller, still sounds astonished
when he talks of how much the FDA learned from the companies,
and how fast.

"Because the companies were so worried about the ABC report — they seemed very defensive — I think they welcomed the opportunity to explain themselves. Philip Morris called up and asked us to come down to their plants in Richmond. I believe they thought that the kind of 'spiking' mentioned in the ABC report was the center of our investigation. It wasn't."

In response to the companies' own worries about "spiking," they gave the FDA investigators a clear picture of the industry's central method of controlling nicotine, the blending of tobaccos of different nicotine concentrations. And crucial to the blending of tobacco and maintaining of nicotine levels, they found, was stalk position.

On the tobacco plant, there are perhaps two dozen leaves or more, and they are not all equal in taste, sugar content, or nicotine level. The sun-starved leaves on the bottom third of the plant are underdeveloped, and have less nicotine. Those in the middle are the tastiest and have a robust dose of "alkaloids," the word used to refer to nicotine. There is actually more than one of these substances in the leaf, but nicotine comprises more than 90 percent of the alkaloids in the plant.

The companies showed the wide-eyed FDA investigators diagrams of tobacco plants, showing that the dozen or so leaves at the middle to top of the plant are the choicest, and showing that these leaf positions all have "codes" — numbers identifying their rank on the plant as well as the tobacco type and the region from which the tobacco comes.

They showed FDA investigators drawings of each major variety of tobacco: basically three varieties, and about ten to fifteen stalk positions. In addition, they store three to six different crop-years in the warehouses. In one plant, investigators were shown what was described as a typical bale of tobacco leaves — about 2,000 pounds of leaves bound together in a great, brown, aromatic bundle.

For each bundle, the companies have accurate measurements — up to four decimal places, of the moisture, sugar, and nicotine in the bundle.

The major companies have computer databases where they keep the data on each bundle of tobacco, and so as a result have dozens of different, graded nicotine levels to choose from.

The blenders, the venerated alchemists of the industry, thus can survey and choose among many possibilities to achieve the needed mix from the flavorful Orientals to the higher-nicotine, heat-cured American leaves.

As filters have taken out more tar, the tobaccos used have included increasingly more potent leaves to compensate for the lost nicotine.

One of the investigative forays by the FDA on the trail of nicotine is the story of Brown and Williamson's "Y-1" super-nicotine tobacco.

After the hearings in March but before the tide of escaping documents, the agency got a telephone tip to look at patents on Brown and Williamson company's efforts to breed a special tobacco, one with stunningly high levels of nicotine.

One FDA investigator began to sift through patent records — if the company had a new breed, a genetically-altered strain of tobacco that had high nicotine levels, they must have patented it. The American patent records were blank. The records of company affiliates in Britain were blank.

But in scanning through the pile of documents, the investigator saw the key symbols displayed on an otherwise completely uninterpretable patent. It was in Portuguese.

The figures Y-1 and 6 percent nicotine stood out. The names on the patent were not employees of Brown and Williamson, nor were they Brazilian, though the plants were grown there. At the bottom of the Portuguese patent were the names of two scientists who were later found to work for a small company in New Jersey — DNA Plant Technology.

Zeller and another investigator drove up from Washington to New Jersey, where they had found the home address of one of the scientists on the patent, Janice Bravo.

They got lost, and as they came near Bravo's home it was pouring rain, very heavily. The FDA officials thought as they went up to the house that they would be taken for insurance salesmen or worse — it was an unannounced visit at night from two guys in dark suits who were getting out of a nondescript, dark-colored car.

Janice did not answer the door; her husband did, and immediately took pity on the soaked visitors. "Come on in out of the rain. . . ."

Though she had only a slender window looking out on the whole scene, she described to the investigators the development the company had done of a variety of tobacco that contained 6 percent nicotine — more than double the usual amount among the already high-nicotine American varieties.

Tobacco with this level of nicotine could not be grown in commercial quantities in the U.S. Contracts among the companies and the farmers to maintain quality standards state that no tobacco over 4.5 percent nicotine can be grown for sale here. Further, seeds in commercial quantities could not be shipped out of the U.S. without specific approval because of regulations of the Agriculture Department. So the whole operation seemed odd and maybe more than odd.

At least fifteen pounds of the extraordinarily tiny tobacco seeds, the investigators were told, had been shipped to Brazil. That would yield between one and two million pounds of high-nicotine tobacco: hardly an experimental quantity.

Reporters following the issues realized immediately that there could be only one reason for this — that the company was trying this method of compensating for the reduced nicotine in cigarettes that had come with the necessary reductions in tar.

If it could be demonstrated that the companies had greatly reduced tar, lawyers said, and worked hard to keep the nicotine levels closer to their original levels as the tar dropped, that would be critical evidence needed to show that the companies intended to use nicotine as a drug.

With this trip, the FDA investigators had established that one company was so concerned about keeping the nicotine levels up that it was breeding a wholly new tobacco plant with very great nicotine levels.

In combing through records of agricultural imports, an agency investigator had found an invoice from a Brazilian Company, Souza Cruz, to Brown and Williamson, for half a million pounds of Y-1 tobacco.

Putting the evidence together, the FDA had found that the research was done, that the tobacco plant seeds were produced, and that tobacco in commercial quantities had been shipped from Brazil to the U.S.

"But, still," Zeller said, "we had no evidence this tobacco was ever actually used commercially. We still could not name the brand that it showed up in."

Eventually, the FDA brought the company to a meeting in

Rockville, Maryland, just up the freeway from Washington, on June 17, 1994.

The story that emerged from the company officials was that there were efforts beginning in the early 1970s to raise nicotine levels, but the plants that had been developed, while high in nicotine, were not hardy. They ended up with a variety that bent down in rain and wind. In the 1980s, however, two scientists working at the Jones farm in Wilson, North Carolina, had worked through a list of tobacco breeds. There were five types being worked on, and these were soon winnowed to two types, which just happened to fall under the letter Y in the grower's notebook, so they became Y-1 and Y-2. Both were high in nicotine and could survive a rainy season in the field. But Y-2, when burned, smelled "like dirty socks," the tobacco company officials said.

So, Y-1 was the breed of choice. The officials said that after using the new tobacco in five different brands on the market, they still had 3.5 to 4 million pounds on hand in 1993.

Asked the reason for creating the breed in the first place, the company's chief product developer said, "It was going to be a blending tool, so that when we lowered the tar we could maintain the nicotine level."

FDA officials were dumbfounded. "This was a fantastic admission," one official said, "because it flies in the face of everything they have said. They have said over and over that nicotine is not set, but it follows the tar levels. Now we had a top product developer for the world's third largest company telling us that what they had said in public was not true."

Oddly enough, many of the executives in the company had told CEO Tommy Sandefur that the high-nicotine tobacco was a scheme that would not work. When too much nicotine is added, the smoke becomes very harsh, and so the new tobacco could be used only in very small quantities in any blend, for fear of making the cigarettes unsmokable. But with the enthusiasm of Sandefur behind it, the program went ahead. It was largely unsuccessful, but it was a lovely indication of what the company's intentions were.

For Kessler it was a turning point. This was concrete evidence of manipulation and control of nicotine. "You don't insert a gene for nicotine without the intent to control it," he said to his colleagues.

Again, it was not that the FDA could not guess the companies' intent, but that proof from their behavior was needed.

As the investigation wore on, the pressure was rising. Half a dozen newspapers, as well as National Public Radio and CBS were now under threat of subpoena from the tobacco companies, and ABC was already in court. At the first Waxman hearing of the year, a couple of Democrats had shown up, but for the Republicans, it had only been the last linebacker, Rep. Tom Bliley of Richmond (who had received tens of thousands of dollars of regular contributions as well as a long list of favors and perks, from the companies). But by the hearings on Y-1 high-nicotine tobacco, the full roster of Republicans appeared and had begun making threatening sounds about FDA. Rep. Dennis Hastert, whose understanding of the separation of powers in government is a little weak, suggested that Kessler should be held in contempt of Congress for carrying out the Y-1 investigation without telling Congress the details.

By the end of the summer, the agency had thousands of pages of explicit evidence of what the major companies were doing. They even had in hand a manual from Brown and Williamson, explaining to those learning tobacco blending just how to control nicotine and how to boost its effect by adding ammonia to the mix.

The top staff who had been working on tobacco and nicotine at the FDA was beginning to sort out just what kind of regulation of tobacco might work. What would be reasonable, but also effective in reducing the nation's tobacco problem?

Two groups were formed at that point — one to work on the investigation and turn it into a strong legal paper that would lay out the basis in law for regulating tobacco, and the second to investigate policies that might work, including looking at all the regulation of various kinds in other countries that had succeeded or failed.

The idea of banning tobacco or smoking was never an option, and did not come up. Outside the agency, a new idea was being entertained, that the government could require tobacco companies to reduce nicotine over many years, a bit each year, until it fell below the levels at which people become addicted. But this option was not considered, Kessler said, because it was plainly experimental. It could lead to people smoking more as well as people smoking less. "You can't do public policy based on a hypothesis," he said.

What they wanted was approaches that had worked somewhere else, that had some evidence for being useful, and that would not create needless trouble for the millions of citizens who are already addicted.

The single most important piece of information in shaping the proposal that the agency finally came up with was the fact that smoking is not an addiction of adulthood, but occurs almost exclusively in children. As Dr. John Slade of New Jersey, an expert on nicotine and addiction, said, it was essentially a "pediatric disease."

After reading the papers from the Canadian tobacco companies' work with children, Kessler said, it became clear. "Only after they are addicted do children realize what has happened to them. Before, they say it won't happen to me. This is what is different about kids and adults. They act, then regret it at age 17," he said.

So, the emphasis would be on children, to help them avoid addiction in the first place. It is not possible to simply stop children from smoking, but you can begin to convince them, and set up both obstacles and incentives. That is, after all, the limit of what the government should be doing in any case.

Then, after talking to tobacco control experts around the world, the object was to design a program that might have some real effect, that is, might actually result in decreased starting among children.

The main advice from those who have established programs around the world is that whatever program you try, it cannot be narrow. It must include all the important elements at once. It is important to work on each of the following issues: limiting children's access to purchase cigarettes; limiting their advertising exposure; educating them about not only the dangers of smoking but the social impulses that lead them to smoke; and increasing the taxes on tobacco.

As the FDA has no taxing powers, their proposal outlined steps in each of the other three areas and proposed putting those into effect first, followed by a review in a few years to see if they had worked. If they had, they would continue; if not, they would be changed. The idea was to set up a series of goals to meet, and empirical tests to assure that they were met.

When the Republicans were in control in Congress, it was common wisdom in Washington that tobacco regulation simply wouldn't happen. The FDA couldn't afford to try it, and the Administration would be crazy to take on more trouble than it already had (Whitewater, firing travel officers, and so on).

Nine months after the Republican sweep in the election, the news broke in the *Wall Street Journal* and in my story in the *Times* that the FDA had submitted a proposal to the White House officially declaring nicotine a drug and proposing regulations for tobacco, the first substantive rules ever proposed by the government on tobacco in America.

The rule would ban vending machines (used by less than 2 percent of adults, but the source of about a quarter of the cigarettes used by 13-year-olds). It would prohibit advertising in media that have audiences with substantial numbers of young people, and would ban the use of promotional gimmicks like hats and tee shirts. It would also require manufacturers to pay for a federally-designed public education campaign aimed at children, to counter the positive image of smoking in company ads. The most important provision, the last, states that if adolescent smoking does not decline by half in 7 years, additional measures will be taken.

In Congress, the reaction was predictable — those who accepted large amounts of tobacco money were opposed to FDA regulation. Newt Gingrich, for example, in his typical style, said Kessler was "out of his mind." He suggested that the agency should be paying attention to more serious problems like cocaine and other drug abuse, apparently unaware that the FDA does not work on drugs that are on the controlled substances list.

A number of Democrats as well backed away quickly from the FDA and the Administration. Tom Daschle, (at least $21,000 from tobacco), David Bonior ($54,000), and Missouri Rep. Dick Gephardt ($76,000), who are otherwise counted as progressive Democrats, support the industry.

At the same time, the industry went to work immediately putting pressure on the White House to dump the proposal. The chief emissaries were Governor James Hunt of North Carolina, friend of the President, and Senator Wendell Ford of Kentucky. A couple of different proposals were suggested to the White House by the industry, both of them offering to have the industry regulate itself.

One proposal suggested a voluntary program in which the companies would pay $100 million or more to educate children about tobacco and curtail the worst abuses of tobacco advertising (their own!). Ultimately the companies could not agree among themselves whether this proposal was a good idea, and it was dropped.

For weeks, the struggle for the heart of the White House went on, and at different points each side seemed to have the edge. The White House had not only read the polls, but had commissioned its own surveys in the Southern states on tobacco regulation. All the surveys were clear: about two-thirds of the voters wanted some kind of tobacco regulation, especially if it would be aimed at protecting children.

Finally, the decision was in the hands of Clinton himself.

One White House insider described a meeting in which the President, Vice President, and Secretary Shalala met with Commissioner Kessler, just before the President's decision. It is not clear how much Clinton's mind was made up before that, or at that moment.

Dr. Kessler and Secretary Shalala went into the White House through the back entrance so they wouldn't be spotted by reporters. They were led up to the Clinton family quarters.

The President said he was familiar with the agency's proposal on tobacco, but asked Kessler to lay out what he had found in the agency's investigation.

Dr. Kessler opened a book of findings and began to read some of the industry's own comments on nicotine and tobacco. He handed the President the brown book.

"These are their words?" Clinton asked.

Vice President Gore opened a recent newspaper and read aloud for Clinton a memorandum by R.J. Reynolds executive Claude Teague. "In a sense the tobacco industry may be thought of as being a specialized, highly ritualized, and stylized segment of the pharmaceutical industry. Tobacco products uniquely contain, and deliver nicotine, a potent drug. . . ."

Kessler said, "Mr. President, it would not be credible for us not to proceed."

13

IN THE BALANCE

We might make a public moan in the newspapers about the decay
of conscience, but in private conversation, no matter what crimes a
man may have committed or how cynically he may have debased
his talent or his friends, variations on the answer, "Yes, but I did it
for the money," satisfy all but the most tiresome objections.
— Lewis Lapham, *Money and Class in America*, 1988

By the time Bill Clinton ended his announcement that the government would, for the first time, try some serious but reasonable
regulation of tobacco, the industry lawyers were at the courthouse
door in Winston-Salem (where they could be assured of a judge
with a full set of loyalties to tobacco). It was too early to sue by
legal rules, as public comment had not even begun. But they were
angry, they believed it was all a conspiracy to ban tobacco from
America, and they wanted no mistakes about their intent: all the
law that money could buy would be put between this proposal and
its enactment.

The public relations experts decided that the best spin for
the companies would be to call the FDA proposal "an illegal
power grab" by a gaggle of senseless Washington bureaucrats. But
in Congress, the comments were strangely muted. The Republicans could have made lengthy, angry speeches, introduced a spate
of bills, held hearings, in sum, turned on the emergency genera-
tors. They didn't; their own poll numbers made it clear that their
constituents were not behind them. The emotions were all against
tobacco, and so, even a small slip could lead to irreparable damage. They had not been shy about taking up the battle for the

wealthy and powerful, but tobacco? The merchants of death? They would be there when needed, but would have to step carefully. Tom Bliley, the new kingpin in the House of Representatives on issues of health and commerce was quiet. He was the one to watch: he spent most of his career representing the district in which the giant Philip Morris industrial complex resides, earning him the nickname the Congressman from Philip Morris. (Among the press corps, the quips got a little nastier. Bliley is an undertaker by trade, a perfect match for the tobacco trade, because he gains both ways—when you smoke and when smoke gets you.) His whole comment, passed through his press assistants, was that they would get to the issue eventually, but for the moment it was an issue for the courts.

The natural end for a tangle like the tobacco wars is in court. Whatever the FDA does, whatever the Congress does, the resolution must finally be in court. That is because the issues are at bottom not just social but criminal issues—fraud and perjury. At least *these* issues must be resolved before we can say that the society has come to live with tobacco or not.

Judges and juries are now presented with a dozen or so important cases of different kinds against the companies, and they now have some reasonable access to the facts, though not all of them, and they must make some choices. Either the company behavior is within the bounds of what can be accepted, or it is not. (There is another possibility, of course, and that is, whether or not the behavior is acceptable, the legal system is unable to cope with a client so rich and powerful that it can not only take advantage of all the rules, but invent them as it goes. I am writing this the year after the O.J. Simpson verdict, as you might guess.) But still, the cases now in hand will settle the matter.

Congress may try to arrange some kind of settlement to rescue the industry, or give it some kind of special dispensation.

The cases arrayed against the industry now are called by veterans "the third wave." The first few suits against the companies were filed in the mid-1950s after the hazards of tobacco first became explicit. Another wave surged up in the mid-1980s, after the beginning of the consumer movement and after toxic substances became a topic for dinner party conversation.

But tobacco has somehow been different. As lawyer George Annas has said, product liability suits have been important in encouraging automobile makers to make safer cars, and drug makers to test their products carefully. But after the more than four hundred suits in those two waves, the industry lawyers like to say that tobacco companies have never paid out a penny to compensate a smoker. There have been no settlements, and no final court awards against them. This is a remarkable record, one that is probably unequaled in American law.

The record may be a little less remarkable when you reflect on some of the cases themselves. Throughout the first and the second wave, each case set a single smoker and his attorney, working out of his own pocket, against an industry that can play high-stakes poker with God. In the game they play, there is no limit to the bluff money, and ties go to the industry. For example, as one saddened and outraged judge in Michigan pointed out, misconduct by either side produces a mistrial, which is a win for tobacco because no plaintiff can afford a second trial and the companies can afford any number of them. Therefore, if nothing else works, the companies can cheat. And there is more than one angry judge who has spoken out from the bench about the seemingly routine misconduct of tobacco company lawyers.

To give an example of the crazy mismatch in the cases, one plaintiff's lawyer, Stanley Rosenblatt in Miami, has written that the average case against tobacco nowadays costs $10,000,000, lasts ten years, and does not typically end with a tobacco victory, but ends when the plaintiff is completely exhausted and can afford not another day in court even though the case is not ended.

In a typical legal case, for example, an important preliminary is to take depositions from those who are likely to testify. They are a sort of dry-run for both sides to see what each witness will offer and what issues the witness will raise. It is not uncommon to take an entire day to depose one witness, or even two or three days, for the most important witnesses in the toughest cases. But like a one-team league, the tobacco companies set records just by stepping on the field. In one case, a scientist who was testifying about the hazards of cigarette smoke for a plaintiff was grilled in deposition for 22 days; when the case ended (an exhausted plaintiff again) the industry lawyers had indicated they were not finished with him. In the same case (called Haines vs. Liggett Group), the industry had taken depositions of plaintiffs' witnesses for 292 days, consuming three years of court time. The judge in that case recalled a quotation from a Reynolds attorney on the strategy being employed: "The aggressive posture we have taken regarding depositions and discovery in general continues to make these cases extremely burdensome and expensive for plaintiffs' lawyers. . . . To paraphrase General Patton, the way we won these cases was not by spending all of RJR's money, but by making that other son of a bitch spend all of his."

At the end of the Haines case the lawyers for the widow of the dead smoker had to quit. They had spent $6.2 million, and ten years, and were not near a conclusion. They offered to turn the whole thing over to a fresh lawyer, and not even ask for expense reimbursement. No attorney could be found to take up the case.

Judge Noel Fox in Michigan, having presided over a similar debacle in his court, realized at the end of the trial there that his own rulings were misused and hopelessly inadequate to the situation. The court had granted a motion, for example, that kept tobacco documents secret during the trial and limited the amount of outside help that the plaintiff could get. At the same time, the company routinely had a dozen experienced defenders in court. The judge said that one more "obvious advantage accrued to Defendant by virtue of its overwhelming superiority of resources. It knew that Plaintiff could not afford the luxury of a mistrial. With such knowledge Defendant could confidently risk tactics that would normally be deterred by this sanction. Plaintiff, on the other hand, knew both that she had to be cautious herself and that, as a practical matter, she would be unable to effectively police Defendant's conduct."

The judge added, "Justice must be made available to all, not only to the strong who can martial the greatest resources, but to the weak and disadvantaged. This goal has been sought for centuries, and bears repetition today when so much of our energy is directed to the quest for social justice."

The whole case, the judge said, seemed to amount to a denial of due process. He ended by saying, "This question, unfortunately, is now moot because Plaintiff cannot afford further proceedings. Therefore, if a denial of due process has in fact occurred, it has at this point slipped past the safeguards existing within the system and cannot be corrected."

It is unusual, I submit, to hear a judge in an official record say that the legal system may simply not be able to provide justice to citizens against a large and continuing wrong.

While pressing plaintiffs, at the same time the companies

have been rather hard for plaintiffs to get hold of. Again and again judges have complained about their unwillingness to produce important documents when ordered to. A good example is the Brown and Williamson papers, which cover many years and all the vital topics on health and tobacco, including all the most important research which informed top executives. Assistant General Counsel of B & W, J. Kendrick Wells (himself the author of the "deadwood" memo on how to get rid of the embarrassing papers) has said that none of the documents have ever been produced by the company in court. The company has been asked for relevant documents in more than 80 cases, according their own lists, but the damaging material was held back.

Early on, during the first wave of anti-tobacco suits, the industry devised methods to keep the papers from causing trouble. The attitudes were described in August, 1970, by David R. Hardy, probably the most important strategist for the combined companies' defense. In a letter labeled "Confidential, for Legal Counsel Only," he wrote that the company narrowly missed serious damage or loss in a tobacco case, and he was worried. He said it would be important to make sure that the remarks made by company officials, especially the scientists, be kept under wraps. He said that in a recent conference, opening talks were duly ambiguous, as they said for the record that "causation" of disease was still an open question. But in the conference itself, the actual attitudes were too obvious, he said: "We note a number of statements or expressions which could be most damaging, notwithstanding the disclaimer in the opening statement. For example: (i) reference is made on page 6 to the fact that research 'will continue in the search for a safer product'; (ii) on page 14 a product is characterized as 'attractive' because less biologically active; (iii) on page 15 the phrase 'biologically active' is used; and (iv) on page 18 reference is made to a 'healthy cigarette.' "

He wrote that, "It is our opinion that statements such as the above constitute a real threat to the continued success in the defense of smoking and health litigation. Of course, we would make every effort to 'explain' such statements if we were confronted with them during a trial, but I seriously doubt that the average juror would follow or accept the subtle distinctions and explanations we would be forced to urge."

Yes, indeed. He said that if all these damaging admissions

ever made it into court (and they have *not* yet by 1996, 26 years after the memo!) it would tend to establish "actual knowledge on the part of the defendant that smoking is generally dangerous to health, that certain ingredients are dangerous to health and should be removed, or that smoking causes a particular disease. This would not only be evidence that would substantially prove a case against the defendant company for compensatory damages, but could be considered as evidence of willfulness or recklessness sufficient to support a claim for punitive damages."

If Mr. Hardy is ready to award punitive damages after seeing the tobacco documents, then the necessary strategy for the company is obvious — scientists and other executives must stop making reckless remarks, and these papers cannot get into the hands of the plaintiffs nor ever be shown to a jury.

With Hardy's aid, companies then devised a series of record-keeping devices which would ensure that the damaging material was always out of bounds to plaintiffs. In court, both sides must have access to all the material relevant to the issue at hand. Documents showing the executives' attitudes and their lawyers conspiring to hide scientific opinions should in general be available, for a jury to see what was going on. However, there are two technical exceptions in law. The discussions between a lawyer and his client need not be brought into court, in order to allow them freely to discuss the case with each other when preparing a defense. Second, and related, is the lawyer's "work product" — his notes and fact gathering done to prepare for a trial are not to be brought into a case. The jury should see everything about what was done by the defendant, and how and when, but the later defense of his actions is not the point, because everyone has a right to defend himself without further incriminating himself.

So the task was to make sure that all the damaging materials could be designated attorney-client or work-product "privileged." It is a bit hard to imagine that scientific research by company workers and conferences about making safer cigarettes could be construed as part of some "attorney-client" dialogue or somehow become notes like "work-products," especially years *after* these papers were created. But that was the tactic.

In another example of the handiwork of J. Kendrick Wells, a memo from June of 1979 outlined a procedure to make sure that the scientific information about cigarettes was hidden. He wrote to Ernest Pepples, the head of litigation, that "The [scientific] material should come to you under a policy statement between you and [the research lab in] Southampton which describes the purpose of developing the documents for B & W and sending them to you as use for defense of potential litigation. It is possible that a system can be devised which would exempt the engineering reports because it might be difficult to maintain a privilege for covering such reports under the potential litigation theory. Continued law department control is essential for the best argument for privilege." He suggested storing the documents in a special file, after looking through them for the most damaging material. Then, only the somewhat less explosive material would be permitted out, even to other company scientists working on the same technical questions.

There was one problem, he noted. The financial agreement under which all the scientific work was done and paid for made it too clear that the work was done for commercial reasons. There was even a business contract which said that the work was commercial. "The cost sharing agreement between B & W and BAT, under which B & W pays for BAT scientific research and receives reports, is an obstacle because as presently written it would probably contradict the position that you were acquiring the reports for purposes of litigation. . . ." He suggested faking a new cost sharing agreement, and making sure that all the scientific reports coming in would first go to someone under law department control.

The industry lawyers were right about the documents. All their fears and machinations began to be realized in one suit, the most important tobacco case to date, brought by a feisty woman in New Jersey, Rose Cipollone, and her husband Antonio. She had started smoking when she was 17, in 1942, and smoked one to two packs a day throughout her life, switching brands as she went looking for the "safest" on the market. She finally quit smoking in 1983, and sued. She died at age 59, just as the case was beginning in 1984.

That was the first case in which a jury got even a good peek at what damaging materials resided in the darks of the company files. Just before the trial began, the chief lawyer for the plaintiffs, Mark Z. Edell, predicted that the case would be different because of what was becoming known about the company behavior. "We believe a jury won't give Rose Cipollone an award just because

she smoked and got lung cancer," he said. "When they understand how the tobacco industry has manipulated the American
people, they'll be incensed and come back with a verdict." In 1988
the jury did award damages for the first time in a tobacco case, to
the family of Mrs. Cipollone. The jury still was not happy about
her choice to smoke, and said that she was 80 percent responsible
for the damage to her health. But the jury did assign some blame
to the industry for failure to do a better job warning the public. It
looked for a time as if that would be the industry's first loss in
court, and the beginning of the end. But in appeals, the companies carried the case to the Supreme Court. The court said that
the industry could get some protection because they had been
forced to put warning labels on their packages: no warnings other
than the ones mandated by Congress could be given, so the
companies were off the hook on that count. They did not have an
obligation to make better warnings. But the Supreme Court made
it clear that there was more to it — plaintiffs could still sue and win
if they could show the companies had committed fraud in what
they told the public and the government. The family might have
gone back into court, but the opinion, issued in 1992, ten years
after the start of the suit, would mean starting over again under the
new rules set out by the Supreme Court. The exhausted plaintiff
and attorneys folded.

Now, the third wave has begun. New and dangerous things
have happened. Over the past forty years, tobacco cases have
turned largely on a single issue. Smoking is hazardous, perhaps,
but whether it is or not, smokers are the ones who go to the store to
buy the cigarettes, and tear open the packs to smoke before they
get home. Juries believe in the voluntary nature of behavior;
humans can choose what they want to do, even if carrying out
their choices is sometimes hard. The juries may or may not be
correct, ultimately, as philosophy and science are at this moment
only beginning to confront this issue with new biological under-
standings in hand.

But it was only in 1988 that the Surgeon General officially
declared nicotine addictive — *after* the Cipollone trial was essentially over. In the next wave, addiction will no doubt become a
much larger part of the trials, especially because, since the Cipollone trial, thousands of pages of material in which company
officials and scientists plainly state that they themselves believe

smoking is addictive have become available. The companies' fixation on nicotine and the extremely careful control of it are now known in great detail, but they are still publicly denied by the companies despite the documentary evidence, a position which juries might well recoil from.

Second-hand smoke had not been an issue either, until now. But in Florida, a class-action suit has begun on behalf of 60,000 flight attendants who were forced to work in the veritable smoke chambers of airline cabins before the ban. Their inhalation was not voluntary; many of them suffer ill effects and will die.

Another new feature of the third wave are the suits, not from individual plaintiffs, but from state governments. Having expended billions of dollars to pay for medical treatment for smokers' illnesses, they want their money back. As the companies have been engaged in a massive fraud to deceive both the public and the government about the hazards of smoking, they ought to be forced to pay for the damage they have done. Again, in these cases, the individual choice to smoke becomes a secondary issue in the face of statewide statistics on just how much damage is done by tobacco.

Charles R. Wall, who is Philip Morris's chief litigation specialist and who formerly worked for Shook, Hardy and Bacon, acknowledges that the situation is rather different, but says that the company hopes to hold cases to the same, basic issue. I talked with him about the cases at the end of 1994, and he said, "Litigation from the plaintiffs' perspective has not been successful, so they are now looking for new things, new ways to approach it, and they have found some. One idea is the class, they say to themselves, if we go at it en masse, maybe we will have better luck. Another idea is to have attorneys general sue in each state," he said. "They are thinking, how can we get this industry? But at the bottom, these are old ideas wrapped up in new dressing. Each is a personal injury case and each one will have to be dealt with on an individual basis." He promised that the companies would not accept group efforts, but would force each of the 50 million potential cases (for the number of smokers left) into a separate trial, one way or another.

But there is one issue that cannot be handled in that way. The companies are trying to hide an elephantine stack of papers under a nod and grin. Whether you believe addiction involves choice or not, you may well believe that the companies have perpetrated a rather bold fraud.

Another new feature of the third wave, and maybe the most important, is that the plaintiffs are no longer poor. Five of the plaintiffs are not individuals at all, but states. Another five cases are class actions, of which the one that is most different from past tobacco cases is Castano *vs.* American Tobacco in New Orleans, the class action filed on behalf of all those addicted to nicotine. The plaintiff in this case is represented by about 100 attorneys, from 60 law firms. The firms have donated enough cash for a $6 million-per-year budget. "We have enough talent and numbers to go toe-to-toe with the tobacco companies for the first time," said John Coale, one of several unusually flamboyant lawyers who have gravitated to the Castano case. "They simply cannot outspend us, and that is important because the history of tobacco litigation is that companies have overwhelmed the plaintiffs." But first, they must get into court.

So the arguments went as the lawyers began to prepare for court appearances in 1996. The back-and-forth of charges and rebuttals went on through the winter of 1995–1996. There were blizzards up and down the east coast week after week, breaking all records for snowfall. And when the weather broke in March of 1996, the tobacco wars also turned. "The tide just went out on the companies," as one lawyer put it.

First came the news that the smallest of the five remaining tobacco companies, Liggett & Myers, was willing to settle the suits against them — the Castano suit and five of the suits brought by states against them. The settlement was weak in that it offered little money to the plaintiffs, and covered only six cases of the dozen or more out there, but it was the first time in 40 years that the solid front of tobacco had broken. Perhaps more significant was the fact that the company officials agreed to produce information and aid in going after the other tobacco companies. The settlement, though it was produced by the selfish business motives of Bennett LeBow, who was trying to rescue the small company under his control from take-over by the giant RJR, was a hopeful turn.

Then, by St. Patrick's Day, 1996, the dam began to break.

Three tobacco company officials, over and above Merrell Williams and Jeffrey Wigand, suddenly agreed to cooperate with the FDA to make truthful statements about their work. All three of them had important jobs in the research production departments, and all three had significant experience with the importance of nicotine in the design and manufacture of cigarettes.

Where the companies had worked hard to discredit first Merrell Williams, and then Jeffrey Wigand, it was no longer possible to imagine discrediting every employee who left the company and was willing to describe his or her work. More would come forward day to day. The operations of the companies now began to be laid bare brick by brick.

The statements of the three were remarkable because they were simple and frank. They were not apologetic about their work, they were fascinated by the science of tobacco and nicotine, from the chemistry of plants to the action at human brain synapses, and they reflected that excitement. If anything, they sounded puzzled by the antics of the top lawyers and executives, who seemed determined to paint the companies into an impossible corner.

The facts were laid out in detail, attacking directly the public statements of company officials. In these documents you can hear again the voice of rationality — cigarettes are a fixture of society, cigarettes are hazardous, and can be made less so, thus, what is logical is open discussion and compromise between federal regulators and the more reasonable people inside the companies.

William A. Farone, a chemist who is now the head of his own company, Applied Power Concepts, wrote the most extensive affidavit. He graduated from the small Clarkson University in upstate New York, and is an inventive man, who is proud of his ability to devise new technology for products, which he did at Lever Brothers and then at PVO International before going to work for Philip Morris in 1976. At Philip Morris he was in a key research job, the Director of Applied Research, for seven years. It is from this position that all the company's knowledge about nicotine gets applied directly in cigarettes. Few people would know more about the subject of nicotine and tar in cigarettes than he.

His statement, written more like an academic paper, with 53 citations on 16 pages of text, may almost be counted as the closest thing to a personal apologia that has come out of the tobacco wars. He is clear, admits everything, and offers a simple rationale for his work.

He opened with a statement that cuts through the verbiage about nicotine: "It is well recognized within the cigarette industry that there is one principle reason why people smoke — to experience the effects of nicotine. . . . Clearly, by the 1970s and early 1980s the tobacco industry had established that smokers required a minimal level of nicotine within a cigarette. Knowledgeable industry personnel, primarily scientists and blend and development personnel, understood that a level of nicotine had to be present to result in a commercially successful cigarette. As publicly available documents reveal, the tobacco industry began to study how to design and construct cigarettes to ensure acceptable nicotine levels. It was common knowledge within the industry that cigarettes without nicotine would not sell. Nicotine-free cigarettes in the 1950s and 1980s were failures."

He offered a bit of a rationale for what he did, why he did it, and how he thought about the work. A technician's pride rises through the words: "If we accept the premise — as the cigarette industry surely does — that cigarettes are a nicotine delivery system, and that current laws do not forbid the self-administration of nicotine via smoking by adults, then it becomes a desirable technical challenge to decrease the 'tar' in a cigarette while maintaining the delivery of nicotine. This has been a key objective of the cigarette industry over the last 20–30 years, some industry documents now publicly reveal."

Minimizing bad health effects and maintaining the nicotine buzz, he said, "is thus a valid and useful technical challenge that I and many of my former colleagues in the cigarette industry considered a top priority." Maintaining the level of nicotine in the face of constant reduction of tar was "an enormous challenge. It required cigarette manufacturers to deliberately control the levels of nicotine in their products in order to overcome the naturally-occurring variability of nicotine in tobacco plants. Since tobacco is a natural product and the content of nicotine varies from year to year, by type of tobacco, by varieties within types, and from farm to farm, it is also necessary to be able to control nicotine levels and the ratio of nicotine to tar to be able to make a consistent product. . . . Cigarettes manufacturers have invested enormous financial resources to achieve the desired level of control over nicotine and tar in their products."

He went on to say that "The strongly held conviction of most industry scientists and product developers was that nicotine was the primary reason why people smoked. This was sometimes openly expressed. In fact, it was commonly understood within the industry that the smoker's acceptance of a cigarette was related to the amount of nicotine it contained. Extensive, in some cases ground-breaking research by the tobacco industry was necessary to construct a cigarette that ensured an adequate delivery of nicotine as the cigarette market evolved from the traditional full-flavored, unfiltered product of the 1950s to the filtered, low-tar cigarette demanded by many smokers for the last 30–40 years. The objective of industry scientists and product developers, simply stated, was to provide the consumer with the same pharmacological satisfaction derived from nicotine in the natural blends and flavor of the full strength cigarettes of the 1950s as the marketplace shifted to the naturally less flavorful and satisfying low tar and nicotine cigarette demanded by the more health-conscious consumer."

He spoke of one of his mentors, William Dunn, the "nicotine kid" by Dunn's own description. Farone said that "Dunn believed that nicotine was a beneficial component of cigarette smoke . . . [and] the development of low tar cigarettes that gave smokers the nicotine they wanted but exposed them to less tar were considered good research and product development objectives. Industry scientists were proud to be working on the development of these products."

The more difficult issues of why they did not create cigarettes that are much safer rather than only marginally safer if at all, is not addressed.

He wrote in some detail about the great efforts the industry took to understand nicotine, including a broad array of human experiments to find out how it fulfilled smokers' needs, how it affected thinking and physical performance.

He said that products that did not have enough nicotine "impact" were quickly redesigned to add more. "Product developers and blend and leaf specialists were responsible for manipulating and controlling the design and production of cigarettes in order to satisfy the consumer's need for nicotine. . . ."

He explained how the nicotine manipulation — and he used the word "manipulate" as well as the words "deliberately control" more than once — was done, beginning with simple blending tactics. When nicotine dropped too low, some of the Bright tobacco was dropped and a little more Burley put in.

He gave one example, Merit Ultra Light, which he said was introduced in 1981 with an intentionally high nicotine-to-tar ratio. It was necessary, he said, to use extensive expertise from their research on both flavors and smoker behavior to mask the harsh nicotine taste of the cigarette.

He reviewed some of the methods of controlling nicotine — filters that let through more nicotine than tar, reconstituted tobacco sheet with different loads of nicotine, the addition of ammonia to free more nicotine from tobacco. All the components of the cigarette, from the type of tobacco to the ammonia additive, were incorporated in a giant computer program which could predict how various changes would affect the delivery of nicotine to the smoker. The computer models "enabled nicotine and tar deliveries to be successfully predicted and enabled product developers to identify which components were required to produce specific nicotine and tar deliveries."

After all of this and more, Dr. Farone noted that while some of the work inside the tobacco research labs has come to light, "much of the novel and groundbreaking scientific research of the tobacco industry has not come to the public's attention." One can only wonder what other surprises lie still in the Richmond labs.

His final word in his statement was a simple appeal for an "open environment, with cooperation on the nature of cigarette products between the industry and government" in which new, safer products could be made and "agreement between regulators and industry would open up entirely new options for cigarette construction and progress in the industry."

To appreciate just how striking all these admissions are, one needs to bring back what the chief executive of Philip Morris, William I. Campbell, said under oath before Congress.

In the hearing in which seven top executives testified, he said, "Philip Morris does not manipulate nor independently control the level of nicotine in our products . . . nicotine levels are measured at only two points in our manufacturing process, prior to the tobaccos being blended and then 18 months later, when those leaves have been manufactured into finished cigarettes. Although Philip Morris maintains over 400 quality control checkpoints in the manufacturing process, that measure things like moisture, weight, et cetera, none — not one — measure, report or analyze nicotine levels in tobacco."

Compare that to the affidavit of Jerome Rivers, obtained by

the FDA in March, 1996. He had worked at Philip Morris in Richmond for 23 years, in several of the jobs with direct responsibility for the control of nicotine in Philip Morris cigarettes.

"During the manufacture of reconstituted tobacco, we frequently monitored the alkaloid content of the by-products, the slurry, and the final reconstituted tobacco sheet. Alkaloid is another name for nicotine. The alkaloid content would be measured using a gas chromatograph . . . we would measure the alkaloid content of the by-products approximately once a shift. We would measure the alkaloid content of the slurry approximately once per hour. We would also measure the alkaloid content of the final product approximately once per hour.

"The alkaloid measurements would be returned to us soon after we had taken a sample. It generally took only 10 to 15 minutes to get the results back.

"We would record the alkaloid content of the reconstituted tobacco sheet in a computer database. This database recorded the alkaloid content of each time-stamped package of blended leaf.

"Philip Morris established standards, or 'specs' for the alkaloid content of the reconstituted tobacco sheet blended leaf product. If our measurements showed that the product was out-of-spec for alkaloids, we would pull the reconstituted tobacco sheet. . . ."

Rather different from the once-in-18-months that Campbell reported, Rivers' account matches that obtained by ABC lawyers from Philip Morris documents and interviews with current plant operators and manuals.

The third of the statements obtained at the end of the winter, this one from Dr. Ian Uydess, who worked as a researcher with Philip Morris for 11 years, confirmed the statements of the others, and added some significant detail not in the others. He described the pattern of testing cigarettes with several different nicotine levels in order to pick the one that would work best in the market. He also distinguished between two terms that company executives have blurred together. The "impact" of nicotine is the feeling at the back of the throat when a smoker inhales, followed some seconds later by a physiological sensation. This is different from "taste" in the mouth created by the cigarette tars. Nicotine is not really a taste at all, and is handled by different departments in the company. Dr. Uydess said that while both impact and taste are important to the ultimate acceptability of a product, "impact (nicotine) was known to be the more powerful determinant in many of these cases. In the long term, smokers would be more likely to stay with a marginally-tasting product with adequate 'impact,' while they would tend to abandon one of relatively good flavor having no, or insufficient, impact."

Dr. Uydess also recalled a graph used in the company to show how a cigarette's acceptability declined with lower available nicotine. On the chart were two boundary lines: one of the low level below which cigarettes could not be sold, and one of the high level above which cigarettes are too harsh to be tolerated.

And, if there was any doubt that upper management was aware of all this, top executives from New York came down to Richmond at least once a month to review the research and progress in fine detail.

Lawyers looking at the situation began to think that the accumulation of evidence would continue, and began to entertain thoughts that the companies might actually lose in court. If they do, and settlements of billions of dollars are discussed or even ordered, the companies may declare themselves bankrupt, and will have to re-form under new names and begin again. But even if they lose, even if they are forced up against the wall by a jury, they have one final card to play. After all, they *did* succeed in designing safer cigarettes. From the ashes and smoke will certainly rise a new bird.

C H A P T E R

1 4

BEYOND SUSPICION

I reside at Table Mountain, and my name is Truthful James; I am
not up to small deceit, or any sinful games.
— Bret Harte, *The Society Upon the Stanislaus*, 1868

Where I finish is where I started. More than three years ago, when
I was a health and science reporter concentrating on issues of
health policy in Washington and had done virtually no reporting
on tobacco, I was approached by an old friend I used to work with
at the *Washington Post*. We were both science reporters at the
Post, but in the intervening time he had gone to work for a public
relations firm in Washington to make real money. One of his
clients was now R.J. Reynolds.

He called and said he had what he thought was a terrific
story, not just the usual daily material, but something really interesting. Granted, it's the evil empire, but hey, you'll listen to the
idea, right?

I went to dinner with the old *Post* colleague and Thomas C.
Griscom, now a top executive for RJR, but who had before been a
savvy political aide in Washington, working on Capitol Hill for
Senator Howard Baker of Tennessee and in the Reagan and Bush
administrations. We ate pasta, drank wine, and I listened to the
pitch.

The company had a new product, not just a new cigarette,
but a whole new type of cigarette. This one resembled a cigarette
in appearance, and had a taste very much like the average cigarette. But there was virtually no smoke from it, and it would
eliminate the hazardous compounds produced in smoking by far

more than anything ever produced — in fact, people in the factory who had been smoking prototypes for some time looked to their doctors as if they had quit smoking.

I wasn't worried about the seemingly excessive claims — they wouldn't be pitching them to me if they weren't prepared to show me data. That's what I did all day, every day, look at data. I called it an "artificial cigarette" and Griscom blanched, but the proposition that a system to deliver some flavor and nicotine without the same high levels of disease-causing components seemed plausible.

What I really wanted to know was *why* they were leaking the story to me. Whether or not I could participate in writing a story leaked to me by the evil empire would be determined in large part by their motive. I had to know what they were doing, and why.

I gradually sorted out the issues. The reason they wanted to leak it, and this is the usual reason for leaking any story, was that they wanted to select the reporter and the newspaper to handle the story, either to get someone they believed understood the subject, or to get someone who didn't understand the subject, or someone with a particular bias they'd like to exploit. Selecting a reporter wouldn't give them much additional ability to shape the story, but if they were clever, their choice would naturally be an asset. In this case, they wanted my biases — health and science data — and my ignorances — the business picture.

In this case, what they wanted to suggest was that the main issue here was a technical breakthrough which could create a significant health benefit and a product which could conceivably take over the entire cigarette market if things worked out. But that technical and health orientation would not have been of much interest to business reporters, the likely reporters to cover the story, who would think of it as some kind of clever new marketing scheme and focus on the market dynamics. Worse, a previous product, the Premier cigarette which they had launched in 1988 with a similar idea but different cigarette design, had failed utterly as a market ploy. Business reporters would want to analyze that product, compare the two, and spend a fair amount of energy focusing on those issues. All this, of course, is only for the first story, the announcement. After that, all reporters write the story and even the first reporter is influenced by the approach of the others writing the story. But the spin of the first day, old hands will tell you, can make or break a story. It can often set reporters off in a particular direction.

To a reporter about to be manipulated in this old game, these are thoughts not to be taken lightly. After listening to the pitch, will you allow yourself to be used, and to use the source? Is the story and the particular pitch they are offering legitimate? In particular, when working with tobacco companies, the likelihood of attempted deception is very high; I knew that even though at that time I knew essentially nothing of what I have written in this book.

But if I had good access to the people working on it, could get all my questions answered, and had time to study the ways the whole pitch might be legitimate or illegitimate, I felt it was worth doing. Besides, it was a hell of a story.

I spent time in Winston-Salem at the company headquarters, and sitting in on secret tests with smokers in Chattanooga. I reviewed some data and asked scientists and others familiar with the history of "safer" cigarettes about that history.

Ultimately, I came to believe that the story of tobacco, and the crisis the companies had got themselves in by their dishonesty, followed then by their political and social struggle, was one of the great stories of this century in America. The subject, to begin with, was quintessentially American, from the Native Americans to the rescue of the American colonies by this crop, to the discovery of cigarettes. Then, the story was about social mores, and how the nation had learned the hard way during Prohibition that personal vices cannot be eradicated without very great costs. And then finally, the health crisis, when it was discovered that cigarettes had essentially invented a massively lethal disease, creating a pandemic of illness and death where there had been none. In the time after the Vietnam War, when corporations began to get some of the blame they had escaped for social and environmental ills, here was the worst of all offenders, still alive and well and prospering, thank you. An odd story, it is. Now, finally, the industry is contemplating paying attention to its customers' health for the first time, with a new "safer" cigarette. An addictive one, with carefully calibrated amounts of nicotine to keep smokers addicted. But still, one that actually offers a social benefit of some kind. The situation, actually, is comical and absurd. But a great story.

One thing that appealed to me was that if it worked, the cigarette might actually prevent a significant amount of death and illness. Could society pass up that opportunity out of anger at the tobacco companies, or out of suspicion? Or perhaps it would be a good idea to prevent the thing from getting to the market because, if smoking began to seem safe, wouldn't that prevent people from quitting, and maybe even entice some back to smoke who have already gone through the anguish of shedding the habit?

For the company, at the end, it was a very risky, but worthwhile gamble. If it failed, the company had lost perhaps $500 million to $1 billion over a decade or more. Not huge dollars in tobacco industry terms. If it succeeded, the company that had come up with the successful technology that delivered good taste, addiction, and some safety, could take over the world of cigarettes.

And, with the evidence of their perfidy gradually coming to the surface, sooner or later they might be forced by the government or plaintiffs' successes to make a safer cigarette anyway.

So it was that RJR decided to make the bold move that the other four companies with designs for safer cigarettes had decided to forgo. The secret project was announced, and I wrote the story of the new cigarette, after anti-smoking groups in Buffalo had heard of one of the focus groups in which the cigarette was being tested. They even managed to steal one and smuggle it out of the secret sessions, into the hands of Drs. K. Michael Cummings and John Pauly of the Roswell Park Cancer Center. They took the smuggled samples apart and realized it was something significant. After thinking about it, they were strongly ambivalent about the cigarette, but said finally that it might be worth a try on the market, provided the government has some control of it and can get extensive testing done as it is marketed.

What the company is most proud of in the cigarette is its new technology. To make a cigarette is relatively simple; to make this artificial one which looks and tastes like it, while not delivering huge quantities of toxic substances and without eliminating the substantial amounts of nicotine is quite a feat.

The cigarette looks like a standard, white, filtered cigarette. But it includes on the lit end a small piece of charcoal just inside the tip. When you light the cigarette, instead of lighting tobacco and paper, the flame lights this bit of charcoal, not the tobacco behind it. In fact, there is a fiberglass insulator to ensure that the charcoal doesn't set the tobacco on fire. The little piece of charcoal ignites and remains hot while the cigarette is smoked but does not burn down, rather like a barbecue briquette.

The idea is to heat the air coming in the end of the cigarette, and pass that hot air over the tobacco, reconstituted sheet, and puffed tobacco inside the cigarette rod. The steam moves over the tobacco and draws out its flavor and nicotine, somewhat like the way water passes through coffee grounds to make coffee. This sounds simple enough, except that tobacco won't normally yield up its flavors, and certainly not its nicotine, just to passing hot air. What makes it possible is that the "tobacco" in the rod has been loaded with glycerine — about 50 percent by weight. Glycerine vaporizes at temperatures below those that burn tobacco, and when it warms up and leaves the tobacco as a vapor, it carries with it nicotine and tar flavors. There are a thousand small tricks in the manufacture to counter problems that smokers have had with the product. For example, to get the nicotine freed, it is necessary to treat the tobacco ahead of time to ensure that enough will come off into the vapor stream. Also, when the cigarette is lit, if there is only carbon up front, the first drag tastes too much like licking a briquette from the grill. So the company technicians incorporated some tobacco into the tip, just enough to dampen the taste created by the raw charcoal.

The feature first noticed by smokers encountering the cigarette is that it produces very little smoke. There is no noticeable smoke from the lit end, and from the smoker's mouth only a quickly-dissipating steam is seen. The faint smell is also unlike a cigarette. Rather, it smells like woody weeds, or stems, burning. It is a little harder to light and to draw on than standard cigarettes, but the taste is well within the range of usual smokes. It is odd for smokers to deal with a cigarette that has no ash, and does not burn down, so their hand motions are at first disturbingly out-of-sync.

All along, the company had a fear of the FDA, expressed by the executives working with the new cigarette. At the top of the company, Griscom said, was the question of whether to go to the FDA and talk about the product before putting it on the market, or not. The lawyers, of course, were opposed. No concessions, no quarter given or asked.

But at the same time, the Reynolds ads which showed police surrounding a smoker, and saying "Come out with your cigarette over your head," were not just amusing expressions. They pressed the fear of Big Brother, and this neatly fit with the new cigarette. If the FDA were to seize the new cigarette, the images would already have been planted. They had imagined a political confrontation, angry smokers in the streets demanding safer cigarettes, if the FDA did not go along.

There are ironies here. The tobacco people were dishonest in order to try to escape their situation and secretly make a safer cigarette, so that things would be okay in the end. But they soon found they were caught in a web of deception, and found it necessary to carry it on year after year, expending all the trust the society had to offer, to the point that now, when they actually would like to put a safer cigarette out, no one will trust them to do it.

Personally, the tobacco executives are surprised by this. They find it hard to comprehend that people would be so angry and suspicious that they would not even want to hear about the possibility of fewer lung cancers. It is proof, to them, that the "anti" people are not only Puritanical, but cruel, and really have no interest in health, but only in making the companies pay for their sins.

Their arguments about why they do what they do begin with an argument of principle, an argument about personal freedom, if you are willing to indulge them this far. Smoking may be risky, they say, but people have the right to choose their own risks and pleasures. They also feel they are on the side of society's non-conformists and rebels against the all-gray world of the moralists.

In a sense, they are right. If society had made its peace with tobacco, and the companies were open and honest about their intentions and practices, their position would make perfect sense. They would, as compassionate people, have to offer smokers who wanted to quit some help. They would have to offer safer cigarettes of various kinds.

But there is the problem that they have not reached this stage, they still lie about what they do. They rationalize this by saying to themselves that they are forced to it by the extreme attitudes of their opponents. They believe that their opponents want to remove tobacco from society entirely, and will try to do so by force if necessary. They believe in a widespread conspiracy against them. They are forced, they say, to "be careful" about how they say things, and sometimes even to put things in a way which is probably misleading. But everyone knows what the situation is, anyway, they say. It's not as if anyone were actually deceived by the company comments on addiction or the waffling on the hazards of smoke. We only have to speak that way because of what we'll be forced to do in court if we are too open in front of the enemy.

This is the key to the psychology within the companies: they are closed societies. They are isolated and under siege. What makes sense inside the bunker may appear to those of us on the outside as appalling, irrational and rather plainly evil. Within their world, they have a job to do. It is challenging and interesting, and they feel as if they are on the side of the underdogs.

For them, within a day's work, the underlying morals generally do not come up. In his work *The Nazi Doctors*, Robert Jay Lifton attempts to explain in sensible terms how it is possible for ordinary humans to commit monstrous crimes, because, whatever else we would like to deny, we cannot deny that the Nazis were ordinary people with daily routines who had for their work an unspeakable crime. He writes that comfort within the organization is important: "An important part of bureaucratic function is its sealing off of perpetrators from outside influences, so that intrabureaucratic concerns become the entire universe of discourse. What can result has been termed 'group think,' a process by which bureaucracies can make decisions that are disastrous for all concerned and, when viewed retrospectively, wildly inappropriate and irrational . . . there is a powerful impulse, both from without and within, to create absolute barriers of thought and feeling, between itself and the outside world. Only then can the strange assumptions of virtue within the group be maintained."

Within the group, there is a kind of grumbling about the deceit necessary to keep things going — a variant of what we see when Addison Yeaman or Claude Teague suggests breaking out — but when they come to the final question, "How can we be doing this?" there is an answer: Well, people are going to smoke, and there is no reason why they shouldn't choose it if they want to. What's better? Giving people their small risky pleasures, or prohibition and a civil war over morals?

The guards and doctors in the Nazi death camps had similar rituals in which they would talk to one another, and ask how could they be doing what they were doing. They had an answer as well. Whenever a new doctor would arrive at Auschwitz, Lifton writes, "the process was repeated as the newcomer's questions were answered by his more experienced drinking companions. He would ask, 'How can these things be done here?' Then there was something like a general answer . . . which clarified everything. 'What is better for [the prisoner] — whether he croaks in shit or goes to heaven in a cloud of gas?' And that settled the whole matter for the initiates."

As I spent little patches of time with tobacco people in Winston-Salem, in Chattanooga, in Richmond, and in visits with executives elsewhere, I felt myself curious about the accommodations the tobacco people had reached with themselves. I could understand the arguments about personal freedom and maniacal Puritanism. I too believe that smoking is ineradicable, and have even enjoyed it. I shared much of their belief in this way. So I listened for their arguments to themselves, and for the moments they wanted to explain themselves to me.

Lifton writes that the organization helps individuals live with themselves, it aids the distancing and numbing that each individual must do internally to remain in the group. It helps make the consequences of their acts unreal, which they must be. Along with it comes the "de-amplification of language — with its attendant numbing, denial and derealization. . . ."

In tobacco, the distancing euphemisms are crucial, not so much to defend themselves against outside, but to comfort themselves against the harsh effect of plain language descriptions of what they are doing. Things that cause disease become things that are "biologically active." Nicotine becomes "satisfaction." The rank bitterness that indicates how much nicotine a smoker is getting becomes "its impact." Addiction is just "a habit." Toxic chemicals are merely "controversial compounds." Children are "the youth market."

These make it easier. But the center of their accommodation was their willingness to put down the deceits of the past and the excesses of the current lawyers as being something like the activity of a radical fringe, much as I might want to deny that Jenny Jones or the *National Enquirer* are part of the journalism in which I live. I am satisfied if I can keep my own work honest. So in the companies most are all right with themselves if they can believe that, whatever nonsense was done before, now everyone knows how things work, and all is above board.

One instance of this even occurred in the midst of one of the Congressional hearings. Henry Waxman asked Tommy Sandefur about the "deadwood" memo and the heap of damning biological data that had been hidden. Sandefur said he would have made it all public.

I think he may *believe* that he might have made those things public in the old days. Of course, he had been a top executive in the company for a dozen years already in 1994, and had had ample opportunity to make those and other things public. He was still working day to day with the writer of the deadwood memo, J. Kendrick Wells. But I think that he was saying it more to himself than to Congress: No, we're not carrying on the same kind of abuses as in the past. Everyone knows the facts now. We're just carrying on with a legitimate industry here.

The way the executives speak makes it clear that they are living with what Dr. Lifton calls "middle knowledge." They know and don't know. If they were put in a position where they could comfortably answer questions with full frankness, they would display a complete knowledge of the factual details of what they are doing. They are also fully capable of making moral judgments in all other areas of their lives, and capable of teaching their children not to participate in dishonest activities that will hurt other people. But between the two is a short circuit: when the possibility of linking them up arrives, their thoughts are shunted off into a mental eddy, a circular line of thought about freedom and choice, from which the thought never returns to the question. We have a live example or two of people who have been inside, and have come out with their brains unscrambled, and this is what they tell us. They knew but didn't know. They acted; they got caught up in the enterprise. It took personal trauma to bring these people out, to get them to deal with the way they looked to others outside the business. For Victor Crawford, it was throat cancer. For Jeff Wigand it was being fired late in life. Soon, I expect, there will be others.

After two years of working with tobacco and tobacco company people I have heard all the arguments about smoking, and I think it helps get to the heart of the matter by listening to what the company people say. The argument begins with the point that smoking is simply a pleasurable vice, like drinking scotch, and that people ought to be free to choose to use cigarettes. On the matter of disease, they argue that everyone in society is quite aware of the hazards of smoking, and so it is not as if anyone is being caught unaware. Smoking is a choice that people make, just as they choose other risky behavior for pleasure. I am a scuba diver; I accept whatever risks come with it. As for addiction, people are aware that smoking is habit-forming, and still choose to take the risk that they will get the habit. They also say that if people don't like smoking they can quit; 40 million people have quit.

These are the arguments they use both in public and in private, and as far as they go, they are true.

But we are not living in the tobacco world. We can see what the problem is with their argument. They say that people are aware of the hazards and habit-forming properties of smoking. By making this argument they show that they are aware that it would be wrong to push cigarettes if people were *unaware* of the risks. They acknowledge by this statement that smokers must be told. But who tells them? Not the tobacco companies; in fact they work very hard to prevent people from believing in the hazards and the addiction.

So, until they work to inform people themselves, they may not accept credit for the fact that smokers do know something about the hazards. (A second point is that, whether they take credit or not, the point that smokers are aware of the problems of smoking may not be true. For example, the argument that 40 million people have quit suggests that it is relatively easy to do. But if they were to add the other, crucial, fact to the equation — that the rate of quitting among heroin addicts is greater than the rate of quitting among smokers — the statement comes into focus. Yes, people can quit. But it is not as easy to quit smoking as it is to quit heroin or cocaine. Let's get "easy" and "hard" straight before we argue that people understand the hazards of smoking.) More important, the companies must themselves tell smokers what the risks are, or they have no right to sell the product. This is not a radical point; business in all civilized nations is conducted with this understanding. Deception, or silence in the face of hazards, is not permitted. It is not okay to say someone else has informed the public, so you as the manufacturer need not do it.

This is the center of the issue. Allowing companies to behave by a standard different from all other businesses, all of them businesses which create less hazard for their customers, is not only wrong, but corrupting. It discourages the honest. For this reason alone, it should be required that the companies come clean. The reason they don't, of course, is a practical one. They don't want to be blown all over the landscape by the legal actions of angry smokers when they do admit what they have been doing. The fear is understandable, and perhaps there is some way to accommodate both angry smokers and belligerent companies.

But whether there is or not, the companies must own up to their behavior and accept their not very great burden to tell people what smoking is about.

In fact I believe that this single point, that the companies can make use of the public awareness as a defense, is the most important point in the current history of tobacco.

It is what permits the companies to go on day to day, sliding past juries and Congressional committees. It allows editors to say that tobacco stories are boring, and to kill the most aggressive tobacco stories. Because people have learned of the hazards, despite the best efforts of the companies, the companies are now able to say, "Well, after all, people know perfectly well what the risk is," and slip out of the noose. They get credit, and they take credit, for what they have worked against.

The public relations victory for tobacco companies in the beginning had been near total. Deceit and greed have often led to social catastrophes, though not often on the scale that cigarettes did. We should remember, though, that the companies did not CAUSE smoking. It existed; they exploited it by pressing its popularity, and worse, defending it when they knew it could be fatal.

Rick Pollay, marketing professor at the University of British Columbia in Vancouver, in writing about the figure of John Hill and his comrade Edward L. Bernays, raises the crucial question about all this. Bernays said, "The engineering of consent is the very essence of the democratic process, the freedom to persuade and suggest. . . ." But what of a program that gets outsized funding and is based on deceit? Is it not possible to police advertising in order to screen out the untruthful ads?

In a society dependent on open debate, how do we reasonably prevent the engines of deceit from carrying out their work? At what point do we intervene? It is a significant challenge to democracy when heavily monied interests interfere with the natural competition of ideas. It is the tangle of two freedoms, and as referees at this wrestling match, how do we separate the two?

The most elegant solution to the problem is openness: simply forcing open the files of the companies so that we may all know what they were doing, when and why. Once informed, we may decide what to do with the companies and their products through ordinary elective politics. But for other reasons, that solution is one that is slowly becoming closed to us. Courts now routinely permit companies to keep their secrets, even when they are not related to secret formulas and vital competitive practices. Courts and Congress also permit the federal government to use a similar big cloak under which to carry out their business.

A second solution to achieve the same end, that is, to find out whether we are being lied to, would be to strengthen the natural opponents of deceit in the already-existing structure of the government. In this case, that would mean some additional powers for agencies such as the Federal Trade Commission, the Food and Drug Administration, or the Consumer Products Safety Commission.

There must be some limits, ultimately, to the freedom to deceive, and the case of tobacco makes the best case for intervention. It is highly addictive, pleasurable, and deadly.

Fundamentally, this is the social challenge of tobacco: To extract the companies from their continuing need to deceive, to make all the facts clear, to protect the public health, and still allow cigarette smoking for those who want it. The problem is not so much that a group of people from all sides might not meet and decide to do just these things; the problem is that the machinery of politics and law are vastly complex and cannot simply be ordered to produce a sensible result because we happen to know what that result is. There will be a good deal of work to try to get sense out of the machinery. There are obstructionists willing to foul it all for their own reasons, and others who are perfectly sincere but incapable of handling the whole equation that involves elements of both freedom and regulation.

But we now have advantages that were not present before: a company willing to make a safer cigarette, another company willing to settle with plaintiffs, and a government willing to take on the job of rationally regulating big tobacco. If the welter of mutual suspicions between industry and society can be lanced by a jab of honesty in some forum, then a workable social compact on tobacco may be written.

Notes

This book was the result of work beginning in the fall of 1993, and continuing to the present. I have not counted the number of interviews I have done on the topic, but it numbers in the hundreds. Most were on the record, and some were quoted in my stories in the *New York Times*. For the most part, the interviews with tobacco company executives were on a background only basis, or were off the record, because those working in the industry fear reprisals if they speak openly about their work. I have tried not to rely on those interviews and conversations in this book, and refer to them only occasionally. They may have had a strong influence on my thinking about the subject, but the evidence for what is said in this book is virtually all, in one way or another, in the public record now. I hope I have cited enough of it in the text to be convincing. Below are some of the sources for the work in each chapter. I have abbreviated the citations for several caches of papers: BW papers for Brown and Williamson; PM papers for Philip Morris; AT papers for American Tobacco; LM papers for Liggett & Myers; and RJ for R. J. Reynolds.

CHAPTER 1
CANCER AND CRISIS

U.S. Department of Health and Human Services Report to Congress: "Smoking and Health: A National Status Report" 2nd edition, 1990.

Reports of the Surgeon General, U.S. Public Health Service.
"Preventing Tobacco Use Among Young People," 1994.
"The Health Consequences of Smoking: Nicotine Addiction," 1988.

"The Health Benefits of Smoking Cessation," 1990.

"Reducing the Health Consequences of Smoking: 25 Years of Progress," 1989.

"Smoking and Health," 1979.

"Smoking and Health: Report of the Advisory Committee to the Surgeon General of the Public Health Service," 1964.

University of British Columbia, History of Advertising Archives, Richard Pollay, Curator. Materials on advertising, including print and television programs.

Hammond, E.C., "Smoking in Relation to the Death Rates of One Million Men and Women," in Haenzel, W., Ed., *Epidemiological Approaches to the Study of Cancer and Other Diseases*, National Cancer Institute Monograph 19, 1966.

Hammond, E.C. and Horn, D., "Smoking and Death Rates — report on 44 months of follow-up on 187,783 men," *Journal of the American Medical Association*, 166(10): 1159-1172, March 8, 1958.

Royal College of Physicians of London, "Smoking and Health, Report in Relation to Cancer of the Lung and Other Disease" (London, Pitman Publishing, 1962).

Doll, Richard, and Hill, A.B., "A study of the Aetiology of Carcinoma of the Lung," *British Medical Journal*, 2:1271-1286, December 12, 1952.

Doll, Richard, and Hill, A.B., "Lung Cancer and Other Causes of Death in Relation to Smoking, A Second Report on the Mortality of British Doctors," *British Medical Journal*, 2:1071-1081, Nov. 1, 1956.

Wynder, Ernst and Graham, Evarts, "Tobacco Smoking as a Possible Etiologic Factor in Bronchiogenic Carcinoma: a study of six hundred eighty-four proved cases," *Journal of the American Medical Association*, 143(4): 329-336, May 27, 1950.

Broders, A.C. "Squamous-cell epithelioma of the lip," *Journal of the American Medical Association*, 74:656-664, 1920.

Blum, Alan, Special Issue of the *New York State Journal of Medicine*, devoted to tobacco, December, 1983.

Norr, Roy, "Cancer by the Carton," *Reader's Digest*, Vol. 61, December 1952.

Cutlip, Scott M. "The Tobacco Wars: A Matter of Public Relations Ethics," *Journal of Corporate Public Relations*, 1992-1993, Vol. 3. Northwestern University.

Bowling, James C. "Sloan-Kettering Contributions," November 23rd, 1964. From Brown & Williamson papers.

Pollay, Richard W. "Propaganda, Puffing and the Public Interest:

Cigarette Publicity Tactics, Strategies and Effects." *Public Relations Review*, May 1990.

Panorama, British Broadcasting Corporation: "Pack of Lies: A Panorama Special Investigation into the Tobacco Industry." February 19, 1993.

United States House of Representatives, Subcommittee on Health and the Environment, Majority Staff Report: "The Hill and Knowlton Documents: How the Tobacco Industry Launched Its Disinformation Campaign," May 26, 1994.

Hill, John. "The Hill Papers," The John W. Hill Papers are in the Wisconsin State Historical Society in Madison, the Mass Communications History Center. Some of the key memos noted from this collection are:

"Confidential Memo to John Hill" from JJD, December 14, 1953.

"Suggested Approach and Comments Regarding Attacks on Use of Cigarettes," Hill and Knowlton, December 14, 1953.

"Background Material on the Cigarette Industry Client," Bert C. Goss, December 15, 1953.

"Preliminary Recommendations for Cigarette Manufacturers," John W. Hill, December 24, 1953.

"Moves to Counter Anti-Tobacco Blasts," Harry Haller, May 12, 1954.

"Public Relations Report and Recommendations for Tobacco Industry Research Committee," Hill and Knowlton, June 21, 1954.

"Progress Report Through July 31," Carl Thompson, August 15, 1954.

"Proposed Budget for 1955," John W. Hill, November 26, 1954.

"A Scientific Perspective on the Cigarette Controversy," produced by Hill and Knowlton for the Tobacco Industry Research Committee, April 14, 1954.

"Re: Tobacco Institute, Tobacco Industry Research Committee, and Hill and Knowlton," John V. Blalock, June 18, 1963.

"Tobacco Industry Research Committee: Organization and Policy."

Letter from Paul Hahn, President, The American Tobacco Company, to John W. Hill, February 5, 1958.

"Public Relations Report to the Tobacco Industry Research Committee," Hill and Knowlton, April 28, 1955.

CBS Television, *See It Now with Edward R. Murrow*, "Cigarettes and Lung Cancer" June 7, 1955.

Steering Committee of the Coalition on Smoking or Health (Alan Davis, et al). Letter to Congressman John Dingell, July 20, 1992.

Freedman, Alix M. and Cohen, Laurie P., "Smoke and Mirrors: How Cigarette Makers Keep Health Question 'Open' Year After Year," *The Wall Street Journal*, February 11, 1993.

CHAPTER 2
CREATING THE DISINFORMATION MACHINE

Hill, John W. "The Hill Papers," supra.

Warner, Kenneth, "Tobacco Industry Scientific Advisors: Serving Society or Selling Cigarettes?" *American Journal of Public Health*, Vol. 81, No. 7, July 1991.

Cummings, K. Michael, et al., "What Scientists Funded by the Tobacco Industry Believe About the Hazards of Smoking," *American Journal of Public Health*, Vol. 81, No. 7, July, 1991.

Brady, J. M., Memo to C.C. Little of TIRC, "TIRC Program," April 9, 1962. "Historically, it would seem . . ."

O'Shea, Simon, Memo to W.T. Hoyt of TIRC, "Planning," August 18, 1965. "The existence of the Council demonstrates that the industry is acting in good faith . . ."

Pepples, Ernest, Memo to executives of Brown and Williamson, "CTR Budget," April 4, 1978. "Originally, CTR was organized as a public relations effort . . ."

Pepples, Ernest, "Privileged" Memo to C.I. McCarty, untitled, September 29, 1978. ". . . The direct legal protection derived by Brown and Williamson . . ." by CTR.

Waite, C.L., Memo to H.R. Kornegay, "The Addiction Research Foundation," Sept. 19, 1978. "Mr. Cornell's letter referred to . . ."

Yeaman, Addison, quoted in an undated memo in the files of Lorillard chief executive Curtis Judge, "CTR is the best and cheapest insurance the tobacco industry can buy . . ."

Spears, Alexander W. Lorillard scientist, memo to C.H. Judge, chief executive, on the CTR, June 24, 1974. "Historically, the joint industry funded smoking and health research programs have not been selected against specific scientific goals . . ."

Panzer, Fred, of the Tobacco Institute, to Horace Kornegay of the CTR. Memo "The Roper Proposal," May 1, 1972. ". . . Creating doubt about the health charge without actually denying it."

Spach, Jo F. RJR Manager of public information for public relations dept. Letter to the principal of Willow Ridge School, Jan. 11, 1990.

Panorama, British Broadcasting Corporation: "Pack of Lies: A Panorama Special Investigation into the Tobacco Industry." February 19, 1993.

Green, Sidney James. His papers from years of work in the British American Tobacco Company were obtained from the Tobacco Products Liability Project. These quotes are from one article entitled "Smoking, Associated Diseases, and Causality," which is undated. An apparently later version of the paper called "Cigarette Smoking and Causal Relationships" is dated 27 October 1976.

Sarokin, H. Lee, United State District Court for the District of New Jersey, Antonio Cipollone *v.* Liggett Group *et al*, opinion April 21, 1988, and opinion February 6, 1992. "Nothing but a hoax created for public relations purposes . . .".

Pollay, Richard W. "Propaganda, Puffing and the Public Interest: Cigarette Publicity Tactics, Strategies and Effects," *Public Relations Review*, May 1990.

Pollay, Richard W., "Sifting the Ashes: An Intellectual History of Cigarette Advertising Research," Working Paper, History of Advertising Archives, University of British Columbia, April 1994.

CHAPTER 3

THE BURDEN OF KNOWLEDGE

Philip Morris papers. An array of papers, about 2,000 pages, from Philip Morris were given to the *New York Times*, and later entered into the Congressional Record by Rep. Henry Waxman. These and a few other Philip Morris memos made public in the Cipollone case, I refer to them as the PM papers.

PM papers. Mace, C.V., Memo to R. N. DuPuis, untitled, July 24, 1958. "Evidence is building up that heavy cigarette smoking . . ."

Darkis, F.R., Vice-president for research at Liggett and Myers, quoted in minutes of a meeting with Arthur D. Little Inc. staff. "Liggett and Myers Conference" on March 29, 1954. "If Chesterfield turns out to be negative . . ."

Little, Arthur D., Inc., "Confidential Limited" Memo, "L&M — a perspective review," March 15, 1961. "There are biologically active materials present in cigarette tobacco. They are a) cancer causing . . ."

PM papers. DuPuis, Robert N. "Challenges in Tobacco Research," October, 1955. ". . . mouse work may be indicative . . ."

PM papers. Wakeham, Helmut, "Tobacco and Health — R&D Approach," November 16, 1961. " ... TIME MONEY AND UN-FALTERING DETERMINATION."

Brown and Williamson papers. (A full set of these may be obtained from the University of California at San Francisco, or seen on the Internet at http://www.library.ucsf.edu/tobacco.) "Smoking and Health Policy," Minutes of Southampton Research Conference, 1962. Opening remarks by Sir Charles Ellis.

BW papers. "RD 14, Smoke Group Program" memo, March 1, 1957. ". . . zephyr . . ."

BW papers. Yeaman, Addison, memo, "Implications of Batelle Hippo I & II and the Griffith Filter, July 17, 1963.

LM papers. Liggett & Myers report prepared for conference on Nov. 22 and 23, 1955, in which duplication of Dr. Ernst Wynder's results is described and tumors were produced.

Gray, Patricia Bellew, "Smoking Foes Cite New Evidence Emerging in Tobacco-Liability Suit," *The Wall Street Journal*, April 4, 1988.

LM papers. Liggett & Myers Tobacco Company Research Department and Arthur D. Little Inc., "Current Status of Studies on Smoking and Health," paper presented to the U.S Surgeon General, Apr. 1, 1963.

LM papers. Liggett & Myers. Drafts and internal papers prior to delivery of "Current Status of Studies . . ." Including "Suggestions for ADL Presentations to L&M or to the Surgeon General's Committee," January 16, 1963; "Comparison of Smoking and Fatal Motor Accidents as a Public Hazard," March 14, 1963; "Alternative Theories of Carcinogenesis," April 24, 1963; and the undated "Draft of an Outline for a Background Paper on the Smoking Problem To Be Used in Connection with a Presentation of Arguments before the Surgeon General's Committee."

BW papers. The Janus Series of experiments to determine whether cigarette smoke causes cancer. The tests went on between the early 1960s and 1978, and concluded not only that smoke caused tumors in all experiments, but that the rate of tumors was directly related to the amount of smoke condensate applied. Summaries of the Janus series are written up in at least five documents, numbered 1138.01 to 1138.05 in the UCSF numbering system.

BW papers. Wells, J. Kendrick, Memo to file, "Re: Document Retention," January 17, 1985. ". . . deadwood . . ."

Zahn, Leonard, memo on how he prevented Dr. Frederic Homberger from giving his results to reporters. "Confidential Memorandum," April 22, 1974.

PM papers. "Competitive Analysis," memorandum on the design and selling of a "safer" cigarette, code-named Table, by Philip Morris.

CHAPTER 4
NICOTINE FIT

United States House of Representatives, Subcommittee on Health and the Environment, Majority Staff Report: "Evidence of Nicotine Manipulation by the American Tobacco Company," Dec. 20, 1994.

American Tobacco Company papers, "A Summary of Biologic Research on Tobacco," Sixth Printing, April, 1962. Additional supplements to April, 1971. In addition, American Tobacco supplied the House Subcommittee on Health and the Environment with some internal documents.

AT papers. Johnston, Donald, American Tobacco Company letter to Rep. Henry Waxman, Oct. 14, 1994.

AT papers. Irby, R. M., memo on "our current knowledge regarding increasing the nicotine content of reconstituted tobacco." June 5, 1974.

AT papers. "Tobacco Blends for Filter Cigarettes: Effect of Increasing the Concentration of Burley Tobacco in a Blend," June 21, 1963. "The selection of types and grades of tobacco can control the amount of nicotine."

AT papers. Memo on "Compound W," May 14, 1969.

AT papers. Memos, "The Effect of the Addition of 1% Nicotine on the quality of RC tobacco," Oct. 8, 1963, and "Evaluation of Nicotine-fortified RC-A Tobacco," May 2, 1968.

BW papers. Griffith, R.B. "Report to Executive Committee," July, 1965. ". . . find ways of obtaining maximum nicotine for minimum tar . . ."

PM papers. Ryan, F.J., "Bird-I, A study of the quit-smoking campaign of Greenfield, Iowa, in conjunction with the movie, *Cold Turkey*," March 1961.

BW papers. "Project Wheat," 1974. Wood, D.J. and Wilkes, E.B., "Project Wheat, Part I — Cluster Profiles of UK male smokers and Their General Smoking Habits," 1975, and "Project Wheat, Part II — UK Male Smokers: Their Reactions to Cigarettes of Different Nicotine Delivery as Influenced by Inner Need," 1976.

PM papers. Dunn, William J. Paper prepared for presentation at meeting in St. Maarten, "Motives and Incentives in Cigarette Smoking," 1971.

Waxman, Henry, Statement on the floor of the House of Representatives, July 21, 1995.

Humphrey, Hubert III, Working Group of State Attorneys General, "No Sale: Youth, Tobacco and Responsible Retailing," December, 1994.

Freedman, Alix M. "Tobacco Firm Shows How Ammonia Spurs Delivery of Nicotine," *Wall Street Journal*, October 18, 1995, p.1.

Henningfield, Jack E. et al., "Pharmacological Determinants of Cigarette Smoking," In Clarke, P.B.S., et al., *Effects of Nicotine on Biological Systems* (Basel: Birkhauser Verlag, 1995).

Henningfield, Jack E., Statement before the House Subcommittee on Health and the Environment, November 29, 1994.

Henningfield, Jack E., "Cigarettes and Addiction," *British Medical Journal*, vol. 310, p. 1082, April 29, 1995.

BW papers. McGraw, Mick, memo to Tommy Sandefur, "Nicotine Delivery Systems," April 24, 1992.

CHAPTER 5
DEATH OF THE CIGARETTE

Browne, Colin L., *The Design of Cigarettes*, Third Edition, (North Carolina: Hoechst Celanese, 1990).

Grise, Verner, "The Changing Tobacco User's Dollar," in U.S. Department of Agriculture's *Tobacco Situation and Outlook, 1992*, an update of "The Tobacco User's Dollar — Trends and Prospects," TS-199, June 1987 and "The Changing Cigarette Dollar," Agricultural Outlook, AO-147, November 1988.

Clauson, Annette and Grise, Verner, *Flue-Cured Tobacco Farming: Two Decades of Change*, Washington DC, U.S. Department of Agriculture, AER-692, August 1994.

U.S. Department of Health and Human Services, Public Health Service, *The Changing Cigarette, A Report of the Surgeon General*, 1981.

Creek, Laverne, et al., *U.S. Tobacco Statistics, 1935-1992*, U.S. Department of Agriculture, SB-869, April, 1994.

Cohen, Marc and Launder, Gavin, *The Tobacco Handbook*, financial analysis of the tobacco companies, April, 1994. Goldman Sachs International.

CHAPTER 6
FOR STARTERS

Pollay, Richard W. "Promises, Promises: Self-regulation of US Cigarette Broadcast Advertising in the 1960s," *Tobacco Control*, summer 1994.

Lewis, Karen, "Addicting the Young: Tobacco Pushers and Kids," *Multinational Monitor*, Jan.-Feb. 1992.

Johnson, F. Ross, quoted in *Wall Street Journal*, October 6, 1994, p.1.

Pollay, Richard W. and Lavack, Anne M., "The Targeting of Youth by Cigarette Marketers: Archival Evidence on Trial," *Advances in Consumer Research*, vol. 20, 1993.

Pollay, Richard W. "Targeting Tactics in Selling Smoke: Youthful Aspects of 20th Century Cigarette Advertising," *Journal of Marketing Theory and Practice*, Special Issue, Vol. 3, No. 1, Winter, 1995.

Food and Drug Administration, "Regulations Restricting the Sale and Distribution of Cigarettes and Smokeless Tobacco Products to Protect Children and Adolescents," 1995.

Bart, Peter, "Cigarette Makers Adopted an Industry Code for Ads," *New York Times*, Apr. 28, 1964, p.1.

Tobacco Institute. "Tobacco Industry Voluntary Code," 1964 and revised periodically afterward, finally to "Cigarette Advertising and Promotion Code," December, 1990.

RJ papers. Teague, Claude E. Jr., "Research Planning Memorandum on Some Thoughts About New Brands of Cigarettes for the Youth Market," February 2, 1973.

RJ papers. Teague, Claude E. Jr., "Research Planning Memorandum on the Nature of the Tobacco Business and the Crucial Role of Nicotine Therein," April 14, 1972.

RJ Papers. McMahon, J.P., Division manager in RJR Sales, Sarasota, Florida, Memo to Sales Reps, "Young Adult Market," January 10, 1990.

RJ Papers. Warlick, R.G., Division manager in RJR Sales, Moore, Oklahoma, Memo to sales reps, "Young Adult Market SIS Account Grouping," April 5, 1990.

RJ Papers. Research Department, "Planning Assumptions and Forecast for the Period 1977-1986+" May 17, 1976.

RJ papers. Bender, L. L., memo on how to describe the targeting of Dakota cigarette, "Dakota Target Redefinition," January 25, 1990.

RJ papers. Faggert, T.L. "Advertising Research Report, 1990 Perception Tracking Study, Camel: 18-24 males: Emphasis vs. Opportunity Markets," July 19, 1990.

RJ papers. Advertising Department, "Consumer Research Proposal Addendum," discussing the work with focus groups age 18-24. November 11, 1991.

RJ papers. Advertising Department, "Camel Target Smoker Groups Summary Description," September, 1991.

RJ papers. Marketing Department, "Camel 1990 Business Plan," October 9, 1989.

RJ papers. Unsigned, undated memo stamped "RJR CONFIDENTIAL," and titled "Analysis of the Virile Segment," discussing sales among FUBYAS, or the First Usual Brand of Young Adult Smokers.

United States Tobacco Company, series of memos on Project Lotus obtained from court cases, in which the company plans a range of products, from high to low nicotine, from strong to sweet flavor, and specifically targets children under 18 years old. "We must sell the use of tobacco in the mouth, and appeal to young people." Documents from 1968 to 1972.

Evans, Nicola, et al., "Influence of Tobacco Marketing and Exposure to Smokers on Adolescent Susceptibility to Smoking," *Journal of the National Cancer Institute*, vol. 87, No. 20, October 18, 1995.

Imperial Tobacco Limited, "Projects Stereo/Phoenix Final Report," February, 1985.

Imperial Tobacco Limited, report from Kwechansky Marketing Research, Inc. "Project 16," October 18, 1977.

Imperial Tobacco Limited, report from Kwechansky Marketing Research, Inc., "Project Plus/Minus," May 7, 1982.

Imperial Tobacco Limited, report from Spitzer, Mills & Bates, "Media Planning, Fiscal 78," 1978.

Imperial Tobacco Limited, report from Spitzer, Mills & Bates, "Operation Memo re: Players Light Media Brief, 1977–78," March 10, 1977.

Imperial Tobacco Limited, report from Spitzer, Mills & Bates, "The Players Family: A Working Paper," March 25, 1977.

Imperial Tobacco Limited, report from Spitzer, Mills & Bates, "Advertising Strategy Paper Regarding Players Light," October 20, 1977.

Imperial Tobacco Limited, report from Spitzer, Mills & Bates, "Players Light Creative Development," January 20, 1978.

Imperial Tobacco Limited, "Fiscal 81 National Media Plans," 1979.

Imperial Tobacco Limited, report from The Creative Research Group, "Project Viking, volume II: An Attitudinal Model of Smoking," Dec. 3, 1986.

U.S. Department of Health and Human Services, Public Health Service, Centers for Disease Control, "Changes in Cigarette Smoking Brand Preferences of Adolescent Smokers — U.S., 1989-93," Morbidity and Mortality Weekly Report, Vol. 43, No. 32, August 19, 1994.

Cohen, Joel B. "Effects of Cigarette Advertising on Consumer Behavior," a report to the Canadian Attorney General, 1991.

Philip Morris USA, "Philip Morris Announces Initiative Against Youth Smoking," press packet announcing the program called "Action Against Access," June 27, 1995.

DiFranza, J.R., et al, "Who Profits From Tobacco Sales to Children?" *Journal of the American Medical Association*, vol 263, No. 20, 1990.

DiFranza, J. R. et al, "RJ Reynolds-Nabisco's Cartoon Camel Promotes Camel Cigarettes to Children," *Journal of the American Medical Association*, 266: 3149-3153, 1991.

Blum, Alan, "Role of the Health Professional in Ending the Tobacco Pandemic: Clinic, Classroom, Community," *Journal of the National Cancer Institute*, monograph No. 12, 1992.

Pierce, John P., et al, "Does Tobacco Advertising Target Young People to Start Smoking?" *Journal of the American Medical Association*, vol 266, No. 22, 1991.

Pierce, John P. et al, "Trends in Cigarette Smoking in the United States, Projections to the Year 2000," *Journal of the American Medical Association*, vol. 261, No. 1, 1989.

Pierce, John P. et al, " Tobacco Use in California, An evaluation of the Tobacco Control Program 1989-1993." UCSD, 1994.

Pierce, John P. et al, "Smoking Initiation by Adolescent Girls, 1944 through 1988," *Journal of the American Medical Association*, vol. 271, No. 8, 1994.

Pierce, John P. et al, "Tobacco use in California, 1992: A Focus on Preventing Uptake in Adolescents," Sacramento, Calif., California Department of Health Services, 1993.

Pierce, John and Gilpin, Elizabeth, "A Historical Analysis of Tobacco Marketing and the Uptake of Smoking by Youth in the United States, 1890-1977," *Health Psychology*, in press, 1995.

U.S. Department of Health and Human Services, *Preventing Tobacco Use Among Young People: A Report of the Surgeon General.* Atlanta, Georgia, Centers for Disease Control, Office on Smoking and Health, 1994.

Burnett, Leo, *Communications of an Advertising Man*, (Chicago: Leo Burnett Co., 1961), quoted from Pollay, supra.

Fischer, P.M. et al, "Brand Logo Recognition by Children Aged 3 to 6 Years, Mickey Mouse v. Joe Camel," *Journal of the American Medical Association*, vol. 266, No. 22, 1991.

Davis, Ronald M. "The effects of Tobacco Advertising: Brand Loyalty, Brand Switching, or Market Expansion?" Guest editorial, *American Journal of Preventive Medicine*, vol. 12, no. 1, March, 1996.

Siegal, Michael et al, "The Extent of Cigarette Brand and Company Switching: Results from the Adult Use-of-Tobacco Survey," *American Journal of Preventive Medicine*, vol. 12, no. 1, March, 1996.

California Department of Health Services, "Operation Storefront," a project in which 700 volunteers surveyed 5,773 retailers in 52 California counties to see what tobacco advertising was placed in stores. August 2, 1995.

Wolfson, Andrew, "Tobacco Industry Actions Belie Its Statements," *Louisville Courier-Journal*, November 13, 1994.

Wolfson, Andrew, "Law Fails to Keep Teens from Buying Cigarettes," *Louisville Courier-Journal*, November 13, 1994.

CHAPTER 7

THE TOBACCO WARS

Environmental Protection Agency, Office of Radiation and Indoor Air, "The Costs and Benefits of Smoking Restrictions, an Assessment of the Smoke Free Environment Act of 1993," April, 1994.

Environmental Protection Agency, "Respiratory Health Effects of Passive Smoking: Lung Cancer and Other Disorders," EPA -600-6-90-006F, Washington, DC December, 1992.

Environmental Protection Agency, "Second Hand Smoke: What You Can Do about Second Hand Smoke as Parents, Decision Makers, and Building Occupants," 402-f-93-004, Washington DC, July, 1993.

Bero, Lisa, and Glantz, Stanton, "Tobacco Industry Response to a Risk Assessment of Environmental Tobacco Smoke," *Tobacco Control*, vol. 2: 103-113,1993.

Bero, Lisa, et al, "Publication Bias and Public Health Policy on Environmental Tobacco Smoke," conference proceedings, Second International Conference on Peer Review in Biomedical Publication, 1993.

Bero, Lisa, et al, "Sponsored Symposia on Environmental Tobacco Smoke," *Journal of the American Medical Association*, vol. 271, No. 8, Feb. 23, 1994.

U.S. House of Representatives, Majority Staff of the Health and Environment Subcommittee, "The Survey of the Science Advisory Board of the Center for Indoor Air Research," July 22, 1994.

U.S. House of Representatives, Majority Staff of the Health and Environment Subcommittee, "ETS Facts, the Tobacco Industry's Misinformation Campaign," July 22, 1994.

U.S. House of Representatives, Majority Staff of the Health and Environment Subcommittee, "ETS Facts, Background Information," July 12, 1994, Jan. 31, 1994, Feb 10, 1994, Mar. 3, 1994, Aug. 2, 1994.

Fontham, Elizabeth, et al., "Environmental Tobacco Smoke and Lung Cancer in Non-smoking Women," *Journal of the American Medical Association*, vol. 271, No. 22, June 8, 1994.

Sullum, Jacob, "Passive Reporting on Passive Smoke," *Forbes* Mediacritic, and "Smoke and Mirrors," *Reason* magazine, February, 1991.

Spitzer, Walter O., et al, "Links between Passive Smoking and Disease: A Best-evidence Synthesis," *Clinical and Investigative Medicine*, vol. 13, No. 1, 1990.

Radio TV Reports, transcript of ABC network's *Day One* program, Feb. 28, 1994.

Weinberg, Steve, "Smoking Guns: ABC, Philip Morris, and the Infamous Apology," *Columbia Journalism Review*, November/December, 1995.

Weinberg, Steve, "Inside Smoke Screen, Walt Bogdanich's Affidavit for His Defense Against the Tobacco Industry Serves as a Primer for Journalists," *The Investigative Reporters and Editors Journal*, January–February, 1996.

Markow, Judge Theodore J., Circuit Court of the City of Richmond, ruling in Philip Morris *v.* ABC, December 30, 1994.

Kessler, David A. "Statement on Nicotine-Containing Cigarettes," delivered before the U.S. House of Representatives Subcommittee on Health and the Environment, March 25, 1994.

R.J. Reynolds Tobacco Company, "Statement before the U.S. House of Representatives Committee on Energy and Commerce, Subcommittee on Health and the Environment, Concerning Whether the Food and Drug Administration Has Jurisdiction to Regulate and Therefore Ban Cigarettes," April 14, 1994.

R.J. Reynolds Tobacco Company, "Statement before the U.S. House of Representatives Committee on Energy and Commerce, Subcommittee on Health and the Environment, Concerning the Jurisdiction of the Food and Drug Administration Over the Manufacture of Cigarettes," March 25, 1994.

Spears, Alexander, and Jones, S.T. of the Lorillard Tobacco Company, "Analysis of Chemical and Physical Criteria for Tobacco Leaf of Modern Day Cigarettes," paper presented at the 35th Tobacco Chemists Research Conference, 1981.

Spears, Alexander, statement before the U.S. House of Representatives Committee on Energy and Commerce, Subcommittee on Health and the Environment, March 25, 1994.

Spears, Alexander, statement before the U.S. House of Representatives Committee on Energy and Commerce, Subcommittee on Health and the Environment, April 14, 1994.

Kozlowski, Lynn T., Pennsylvania State University, letter to Rep. Henry A. Waxman, July 28, 1995.

Robertson, Gray, president of Healthy Buildings International, statement before the U.S. House of Representatives Committee on Energy and Commerce, Subcommittee on Health and the Environment, March 17, 1994.

Neuberger, Maurine, *Smokescreen*, book cite on pharmacopoeia

Applied Litigation Research Co., research done for ABC, giving "mock trial data" from two focus groups in Richmond, December 14, 1994.

American Broadcasting Company, "Defendants' Memorandum in Support of Summary Judgment," July 10, 1995, in Philip Morris *v.* ABC, Richmond, Virginia.

CHAPTER 8
IN CAMERA

Most of the material for this chapter comes directly from my experience in covering the tobacco hearings of 1994.

CHAPTER 9
DR. WILLIAMS

This chapter is the result of numerous interviews with Merrell Williams during 1994 and 1995, in addition to the reading of the B&W papers which he brought out of the company.

CHAPTER 10
UNDER OATH

The sources of information on Thomas Sandefur include a survey of newspaper and magazine stories, interviews with executives from Brown and Williamson, and transcripts of Mr. Sandefur's appearances before Congress and in court.

Transcript of Wigand deposition taken from the Internet.

Wigand, Jeffrey, "Deposition of Jeffrey Wigand," as reproduced on the Internet by the *Wall Street Journal*. From a pretrial deposition on November 29, 1995 in Mississippi.

Hwang, Suein L. and Geyelin, Milo, "Brown & Williamson Has 500 Page Dossier Attacking Chief Critic," *Wall Street Journal*, February 1, 1996.

CHAPTER 11
CASH CROP

Mierzwinski, Ed, "Smoking Them Out, Campaign Contributions by the Dirty Dozen Tobacco PACs, January 1987 to July 1994," U.S. Public Interest Research Group, September, 1994.

Mierzwinski, Ed, "Smoking Them Out, Tobacco PAC Contributions 1986-1995," U.S. Public Interest Research Group, March, 1996.

Moore, Stephen, et al., "Contributing to Death, the Influence of Tobacco Money on the U.S. Congress," a report by the Public Citizen's Health Research Group, October, 1993.

Wolfe, Sidney and Douglas, Clifford, et al., "The Congressional Addiction to Tobacco: How the Tobacco Lobby Suffocates Federal Health Policy," a report by Public Citizen's Health Research Group and the Advocacy Institute, October, 1992.

Samuels, Bruce et al., "Tobacco Money, Tobacco People, Tobacco Policies, How millions of Tobacco Dollars and Tobacco People in High Places Drive White House Pro-tobacco-industry Policies," a report by the Public Citizen's Health Research Group and the Advocacy Institute, August, 1992.

Moore, Stephen, et al., "Epidemiology of Failed Tobacco Control Legislation," *Journal of the American Medical Association*, vol. 272, no. 15, October 19, 1994.

Mintz, Morton, "The Smoking Files, A Year in the Life of Philip Morris's Washington Lobbyists," *Washington Post Sunday Magazine*, December 3, 1995.

CHAPTER 12

PRESIDENTIAL SEAL

Most of the information in this chapter came from interviews with White House and FDA officials, including interviews with Dr. David Kessler, Mitch Zeller and Philip Barnett.

CHAPTER 13

IN THE BALANCE

Daynard, Richard, Tobacco Products Liability Project, Northeastern University. This project puts out books of documents obtained from tobacco companies in court, chiefly the three-volume "Document packet #7-15-92." The central set of documents are the papers from the Cippollone *v.* Liggett Group case which ended in 1988. The liability project is a resource for plaintiffs who are suing tobacco companies, and also holds conferences outlining the coming issues in litigation.

Rosenblatt, Stanley, "A Brief History of Tobacco Litigation," from Rosenblatt's complaint in the Florida case of Engle v. R.J. Reynolds, October 28, 1994.

Annas, George J. "Health Warnings, Smoking and Cancer," *New England Journal of Medicine*, vol. 327, No. 22, Nov. 26, 1992.

BW papers. Wells, J. Kendrick, "Document Retention," the "deadwood" memo, January 17, 1985.

BW papers. Wells, J. Kendrick, "BAT Science," memo suggesting care in permitting damaging scientific documents to come in from the British parent company, and listing some that should not be permitted to remain in the files. February 17, 1986.

BW papers. Wells, J. Kendrick. "Procedure for Handling BAT Scientific Documents," on how to claim privilege for damaging scientific documents, so they need not be given to plaintiffs in court. November 9, 1979.

BW papers. Wells, J. Kendrick, "Conference with BAT Legal on U.S. Products Liability Litigation," June 12, 1984.

BW papers. Wells, J. Kendrick, "Southampton Smoking and Health Material," a memo noting "Continued law department control [of scientific papers] is essential for the best argument for privilege." June 15, 1979.

Hardy, David R. confidential letter to DeBaun Bryant, General Counsel of B & W, dated August 20, 1970.

Food and Drug Administration, copies of two affidavits and one signed statement by former Philip Morris executives, entered into the public record, March, 1996. "Declaration of Ian Uydess, 29 February 1996," "Declaration of Jerome Rivers," and "The Manipulation and Control of Nicotine and Tar in the Design and Manufacture of Cigarettes: A Scientific Perspective, by William A. Farone, Ph.D."

CHAPTER 14

BEYOND SUSPICION

The source of the material for this chapter was largely personal interviews with scientists and executives at R.J. Reynolds during 1993, 1994, and 1995.

Rosenblatt, Roger, "How Do They Live with Themselves?" *New York Times Magazine*, March 20, 1994.

Gori, Gio B. and Bock, Fred G., editors, *A Safe Cigarette?* Banbury Conference report number 3, Cold Spring Harbor Laboratory, 1989.

R.J. Reynolds Tobacco Company, *Chemical and Biological Studies New Cigarette Prototypes That Heat Instead of Burn Tobacco*, Winston-Salem, North Carolina, 1988.

Bibliography

Blum, Alan. *The Cigarette Underworld: a Front-Line Report on the War Against Your Lungs*. New Jersey: Lyle Stuart, 1983.

Buckley, Christopher. *Thank You For Smoking*. New York: Random House, 1995.

Burrough, Bryan and Helyar, John. *Barbarians at the Gate*. New York: Harper Perennial, 1991.

Cairns, John. *Cancer, Science and Society*. San Francisco: W.H. Freeman, 1978.

Doron, Gideon. *The Smoking Paradox: Public Regulation in the Cigarette Industry*. Cambridge, Mass.: Abt Books, 1979.

Glantz, Stanton, et al. *The Cigarette Papers*. University of California Press, Spring 1996, in press.

Goodman, Jordan. *Tobacco in History: The Cultures of Dependence*. London: Routledge, 1993.

Gori, Gio B., and Bock, Fred G., eds. *A Safe Cigarette?* Banbury Conference report number 3, Cold Spring Harbor Laboratory, 1989.

Klein, Richard. *Cigarettes Are Sublime*. Durham, N.C.: Duke University Press, 1993.

Knight, Joseph. *Pipe and Pouch, the Smoker's Own Book of Poetry*. Freeport, N.Y.: Books for Libraries Press, first published 1894, reprinted 1970.

Johnson, Paul R. *The Economics of the Tobacco Industry*. New York: Praeger, 1984.

Krogh, David. *Smoking, the Artificial Passion*. San Francisco: W. H. Freeman, 1991.

Lifton, Robert Jay. *The Nazi Doctors*. New York: Basic Books, 1986.

Middleton, Arthur Pierce. *Tobacco Coast*. Baltimore: Johns Hopkins University Press, 1984.

Pertchuk, Michael. *Giant Killers*. New York: W. W. Norton, 1986.

Reports of the Surgeon General, U.S. Public Health Service.
"Preventing Tobacco Use Among Young People," 1994
"The Health Consequences of Smoking: Nicotine Addiction," 1988
"The Health Benefits of Smoking Cessation," 1990
"Reducing the Health Consequences of Smoking: 25 Years of Progress," 1989
"Smoking and Health," 1979
"Smoking and Health: Report of the Advisory Committee to the Surgeon General of the Public Health Service," 1964

Reynolds, Patrick and Schactman, Tom. *The Gilded Leaf: Triumph, Tragedy and Tobacco — Three Generations of the RJ Reynolds Family and Fortune*. Boston: Little, Brown, 1989.

Robert, Joseph Clarke. *Tobacco Kingdom*. Gloucester, Mass.: Peter Smith Publisher, 1965.

Svevo, Italo. *Confessions of Zeno*. New York: Vintage, 1989.

Swan, Anthony Victor, et al., eds. *Smoking Behavior from Pre-Adolescence to Young Adulthood*. Aldershot, England: Gower Publishing Company, 1991.

Tollison, Robert D. and Wagner, Richard E. *The Economics of Smoking*. Boston: Kluwer Academic Publishers, 1992.

U.S. Department of Health and Human Services Report to Congress. "Smoking and Health: A National Status Report." 2nd edition, 1990.

Voges, Ernst, ed. *Tobacco Encyclopedia*. Mainz, Germany: Tobacco Journal International, 1984.

Ward, Howard H., ed. *Asbestos, Smoking, and Disease: The Scientific Evidence*. Boston: Commercial Union Insurance Companies, 1982.

White, Larry C. *Merchants of Death*. New York: William Morrow, 1988.

Wilbert, Johannes. *Tobacco and Shamanism in South America*. New Haven: Yale University Press, 1987.

Wolinskay, Howard and Brune, Tom. *The Serpent and the Staff, the Unhealthy Politics of the American Medical Association*. New York: Putnam, 1994.

Index